Jefferson, Lincoln, and Wilson

Jefferson, Lincoln, and Wilson

The American Dilemma of Race and Democracy

Edited by
John Milton Cooper Jr.
and Thomas J. Knock

UNIVERSITY OF VIRGINIA PRESS / CHARLOTTESVILLE AND LONDON

University of Virginia Press
© 2010 by the Rector and Visitors of the University of Virginia
All rights reserved
Printed in the United States of America on acid-free paper

First published 2010

9 8 7 6 5 4 3 2 1

LIBRARY OF CONGRESS CATALOGING-IN-PUBLICATION DATA

Jefferson, Lincoln, and Wilson : the American dilemma of race and democracy /
edited by John Milton Cooper Jr. and Thomas J. Knock.
     p. cm.
  Includes bibliographical references and index.
  ISBN 978-0-8139-3004-6 (cloth : alk. paper)
    1. Jefferson, Thomas, 1743–1826—Political and social views. 2. Lincoln, Abraham,
1809–1865—Political and social views. 3. Wilson, Woodrow, 1856–1924—Political
and social views. 4. Race—Political aspects—United States—History.
5. Democracy—United States—History. 6. United States—Race relations—
History. 7. Slavery—Political aspects—United States—History—19th century.
8. Presidents—United States—Biography. I. Cooper, John Milton. II. Knock,
Thomas J.
  E332.2.J474 2010
  305.800973—dc22

                                                              2009049767

Contents

Foreword

This collection of essays is the result of "Jefferson, Lincoln, and Wilson: The American Dilemma of Race and Democracy," the Fourth Biennial Woodrow Wilson National Symposium held by the Woodrow Wilson Presidential Library, September 14–16, 2006, in Staunton, Virginia. The symposium was generously funded by the Carnegie Corporation, the Jessie Ball DuPont Fund, and the Family of Dr. Frank R. Pancake. In addition to the authors of the essays and the volume's editors, other participants in the symposium were Mary Frances Berry, Andrew O'Shaughnessy, and Reginald Butler. The volume could not have been realized without the expertise and work of its contributing authors or its editors, John Milton Cooper Jr. and Thomas J. Knock. The Library also wishes to thank its former Executive Director, Eric J. Vettel, for his organizational efforts early in the planning of both the conference and this publication; Joel Hodson, Director of Education at the Library, for his logistical work in setting the conference in motion and his assistance to the editors; and, at the University of Virginia Press, Richard Holway, Raennah Mitchell, and especially Ruth Steinberg for their guidance along the way. Finally, Hampden H. Smith III, Associate Trustee and former Chair of the Library's Education Committee, played a crucial and tireless role in coordinating various aspects of this publishing enterprise, for which both the editors of the volume and the Library are deeply grateful.

Dr. Don W. Wilson
President and CEO
Woodrow Wilson Presidential Library Foundation

Introduction

JOHN MILTON COOPER JR.

John Milton Cooper Jr.
and Thomas J. Knock

In his classic work *The Souls of Black Folk,* published in 1903, W. E. B. Du Bois stated, "The problem of the twentieth century is the problem of the color line." One of a handful of truly great minds that America has produced, Du Bois wrote about race with deeper understanding, keener insight, and broader perspective than almost anyone else. Indeed, his statement proved prophetic. Again and again throughout the twentieth century, racial antipathies between African Americans and whites pushed themselves into the center of the nation's life, both in forms of discrimination and violence and in efforts to overcome barriers to equality and harmony between people of color and majority groups. Yet, for perhaps the only time in his long life and brilliant commentary, Du Bois may have understated his argument. One way or another, the color line has been "the problem" of all the centuries since the European settlement of the Americas. It arose with the first contact between Native peoples and the explorers, conquerors, and settlers from across the Atlantic. Thus, the collision of races was embedded in the core of the political culture and society of what became the United States long before its inception.

The color line existed everywhere the Europeans went in the New World, in the various nations' colonies and successor countries in the Caribbean and in North, South, and Central America. For those who formed the English colonies of North America, the color line took on its largest and most troubling dimension with the importation of Africans as slaves into Virginia in 1619. Once those colonies had won their independence in the American Revolution, however, black-white relations took on a special dimension that did not obtain elsewhere, or at least not so soon. For the founding document of the United States boldly states, "We hold these truths to be self-evident: That all men are created equal; that they are endowed by their Creator with certain unalienable rights; that among these are life, liberty, and the pursuit of happiness."

Those words of the document's principal author, Thomas Jefferson, set forth more than a case for the independence of a particular people: they laid down a charter for human liberty. But two great contradictions inhered in the Declaration of Independence from the beginning. One was gender. Although "men" was used at that time to include both genders, the fact remained that males enjoyed far more rights and privileges than females. The other contradiction, of course, was race. Almost nowhere in the new nation did African Americans enjoy the same rights and privileges as whites. In fact, the great majority of them were slaves, and slavery existed in all the new states. Moreover, many of the new nation's leaders owned slaves: the list included George Washington, the military leader of the Revolution and the first president under the Constitution; James Madison, the "father" of the Constitution; and, with greater notoriety than the rest, Thomas Jefferson. How to overcome these limitations of race and gender would remain central to the social and political life of America from the founding of the nation forward. Of the two, the matter of race would prove the more enduring and divisive, to the point of causing an attempt to dismember the United States and precipitating the bloodiest war the nation has ever waged (the only full-scale conflict ever fought on its own soil), not to mention intermittent deadly race riots since then and into the present day. How to reconcile what Lincoln in 1862 called "the last best hope on earth" with the glaring injustices caused by the color line has never ceased to haunt the self-proclaimed exemplar of liberty, justice, and equality.

This volume of essays seeks to explore how this struggle has shaped American democracy in the lives, thought, and actions of three of the nation's most important presidents—Thomas Jefferson, Abraham Lincoln, and Woodrow Wilson. Each man led the nation in a different epoch, and each epoch had its own set of historical circumstances that shaped constructions of race: Jefferson at the very beginning of the Republic, as the nineteenth century dawned and the institution of slavery flourished; Lincoln when the country had expanded into a continental empire and fell into civil war over slavery; and Wilson at a time when, simultaneously, the United

States emerged as a leader on the world stage and consolidated legally sanctioned apartheid at home. As great and brilliant presidents, they constitute a kind of trinity, partly because no other chief executives have communicated more effectively or so eloquently to both their fellow citizens and the peoples of the world the ideals of democracy, even as they violated principles for which they ostensibly stood. For all of them, race was at the center of the major events and decisions of their lives.

Of the three, Jefferson remains arguably the most perplexing for Americans of the twenty-first century. To be sure, Jefferson wrote celebrated historic lines about liberty and equality, defining the very purpose of the American Revolution, as well as significant discourses on the rights of citizens in a republic and on the prohibition of slavery in the Northwest Territory. Yet he encouraged the expansion of slavery into Louisiana and the Spanish Borderlands and counted some two hundred slaves among his personal property at Monticello, of whom none save five were granted freedom in the president's last will and testament. These are among the contradictions and hypocrisies that the essays of the opening section confront and elucidate as they examine Jefferson in context, from the time that his father gave him an enslaved child as a boyhood companion, to his final contemplations on colonization in the last months of his life. The authors pay no heed to the injunction of Henry Adams—John Adams's great-grandson and a chronicler of the early republic—to his brother Brooks: "For God Almighty's sake, leave Jefferson alone!"

In the first essay, "Thomas Jefferson and St. George Tucker: The Makings of Revolutionary Slaveholders," Annette Gordon-Reed begins by drawing together the presidents of the Founding generation, slaveholders and Virginians all, excepting Adams; only Jefferson, she reminds us, made a display of his antislavery position. But she opens up a wider perspective by setting him alongside his far less known friend and fellow lawyer, St. George Tucker of the College of William and Mary, as the means of understanding "how and why revolutionary slaveholders talked their way out of their pronounced ideals about slavery and moved toward making peace with the institution that they both claimed they wanted to see destroyed." This unsettling process went through three stages, which Gordon-Reed describes as engagement, acquiescence, and alarm and despair. Although Tucker's antislavery ardor was the more consistent, and was more forcefully expressed in a dissertation he turned into a pamphlet, it was "fear of retribution" (i.e., the contagion of revolts in Haiti and Santo Domingo) that helped to activate the two correspondents' engagement with the necessity of emancipation. Yet, later, both men would allow other concerns to trump moral principles—their children's financial legacy, for example, as each of them broke up slave families in order to enrich their daughters' dowries. (In Jefferson's case, political ambition also contributed to acquiescence in the status quo.) The portent of sectional strife in the crisis of 1819–21 subsequently threw the retired president into alarm and despair; his design for emancipation through colonization left the vast majority of Southern slaveholders cold and skeptical and, notwithstanding the Missouri Compromise, the nation's future seemed to him uncertain. Gordon-Reed leaves Jefferson near life's end not really knowing what to do about slavery and "*truly* in agony."

In "Domesticating the Captive Nation: Thomas Jefferson and the Problem of Slavery," Peter Onuf initially approaches his subject's dilemma from the standpoint of his democratic theory. This was predicated, Onuf explains, on what Jefferson called a "graduation of authorities," or a series of republics, "from the great national one, down through all its subordinations, until it ends in the administration of every man's farm by himself." Herein lay the key to Jefferson's antislavery views. If, as he wrote, the "true foundation of republican government is the equal right of every citizen, in his personal property, and in their management," then to interfere in any way with that prerogative, much less to *impose* emancipation on slaveholders, was to violate republican self-government. And so, in advocating emancipation, Jefferson came to insist that it must take the form of wholesale colonization of African American slaves to some faraway place; but, crucially, this could be accomplished only on a voluntary basis on the part of *uncoerced* slaveholders. In the meantime, until a "revolution in public opinion" made them feel utterly secure in their right to property, and therefore enabled them to undertake this solution, their enlightened duty was to ameliorate the condition of slavery by attending to the material well-being of their slaves—or, rather, to their *happiness* (even though they were not free to pursue it on their own). This was chiefly what Jefferson meant by "domesticating the captive nation," and he tried to set the right example. By the 1820s, however, as emancipation seemed ever more remote, his only alternative was to defend amelioration as at least superior to the condition of Europe's serfs and wage laborers—and its soldiers and sailors, too.

Rounding out the picture, Lucia Stanton scrutinizes social-historical aspects of the foregoing enterprise in "Perfecting Slavery: Rational Plantation Management at Monticello." During the period between his service as secretary of state and vice-president, the sage (and master) of Monticello conducted an experiment manifestly based on his prescription for domestication, and on the notion that an enlightened planter should stay close to the work of farming and "watch for the happiness" of his slaves. For about three years, Jefferson, in Stanton's phrase, conducted "a kind of academy on the mountaintop," as he humanely and efficiently managed his labor force, banishing the lash in favor of "reason and comity" and permitting some autonomy in the performance of the work. In this way, he promoted *esprit de corps* and friendly competition and even granted gratuities. His new nailery, where the teenaged boys toiled, especially pleased him; monitoring the youths daily, imparting skills and inculcating character, he was schoolmaster and prison warden alike. If "democracy" was not quite his aim, Jefferson did nonetheless once aver: "The mind . . . of a slave is to be prepared by instruction and habit for self-government." Thus, he strained to prepare his slaves for the day of emancipation and repatriation. Alas, the project ultimately went to seed, a reflection, Stanton concludes, of its fragility and improbability as a means of achieving liberty for blacks. In 1797, Jefferson abandoned the farm experiment to resume his political career, and the fate of his slaves remained unmitigated after all.

For battling against racial inequality, no American president has enjoyed a more shining reputation than Abraham Lincoln—and deservedly so. Not only did he play the greatest role of any American in the abolition of slavery and the commencement of a long march toward racial equality and justice, but he prevented the establishment of a separate nation based on slavery, and preserved the political and judicial forum for the pursuit of that equality and justice. For this Lincoln enjoys the status of icon, as epitomized by the giant, brooding sculpture inside the national memorial dedicated to him in Washington, which has witnessed two of the greatest moments in the African American struggle—the concert by Marian Anderson in April 1939 and Martin Luther King Jr.'s "I Have a Dream" speech in August 1963. Yet, as the second set of essays suggests, that iconic status also impedes a finer appreciation of the varied and often painful ways in which Lincoln endeavored to reconcile race and democracy. To cite but one example, Lincoln's early solution—colonization—was scarcely distinguishable from that of the tortured Jefferson. What set Lincoln apart is the focus of all three essays in Part II.

In "Personal Encounters: Abraham Lincoln and African Americans," an examination of his direct interactions with slavery and African Americans from his youth onward, Jean Baker demonstrates that the personal was the political for the sixteenth president. "Through his observance of slavery," she states, "he had come to understand its maximal contradiction—democracy." As early as his adolescence in rural Indiana, Lincoln had begun to harbor antislavery views on the basis of several close encounters—for example, traveling to New Orleans on the Mississippi River, he remarked on the "torment that . . . slaves shackled together in irons" endured onboard the riverboat. (In time he would come to declare that slavery "deprives our republican example of its just influence in the world.") During his twenty-five years in Springfield, Illinois, where the law severely crimped the rights and privileges of free blacks, Lincoln's contacts were not necessarily limited to servants: twenty-one African American families lived within a three-block radius of his home, and he had cordial relationships with many of them of various trades and talents. Yet not until his forties did he make any notable public utterance about slavery; as Baker reminds us, "His was a democracy of white males." (Physical differences, Lincoln averred in 1858, "will forever forbid the two races living together on terms of social and political equality.") Once he moved to Washington, however, where 20 percent of the population was black, Lincoln met with an increasing number and diversity of African Americans, in the White House and elsewhere. Encounters with obviously highly impressive people like Frederick Douglass and Sojourner Truth helped to expand his views on such important matters as who might be worthy of the vote among freedmen: the "very intelligent," for instance, and "those who have fought gallantly." With Lincoln, there was always a core of direct human feeling on behalf of the individual people subjected to slavery. Even so, as of April 1865, as Baker notes and as Douglass well knew, he had hardly become a crusader for civil rights.

In "Lincoln and Colonization," Eric Foner explores how the president tried to settle the contradictions—that is, how he came to abandon the panacea of colonization and began forthrightly to embrace a biracial society. As an aspiring politician of the 1850s, Lincoln attempted to square his antislavery views with the greatest perceived barrier to abolition—namely, white revulsion, in the North and West as well as the South, at the prospect of having several million free blacks living among them. For him, and other sincere opponents of slavery, the repatriation of freed slaves to Africa offered a way of taking the sting out of emancipation—but it also compromised his vision of a new nation dedicated to the proposition that all men were created equal. Unlike many writers, Foner takes Lincoln at his word concerning colonization. Indeed, the plan sprang from sincere belief, not merely political tactics, and the president persisted in his advocacy well into the Civil War, even asking Congress to appropriate money for it. Moreover, just months before he issued the Emancipation Proclamation, he told a delegation of black leaders, "You and we are a different race. . . . It is better for us both, therefore, to be separated." As Foner shows, the Emancipation Proclamation marked the great divide in the evolution of Lincoln's views on African Americans and race relations: "For the first time, Lincoln began to think seriously of the role blacks would play in a post-slavery world."

It is a matter of debate whether Secretary of War Edwin Stanton really said when Lincoln died, "Now he belongs to the ages." But it is beyond dispute that, to a far greater extent than with any other president, Lincoln's spirit and example have lived on and inspired leaders who followed him. In "The Theft of Lincoln in Scholarship, Politics, and Public Memory," David Blight examines the uses and misuses of Lincoln's example and legacy. As he emphasizes, these have never been simple matters. For all public figures who have invoked him, the question has always been, *which* Lincoln? In 1912, for instance, Theodore Roosevelt and Woodrow Wilson attempted to seize his mantle for themselves. But it was not Lincoln, the Great Emancipator, over whom they vied in their quest for the presidency, for neither of them addressed race in a very direct way.

Throughout the twentieth century and into the twenty-first, some politicians have appealed to the spirit and example of the Emancipator, while others have avoided that legacy. Yet, in one of the greatest ironies of American political history, Blight suggests, those who once proudly proclaimed themselves the "Party of Lincoln" (and sometimes still do) became the party of the white South; indeed, after the 1980s, the region emerged as the Republicans' bedrock of electoral strength, just as it once had been for the Democrats. By contrast, the Democrats, formerly the "White Man's Party," became the home of the overwhelming majority of African Americans and, in 2008, the first party to choose an African American as their presidential nominee and go on to elect him. In all of this, Lincoln has continued to serve as a political football. As Blight points out, even while conservative economists and advocates of states' rights have excoriated Lincoln in recent years, right-wing organizations have touted him as the paragon of "color-blind conservatism" and smaller government. Likewise, twice, Barack Obama chose Springfield, Illinois, as the place to launch his drive for his party's nomination, and to introduce his choice for running mate.

If Lincoln ranks among the few presidential heroes in the quest for racial justice and equality, Woodrow Wilson often ranks among the villains. Attended by household slaves as a little boy, as Jefferson had been, and the first Southern-born person to be elected president after the Civil War, Wilson brought an undeniably Southern-white flavor to the presidency. Not surprisingly, a majority of his Cabinet were natives of the Old Confederacy. But his administration had more than a Southern-white tone. It tried to introduce racial segregation into the offices of the federal government (the U.S. Postal Service and the Treasury Department in particular) and greatly reduced the percentage of African Americans employed in those offices. The administration, and Wilson himself, likewise generally turned a blind eye to the rising tide of racist demagoguery and white violence against blacks, including lynching. It was indeed "an irony of fate," to quote Wilson in another context, that he should inhabit the White House in 1915, the year that marked, coincidentally, the fiftieth-anniversary celebration of the end of the Civil War, the release of D. W. Griffith's landmark motion picture "The Birth of a Nation," and the death of Booker T. Washington. In all, the eight years of Wilson's presidency composed part of what the historian Rayford Logan has termed the "nadir" in African American life since the end of slavery.

In "American Sphinx: Woodrow Wilson and Race," John Milton Cooper Jr. confronts both Wilson's thought on race and his lack of thought about it. Far from being a typical white Southerner of his time, Cooper argues, Wilson displayed a surprising indifference toward race. This could sometimes lead to courteous gestures, such as inviting Booker T. Washington to attend and speak at his inauguration as president of Princeton University. For the most part, however, Wilson's indifference abetted the discriminatory practices that Southern whites in his administration pursued and enabled him simply to ignore the awful state of the country's race relations. In those attitudes Wilson resembled Northern whites of his era rather than his fellow Southerners. The Southern tone of his administration troubled him, therefore, because he aspired to national leadership for his party and worried that Confederate connotations might alienate Northern white voters.

The racial violence that exploded during World War I finally moved him to issue a statement denouncing lynching—after prodding from African American leaders and some Democrats: "I say plainly that every American who takes part in the action of a mob or gives it any sort of countenance is no true son of this great Democracy, but its betrayer. . . . How shall we commend democracy to the acceptance of other peoples, if we disgrace our own by proving that it is, after all, no protector to the weak?" That statement showed what an eloquent spokesman for racial justice Wilson could have been. Except for that one time, though, he kept his distance from all efforts to combat racial inequality and injustice, even while he championed economic and social emancipation for others, including, belatedly, women.

In "W. E. B. Du Bois: Black 'Radical Democracy' during Wilson's Progressive Era," Manning Marable considers the strained relations between African American leaders and the Wilson administration. The central figure in this story is none other than Du Bois, who joined other prominent blacks to support Wilson in the 1912 election. For him, this was no inconsequential departure. A sometime member of the Socialist Party of America and an admirer of Eugene Debs (its nominee for president), Du Bois nonetheless felt uncomfortable with the racial condescension he often encountered among white radicals; then, too, he resented the way Republicans either took black support for granted or sought their own following among white Southerners. Du Bois thus had high hopes for his fellow scholar Wilson.

The hope soon turned into bitter disappointment. Yet it was a tribute to Du Bois's historical insights and breadth of mind that he never completely broke with the president. Like many leaders of the National Association for the Advancement of Colored People, for instance, he supported American intervention in World War I. Participation in the patriotic effort, especially in the armed forces, he believed, would advance the cause of black liberation. (Of his own enlistment he later wrote, "I became during the World War nearer to feeling myself a real and full American than ever before or since.") Foreign policy offered another good reason to stick with Wilson.

Du Bois perceived that the president's internationalist vision would help to end European colonialism and white domination over African and Asian peoples, however far into the future their termination might appear.

It was in the realm of international relations, of course, that Wilson carved out his most monumental legacy, which rests mainly on his pilot authorship of the Fourteen Points and the Covenant of the League of Nations. The racial impact of that facet of his leadership is the subject of Erez Manela's essay, "'Peoples of Many Races': The World beyond Europe in the Wilsonian Imagination." Although Wilson did not coin the term "self-determination," and deployed it only circumspectly, Manela observes, the vistas of independence and equality ignited aspirations among peoples all over the world. But much of this light shone in spite of Wilson, and in ways he did not intend it to; depending on the circumstances, his responses to demands for self-determination were alternately attuned to his own racial indifference or to the sensitivities of the colonial powers at whom his words of divestment were aimed.

Yet, within these limitations, Wilson did expand his ideas regarding which peoples could enjoy the blessings of freedom and independence. Before the war had ended, it was his conception of the United States as the leader of a new world order that also caused him to discard the notion of America as a nation that had to be led by white Protestants. In London, on the eve of the Paris peace conference in December 1918, he privately told a British leader, "You must not speak of us who come over here as cousins, still less as brothers; we are neither. Neither must you think of us as Anglo-Saxons, for that term can no longer be rightly applied to the people of the United States." Publicly, he proclaimed at the same time, "Any influence that the American people have over the affairs of the world is measured by their sympathy with the aspirations of men everywhere."

Taken together, these nine essays attempt to convey comparative insights into the complexities of the politics of the color line across a broad swath of the history of the United States. Three of the deepest thinkers and most significant leaders among the nation's presidents grappled with trying to reconcile race in the evolution of American democracy. Their respective evasions, failures, and successes illuminate the anguished and profound nature of that effort. In this regard, the felicity of one of the connections between the beginning and the end of this collection should not go unappreciated—

which is to observe that young Joseph Fossett, who labored in Monticello's nailery and numbered among the five slaves Jefferson deigned to free, afterward moved north and prospered as a blacksmith in Cincinnati; that Fosset's children worked in the Underground Railroad and agitated for racial integration in the great river city, and that one among their offspring was William Monroe Trotter; and that this great-grandson of Jefferson's slave went on to graduate from Harvard, became a civil rights activist, and, during an audience at the White House in 1914, personally upbraided Woodrow Wilson for the new federal segregation and for breaking his campaign promise to be "president of all the people."

I JEFFERSON

Thomas Jefferson and St. George Tucker

The Makings of Revolutionary Slaveholders

✳   ✳   ✳   Annette Gordon-Reed

Very few topics have received more considered attention and comment than the response of eighteenth-century American revolutionaries to their country's deep involvement with the institution of slavery. Samuel Johnson's justly famous query in *Taxation No Tyranny*, "How is it we hear the loudest yelps for liberty from the drivers of negroes?" has echoed across the years in dozens of historical works. Johnson, as was his wont, went straight to the heart of the matter, and much of the writing about slavery among the founding generation attempts to answer, insofar as that ever can be done, his dead-on query.

Of all the members of America's generation of Revolutionary slaveholders, Thomas Jefferson has seemed the most problematic. Because he was the principal author of the Declaration of Independence, often seen as the foundational document in the creation of American freedom, he has been, both justly and unjustly, set apart from other Virginians in his Revolutionary cohort. According to conventional wisdom, Jefferson's drafting of the Declaration imposed on him a special duty to rise above the practices and mores of his society on the question of slavery and the related question of race. Because he was an exceptional man in some ways, he was supposed to be exceptional in all ways—particularly in the areas that he spoke or wrote about, and on the issues of primary concern to us today. Despite his really intermittent intellectual offerings on the subject of the peculiar institution, Jefferson had no answer to the problem of what to do about slavery in the United States. One should say more accurately that he had no *workable* solution to the problem of slavery in a society whose economy depended upon enslaved labor and in which the people who would be emancipated were of African descent and made up nearly half the population. That Jefferson had no real solution should not surprise. With the normal caveats about the dangers of seeing any outcome as inevitable, it is a safe assumption that the problem of American slavery could only have been solved in the way it was ultimately solved: through bloody conflict and strife.

It is not, however, simply Jefferson's connection to the Declaration of Independence that has shaped attitudes about his status as a lifelong slave holder. A plethora of Jefferson biographies have highlighted his characteristic optimism—his "we will carry on" demeanor in the face of family deaths, burned houses, destroyed dams, and impending financial ruin. Right up until his last days, when he faced the loss of everything and was trying desperately to think of plans to stay afloat, he was still able to say "I am confident," when expressing how things would work themselves out after he had gotten past his latest crisis with his creditors. That eerie confidence and optimism—some might say capacity for self-delusion—ultimately failed him when it came to thinking about slavery and the black presence in American society. There were many reasons for this, not the least of which was his own mismanagement of his financial affairs and the fact that slavery was never as serious an issue for Jefferson as it is to those who study him today. Building his version of the United States of America was Jefferson's true obsession, not the end of slavery in the country or on his plantation.

The tendency to compare Jefferson to other members of the Revolutionary generation is irresistible, and perhaps even necessary, so long as apples are compared to apples. We think first of people of similar historical stature, such as John Adams, Benjamin Franklin, George Washington, James Madison, and James Monroe. The comparison to Adams is nearly useless, for he did not live in a slave society and Massachusetts' small black population could in no way have been considered a racial threat to whites in that colony, and then state. The question was never whether whites could tolerate living with a relatively small number of blacks in their midst under circumstances where whites were in clear legal, social, and economic control of the society. The question was (still is) the extent to which whites were willing to live alongside, and share power with, an almost equal number of blacks over whom they had no firm control. Nearly every Revolutionary figure below the Mason-Dixon line who expressed himself on this point expressed doubts about the efficacy of a multiracial America: Jefferson,

Marshall, Madison, Monroe. The latter three men all joined the American Colonization Society.[1]

Although Benjamin Franklin ended life as a member of the Pennsylvania Abolition Society, he presents no great credentials as an antislavery crusader. And, if he had been, he would not have been going against the grain of his neighbors and community. Unlike Virginia, Franklin's home state of Pennsylvania had a substantial, ready-made, and very influential body of people devoted to the cause of the abolition of slavery: the Quakers. Quakers and their supporters had enough power to bring about a legislative end to slavery with the passage of the flawed, but still extremely important, Gradual Emancipation Act of 1780,[2] a development that almost certainly could not have happened in Jefferson's Virginia at that same time.

The person to whom Jefferson is most often, and more fairly, compared is George Washington. Washington wrote no stirring words that raised the question, *"Well, what about the slaves?"* Or, *"What about black people? Are they created equal? Do they have the right to life, liberty and the pursuit of happiness?"* Even though Washington during his time as the first president of the United States had a level of political capital that no occupant of the office has ever approached since, he was unwilling to spend any of that capital on the question of the abolition of slavery. What a thing it would have been to have had the most-esteemed "Father of His Country" speak from the office of the presidency about America's need to rid itself of chattel slavery, immediately or even gradually! In contrast to Jefferson, Washington created no expectations on the matter through his actions as a public man, and made no representations about the position the country should take on the subject. In the end, however, Washington did perform the important private action of freeing the people he enslaved. Even though he did so reluctantly, dithering about it almost to the day he died and only after he and his wife had had their fill of using them—he justly receives credit for ending the bondage of the men, women, and children whom he held as chattel during his lifetime. But for his actions, they probably would have continued in that condition until their deaths, for Martha Washington was not so keen on giving up the family's human property.[3]

The "Father of the Constitution," James Madison, held slaves until the end of his life, too. Although Madison's Constitution set forth the compact between the government and citizens of the United States, the Declaration of Independence offered famous sentiments about the equality of mankind and the right of everyone to life, liberty and the pursuit of happiness—a sort of manifesto of broader reach about the truths of life that transcend any particular form of government. Moreover, the American Constitution was not, until after the Civil War, really about the lives or the citizenship of the enslaved majority of black people in the country at that time. To the extent that blacks were referred to, the pre–Civil War Constitution spoke to reinforce slavery and the absence of citizenship rights of those held in bondage—a world far different from the one in which we live today. For instance, during the congressional hearings into the impeachment of President Richard Nixon after the Watergate scandal in 1974, Barbara Jordan spoke stirringly about her faith in the Constitution. The congresswoman was almost certainly referring to the document that included the Thirteenth, Fourteenth, Fifteenth, and Nineteenth Amendments, which made it possible for her, a black woman, to hold a seat in Congress. That was not James Madison's Constitution. Finally, Madison, unlike Jefferson, did not cultivate a public image of himself as an antislavery advocate in a way that would allow us to attach his private beliefs to his work on the Constitution. He simply cannot be seen as having promised anything to black people or other disaffected groups in America.

Finally, there is James Monroe, who held people as slaves even as he claimed to be against slavery. While Jefferson talked about colonization of blacks after emancipation, he made no moves to do anything about it, not even to join the American Colonization Society (ACS) when his friends and contemporaries in politics were doing just that. Monroe, however, used his position as president of the United States to promote the ACS's efforts to repatriate blacks to Liberia on the African continent. His prominence in the effort, of course, led to the naming of Liberia's capital Monrovia.[4]

Despite the overall dismal story of slavery in the early American republic, and the general failure of leadership on the question—a failure that helped set the stage for the armed conflict of the Civil War—it has been Jefferson who has borne the brunt of modern-day criticism over the issue of slavery. His lived dilemma attracts our notice in part because, of all among his cohort, he set a high standard and then seems to have failed the test that standard posed. What test? The test that Americans expect people to live up to the principles that we like to believe represent the truest and best ideals in American life. Whether or not Jefferson should have to pass such a test is debatable. But for purposes of our consideration, let us take as a given that the notion he has failed a "test" has certainly formed the basis of contemporary discussions of his place in American life.

Perhaps not surprisingly, blacks seemed to key in on Jefferson as a pivotal figure among the Revolutionary generation early on. When Benjamin Banneker wrote to him in August of 1791, he explained his reason for approaching the then secretary of state by saying that he had heard that Jefferson was a "friend" to black people, despite the obvious fact that he held black people in slavery. What could his "friendship" have meant? Banneker did not give the source of his information, or what Jefferson had done to create that impression, but this was clearly about more than what he had written in the Declaration. (Jefferson's authorship of the document was not even generally known at that point.) Although Banneker was in Maryland, the communication networks of the enslaved and free-black communities very famously transmitted information far and wide. That is how enslaved people from Virginia, and other areas of the South, knew to make Philadelphia one of their destinations when they escaped bondage. They also knew whom they were to run to in the city. The homes of free blacks like Bishop Richard Allen and James Forten, and of whites such as Dr. Benjamin Rush, were destinations for newly arrived blacks seeking help.[5]

When Banneker wrote to him, Jefferson was living in Philadelphia with, among other people, James Hemings. James Hemings was an enslaved man, the half-brother to Jefferson's deceased wife, Martha. Jefferson had taken Hemings to Paris with him when he went on a diplomatic mission to France in 1784, where the nineteen-year-old was trained as a French chef. Hemings had returned to America with Jefferson, although he and his sister, Sarah (Sally) Hemings, who arrived later, had for a time considered taking their freedom and remaining in Paris. While in Philadelphia, Jefferson paid Hemings a monthly salary equivalent to that of a white worker. He also had on staff several free-black employees. Hemings had regular contact with them and other members of the free-black community in Philadelphia, including Henrietta Gardiner. Gardiner was Jefferson's laundress during his years as secretary of state and then later when he returned to the city to become vice-president. The black servants at Jefferson's home on High Street were in daily contact with him and knew well his personality and his way of dealing with blacks. Servants tended to gossip about and draw comparisons between one workplace or one employer or master and another. It is possible that any one, or all, of these African Americans was the source of information about Jefferson circulating within the African American community.[6]

Whites, as well, likely contributed to Jefferson's reputation during this period. His great friend Dr. Benjamin Rush (mentioned above) was a well-known supporter of abolition and of individual blacks. He got Jefferson to give money in 1791 to Richard Allen as he began his determined and ultimately successful effort to build the first black church in Philadelphia, which eventually became the African Methodist Episcopal Church. It should be said that, given the tenor of the times, it probably did not take much to be considered a "friend" to black people. Expectations could only have been very low. The simple act of not being hostile might qualify, but that Jefferson gave money to help build a black institution probably shaped members of Philadelphia's black community's view of him. It is likely that the combination of Jefferson's public posture and reputation, deserved or not, as an opponent of slavery and the information about his private interactions with blacks shaped the earliest views of him as a slaveholder.[7]

There were, of course, many other Revolutionary slaveholders besides Jefferson, Madison, and the other more well-known figures of the era. While it is natural to consider Jefferson along with equally famous Founders, a comparison with a less well-known but important figure in Jeffersonian Virginia can also provide instructive insights into Jefferson and his time. St. George Tucker was a professor of law at the College of William and Mary, as well as a noted jurist who sat on the bench of Virginia's highest court and ended his career as a federal district judge.[8] Tucker never held statewide or national political office, and he was never subjected to the level of public scrutiny of the kind that Jefferson was. Yet critical aspects of his personal life resembled Jefferson's much more than the men with whom Jefferson is usually compared. Viewed side by side, the trajectory of these two men's thoughts about slavery (and what position free blacks could have in the country that they had both worked to create) provides a useful way of considering how and why Revolutionary slaveholders talked their way out of their pronounced ideals about slavery and moved toward making peace with the institution that both claimed they wanted to see destroyed. One finds that attitudes and behavior that are often attributed to Jefferson's personality, and offered as examples of his particular weaknesses or failures, were very much a part of Tucker's personality as well. What we see are two men of different ages following the same trajectory in life, meeting up at points, but ending up in the same place. Taken together, Jefferson's and Tucker's responses to the problem of slavery can be divided into three distinct phases: engagement, acquiescence and, finally, alarm and despair.

Engagement

To talk about engagement, a little background is required. Both Jefferson and Tucker began life in prosperous families, albeit in different societies. Jefferson's Virginia beginnings are well known. Born the son of a self-made man, Peter Jefferson, and Jane Randolph Jefferson, a woman from one of the most well-known families in Virginia, Jefferson was a child of privilege from his birth in 1743. His first memory, he said, was of being handed up on a pillow to a slave who was to carry him from the Jefferson family home at Shadwell to Tuckahoe plantation, where he spent his early childhood. Virginia had long since become a slave society, and enslaved African Americans were part of young Tom's existence from the beginning. He and each of his siblings were given an enslaved child as a companion growing up, reinforcing their sense of entitlement and mastery over African Americans. Although he would eventually come to denounce this system of bondage as he began to situate himself as a man of the Enlightenment, ultimately he could not disentangle himself from his emotional and personal commitment to the institution that he had known since infancy.[9]

St. George Tucker, in contrast to Jefferson, was not a native Virginian. He was born in Bermuda, in 1752, nine years after Jefferson's birth. Nine years was not enough of an age gap to put the two men in different generations, but it was enough to ensure that Jefferson would hit significant milestones in life somewhat ahead of Tucker. Tucker immigrated to the Virginia colony in the early 1770s, at age nineteen. The youngest son in a family of six, Tucker had to leave home to seek his fortune. The racial makeup and character of Jefferson's Virginia would have been no shock to the young Bermudan, for he was well used to living in a society with large numbers of black people. During Tucker's youth, Bermuda's population was almost evenly divided between black and white. Thus, slavery, and a sense of the potential for racial conflict, was likely as much a part of his consciousness as it was for Virginians. Like Jefferson, Tucker came to Williamsburg to read law at the College of William and Mary. There he studied with Jefferson's teacher and mentor, George Wythe. If he had not been exposed to antislavery rhetoric in his home territory, one can be certain that Wythe exposed the young man to the concept.[10]

Wythe, a well-known and strong opponent of slavery, took what steps he could to try to strike a blow against the institution. He was not a member of the landed gentry and had no part in plantation slavery. He did free the small number of slaves he possessed, even before his death—which apparently was at the hands of a nephew who was jealous at the bequest Wythe left to his black housekeeper and a young African American boy whom he was mentoring. Wythe clearly influenced Tucker, as he undoubtedly did his earlier pupil Jefferson, on the subject of emancipation. Wythe presented the antislavery position as the enlightened one for all educated and forward-thinking men to take. The Revolution gave both Tucker and Jefferson ample reason to consider what relationship their Revolutionary ideals had to the plight of the people whom they enslaved. This intersection of Revolutionary ideas and slavery was no mere academic exercise. African Americans' response to the conflict, particularly after Lord Dunmore's Proclamation in November of 1775, focused the matter for white Virginians in the clearest way. Many joined the British forces and talked openly about the connection between what white Virginians were fighting for and their own plight as enslaved people. Jefferson experienced this aspect of the Revolution personally. A number of enslaved people from his plantations left, in some cases as whole families, to join the British forces as they marched through Virginia, taking the idea of liberty to its logical conclusion.[11]

Jefferson participated in the Revolution at the very top echelon, serving in the Continental Congress and taking an ill-fated stint as Virginia's Revolutionary War governor, while Tucker contributed to the effort at its most basic level. He enlisted in the Virginia militia in 1779 and actually did battle against British forces. The Tucker family was involved in the shipping trade, and he, along with other family members, helped smuggle goods and provisions into Virginia during the conflict. When the struggle ended, Tucker settled into life at Matoax plantation with a wife and children upon whom he doted.[12]

There is no indication that Tucker had any notion of how much the Revolution he helped to make would transform the basic order of American society. Although he expected that there would be a new republican government, and he spoke of the dawn of a new day in society, Tucker was something less than an ardent democrat. Once the forces of monarchy had been defeated, he believed the same elites who had exercised power in Virginia before the Revolution should continue to govern and manage the republican experiment on behalf of the lower orders. At some point in the 1790s, he was aghast at the extent to which the so-called common people (that is, common white people) actually believed that they were to have some say in the management of the new government. Although he admired Jefferson, Tucker hated the direction that Jefferson's newly formed Republican Party was taking society, and he was dubious about the party's eventual triumph in the election of 1800.[13]

As for Jefferson, because of his own personality, his experience in France, and attention to the French Revolution, he was not as surprised, or as dismayed, by the prospect of different classes of people having a say in the running of the government. While Tucker grumbled in the 1790s about what he took to be the growth of unruly democracy, Jefferson was busy casting aside all public traces of his aristocratic self, changing his manner of dress to reflect republican simplicity and riding out without a servant personally attending him. Jefferson's politics as public theater sent the message that he understood his political fortunes lay with the people whom Tucker so mistrusted.

Among the political changes the American Revolution wrought was a new attitude about slavery in the North and the South. While the Revolution helped bring about the end of slavery in the North, albeit slowly in most places, the South was nowhere near ready to provide for the general emancipation of its principal labor force. However, Revolutionary fervor did motivate Virginia to liberalize the laws regarding emancipation. An Act of 1782 made private emancipations (those without the permission of the state) legal, and a number of Virginians took advantage of the law. Both Tucker and Jefferson supported the measure, but we can see a slight difference in the two men's engagement with the subject of slavery and emancipation during their early years.

Jefferson, in his various capacities as a private lawyer and legislator, took steps to make his antislavery position known in a public fashion, working on freedom suits and supporting measures in the Burgesses and Virginia Assembly. This was something he had been thinking about for a long time. As a young man, many years before he was in the public eye, he had copied into his Memorandum Book passages from an antislavery poem by William Shenstone. He titled it "Inscription for an African Slave" and the part of the poem describes enslaved Africans unjustly ripped from their homeland and made to toil for others in a foreign land. Thus, the slave trade as a focus of evil was very much on Jefferson's mind early on. Just as he had developed an image of himself as a progressive person in terms of science, religion, and education, so too did an antislavery position become a part of his intellectual persona. By the time he was in his early thirties, Jefferson had already staked out a public position on the question.[14]

Tucker did not enter the debate on slavery in a serious fashion until 1795, when he was forty-three years old, in a series of lectures he published as a pamphlet in 1796. Moreover, he did so in reaction to a specific event. Tucker's work, *A Dissertation on Slavery; With a Proposal for the Gradual Abolition of it in the State of Virginia*, was Tucker's *cri de coeur* upon hearing of the slave revolt in Saint-Domingue. When enslaved blacks began the process of creating a free state for themselves by killing or expelling their white masters, whites in America, slaveholders and not, took notice. This is not to say that Tucker did not feel all along the wrongness of slavery. One of his early lectures at the College of William and Mary referred to the disjuncture between Revolutionary values and the way black slaves were treated. It is to say, though, that he was not moved to use his position to take public action on the matter until a specific example of slave-instigated violence spurred him to take a stand. Tucker posed slavery as a matter involving both justice to blacks and self-preservation of whites. These two interests were in great tension in Virginia, as they were in Bermuda and all places where blacks represented a significant portion of the population. Tucker's forceful and aggressive reaction to Saint-Domingue, however, suggests that self-preservation was a bigger spur to his interest in removing the stain of slavery from Virginian society than the will to do justice to black people.[15]

Jefferson, of course, also employed a similar calculus in *Notes on the State of Virginia* and in some of his later comments about slavery in America. Fear of retribution from blacks was clearly on the minds of both men. Tucker, however, seemed in 1796 at least to be more genuinely fearful of blacks. Or, perhaps we can say, Jefferson feared the wrath of white public opinion, which would surely rise up against any serious plan of emancipation, more than he feared that the slaves of Virginia were about to rise up and kill their masters. He was, by the mid–1790s, in full nation-building mode, intent upon getting himself into position in order to shape the new nation in the fashion that he wanted. Slavery was an issue, but nowhere near as important to him as creating the foundation for a republican society.

Jefferson wrote in the *Notes* about the inevitability of blacks and whites engaging in a race war, and the events of Saint-Domingue seemed to bear that out. At first he spoke of the revolt as a part of the wave of revolution sweeping across the world. As events unfolded, however, he became more like his fellow Southern slaveholders—that is, alarmed at the prospect that the contagion of violence would spread from the West Indies into the southern part of the United States. Still, he never took serious steps to save white Virginians from the imagined impending conflagration. When he became president, he gave no support to the blacks fighting for their right to freedom in what was now Haiti, and in fact sought to deprive them of the help they needed.[16] But, as for the idea of emancipating and expatriating Virginia's slaves, he put forth no workable plan, because any effort along those lines would have been, in modern parlance, a non-starter. Even more, pursuit of that quixotic (for its time and place) goal would have jeopardized his ability to become a prime mover in American politics. After his initial flirtation with antislavery rhetoric and positions, which had brought sharp rebukes from some quarters, Jefferson engaged the issue only in ways that did not threaten his political viability.

One wonders whether Tucker's experiences growing up on an island—the vulnerability of being alone in the ocean—made the possibility of slaughter at the hands of blacks more real to him than it was to Jefferson, who could be fairly bloody-minded in a strangely abstract way. Saint-Domingue was an island, like Bermuda. Whites were cut off—literally and symbolically—from ready help from those who would want to come to their rescue should slaves decide to revolt. In contrast to Jefferson's musings about the matter, Tucker made serious efforts to persuade his fellow Virginians in the post–Saint-Domingue world that disaster was at hand and that they had to do something about slavery. In addition to recounting the history of the institution in the Old Dominion and recording views on slavery in England and among the ancients, Tucker's *Dissertation* reproduced passages from Jefferson's antislavery writings in the *Notes on the State of Virginia*. He also adopted some of the proposals that Jefferson had outlined in his emancipation plan. He then sent the pamphlet to the Virginia House of Delegates, whose members reacted in much the same way as Jefferson described the reaction to his own and others' earlier efforts to put emancipation before the people's representatives. Their response was beyond hostile, and Tucker was not at all prepared for the reception. Legislators' "blind fury"—some voted not even to allow the document to be placed on the table—caused him to retreat from active involvement in the cause of emancipation.[17]

Despite his disappointment, the following year Tucker sent three copies of the pamphlet to Jefferson, asking him to send the two additional ones to Madison and Monroe, sensing that all three men were of like mind. The author said next to nothing about the pamphlet in his cover letter, whose main purpose was to serve as an introduction for a friend who would be visiting Monticello. Tucker by then had known Jefferson for some time, and was certainly aware that the elder statesman would be flattered to see his words cited so approvingly in the work. Not long after, he sent another letter on a different topic. Jefferson responded warmly and, for the time being, disregarded the main topics of both of Tucker's missives and immediately noted his "subscription to [the] doctrines" in Tucker's pamphlet. He then went on to say, "As to the mode of emancipation, I am satisfied that must be a matter of compromise between the passions and prejudices, and the real difficulties which will each have their weight in the operation. Perhaps the first chapter of this history, which has begun in St. Domingo, and the next succeeding ones which will recount how all the whites were driven from all the other islands may prepare our minds for a peaceable accommodation between justice, policy, and necessity, and furnish an answer to the difficult question, Whither shall the coloured emigrants go? And the sooner we put some plan under way, the greater hope there is that it may be permitted to proceed to it's [*sic*] ultimate effect. But if something is not done, and soon done, we shall be the murderers of our own children."[18]

Jefferson then went on to speak in one of his nautical and weather metaphors about the winds of change sweeping the globe—as evinced by the French Revolution—that would inevitably make their way to America and presumably move the slaves to seek their freedom. He predicted, morosely, that when that time came, white Virginians would likely be left alone to deal with the matter as best they could, as if to say that white Northerners would tolerate a black state on their borders created after the massacre of other whites. Finally, he addressed the other matters that had been a main focus of Tucker's letters and returned very quickly to the business at hand.[19]

Acquiescence

The business at hand for St. George Tucker, after his ill-fated attempt to convince white Virginians to legislate slavery out of existence, was insuring that his three surviving children were on sound financial footing. Here the dilemma that Tucker and other white Virginians faced was brought into sharp relief. Here, also, is where he and Jefferson had more in common than Jefferson and Washington, for Tucker and Jefferson both had children. Washington had none of his blood; his stepchildren were part of an already wealthy family into which he had married. Washington's relationship to his property—human and otherwise—was quite different from that of men and women who had children of their bodies. In a private-property regime, the right to pass property to one's offspring, and that of offspring to inherit it, are crucial benefits of the system. These attributes of ownership are, for many, the whole point of acquiring property. Disinheriting a George Washington Jr., or a Martha Washington Jr., would have been quite a thing to have done, particularly if their mother were still alive and opposed to the idea.

Moreover, slaves, along with the land they worked, represented the basis of wealth for families like the Tuckers and the Jeffersons. Even as he wrote and tried to promote his plan for emancipation, Tucker was selling slaves in order to increase the material wealth of his children. In 1796, he attempted to sell a group of slaves whom he had hired out before. He complained bitterly that the offered prices were much lower than he expected. His agent explained to Tucker that the buyers looked askance at purchasing enslaved people who had been hired out, because often they were too used to having a measure of freedom. Tucker, an Anglo-American lawyer just as Jefferson had been, had a full understanding of the central role that property played in the lives of their society. Divesting himself and his children of a form of property, no matter how odious, was not an easy thing to do. To put the matter charitably, Tucker seems to have been more acutely aware of, and practical about, his family's financial affairs than Jefferson. He came to believe early on that the old-style plantation system that he had known in Bermuda and that had existed in Virginia would no longer be tenable in the emerging commercial and political world. Property was the key to maintaining wealth and status; and, as Tucker saw the Virginia gentry losing its power and position after the American Revolution, he grew ever more anxious about his children's future. He sought ways to hold on to whatever advantages his kind could expect to have in such a frightening (to him) new world—even if that meant a retrenchment from his position on slavery.[20]

Tucker brought his newfound conservatism on slavery to the bench. In 1806, as a judge on the Court of Appeals, he wrote an opinion in the case of *Hudgins v. Wright,* rejecting the natural-law formulations that had formed the basis of the opinion of his law teacher George Wythe in favoring the freedom of a Native American family. In turning aside Wythe's argument, he was determined not to use the free-and-equal clause of the Virginia constitution (which had figured so prominently in his *Dissertation* on slavery) to strike a blow on behalf of freedom. The clause, he said, did not "overturn the rights of property." During the same era, Jefferson, from his platform as president, had an opportunity to try to prevent the spread of slavery into newly purchased Louisiana. He did not do so, once again letting his hopes for building a nation from sea to shining sea take precedence over engaging with any degree of energy the question of slavery.[21]

From their respective positions, Tucker and Jefferson settled into a period of quiescence on the subject of slavery. They went about their business as public servants and family men, attending to the financial interests of their families, which necessarily included relying on the slave system. Both men bought, sold, and rented slaves as circumstances obliged them. And each of them voiced their abhorrence of the mistreatment of slaves. However, for periods of time, both tolerated overseers who brutalized the slaves on their plantation if they got results that favored the bottom line of their business operations. They also passed slaves among members of their family. For example, when Tucker's daughter married, he gave her slaves to take to her home in Staunton, Virginia, just as Jefferson had done when his daughters married.[22]

There was one major difference: Tucker personally taught several of his slaves to read, and there is no evidence Jefferson ever did. The half-brothers of Jefferson's wife, Martha—Robert, James, and Peter Hemings—knew how to read and write, as did a number of other enslaved people with whom Jefferson had close contact at Monticello. But there is no indication that Jefferson taught them. The Hemings brothers probably learned to read before they came to Monticello. Tucker taught his slaves to read to help him manage his affairs. He was also very keen to facilitate the spread of evangelical Christianity, which increasingly became a part of his life as he grew older. In fact, religion was an extremely important force helping Tucker and his family to accommodate themselves to slavery. Of course, religion played no part in Jefferson's consideration of this issue at all.[23]

Within in two years of one another, in 1812 and 1814, both men experienced somewhat parallel moments of reckoning, and it thus became clear they had strayed far from their early antislavery philosophies. Tucker had derided his emancipation plan as "utopian" as early as 1803. He remarried after his first wife's death and acquired a stepson, Charles Carter. In 1812 Charles decided he wanted to free the slaves he would inherit from his mother and told her of his plan. When Tucker discovered this, he voiced strong opposition. The young man would not relent, however, and approached his mother again about drawing up documents in which he would relinquish his right to inherit the slaves and free them upon his mother's death. Tucker put his objections in writing, noting the practical problem of emancipating the slaves upon the death of the boy's mother. Under those terms, the slaves would have every incentive to kill her to gain their freedom. But he went further—to say that the slaves should NOT be freed, for their own good. In his eyes, they were children who could not take care of themselves. Keeping them in slavery was a way to protect them, a sentiment 180 degrees from what he said about the institution in the 1790s. By the time of his conflict with his stepson, Tucker viewed slavery as an affirmative good for the people enslaved.[24]

Jefferson's well-known moment of reckoning came two years later, when the young Virginian Edward Coles wrote to tell him of his plan to move to Illinois and free his slaves once there. Coles would eventually make the same journey from supporter of blacks' rights to emancipation to disillusionment, but he met Jefferson at the high point of his arc. Like Tucker and his stepson, Jefferson was similarly opposed to the younger man's plan to free slaves, and he tried unsuccessfully to dissuade Coles from taking this principled personal stance on the question of abolition. Both members of the Revolutionary generation faltered when confronted by the convictions of the younger men whom they had inspired. Jefferson, when presented with the end products of that admiration, held out to Coles a "things will work their way out in time" formulation, which offered no real solution to the problem. For his part, Tucker seemed at that moment contented with the idea that slavery might continue indefinitely. Or at least he was not willing, as Jefferson still was, to bring up his old antislavery pronouncements, even if only to cast them aside with the prediction that something might turn up at some future date. Both Tucker and Jefferson had made their peace with the institution.[25]

Alarm and Despair

Yet, Jefferson and Tucker got scared again. The Missouri Crisis of 1819–21 horrified them both in much the same way that events in Saint-Domingue in the 1790s had loomed for them as a threat to whites of the slaveholding South. Jefferson, who had long since left the public stage, wrote some quite stirring language about "firebells in the night" and having a "wolf by the ear" in the midst of his anguish at the prospect of disunion over the sectional dispute. He was *truly* in agony. Jefferson, the proponent of states' rights, had run headlong into Jefferson, the nation-builder. One of his deepest hopes for the United States was that the country would exist apart from the intrigues and the wars that followed from intrigues that had plagued the European continent since time immemorial. As he contemplated the possible separation of the nation, he could not have failed to note that such a split would inevitably invite European meddling in American affairs and put the continent back where it was before the formation of the union. One could only imagine Jefferson's reaction to the Confederacy's hope for an alliance with England against the Union. Everything he had ever hoped for in the formation of a new nation, a new peaceful republic, would be gone. All would be wasted.

Even in the face of the Missouri Crisis, Jefferson was not moved to initiate discussion on the subject of slavery. We know of his thoughts only because people wrote to *him* to ask for them. In his private correspondence, he revisited his plans for emancipation and repatriation to Africa with talk of ways to compensate slave owners for the loss of their property. Jefferson's plan was so wildly improbable that one wonders whether he really believed it could ever happen, or whether he was trying to convince himself that it actually could not—by writing it all down and showing it to someone. He fixed out a recipe for failure that signaled what had been clear all along: he had absolutely no idea what to do about slavery because there *was* nothing that reasonably could be done but what was eventually done—and that was something he could never have let himself contemplate.[26]

The Missouri Crisis also galvanized Tucker and took him back to first principles, or his first enunciation of his principles, his *Dissertation on Slavery*. Once again, the prospect of violent upheaval, this of another sort, spurred him to think about emancipation when the subject had been closed for him for many years. He wrote a *Supplement* to his older work that reiterated his reasons for calling for emancipation and positing that blacks, whom he did not believe could live with whites after emancipation, should go west and settle in their own land and make their home. Unlike Jefferson, Tucker had never planned for the forced removal of blacks. Instead, white Virginians were supposed to mistreat blacks so badly that they would simply leave; they would be given no civil rights, nor the right to own property or bear arms. Tucker apparently never contemplated, as Jefferson must have done, how such an arrangement would degrade the republican experiment. Republican citizens would be required actively to oppress ostensibly "free" people. This time, though, Tucker did not attempt to rouse public support for his plan. He did not publish the *Supplement,* and seems to have worked on it in secret, as if he needed, in his own personal alarm and despair, to be able to tell at least himself that there was some other recourse besides violent struggle. Tucker was wrong, but neither he nor Jefferson would live long enough to find that out.[27]

Notes

1. On Madison's involvement with the American Colonization Society, his belief in the inferiority of blacks, and the need to find some place of "asylum" for emancipated slaves, see Ralph Ketchum, *James Madison: A Biography* (Charlottesville, VA, 1990), 625–28.

2. "The Act for the Gradual Abolition of Slavery Act of March 1, 1780" was revolutionary for its time, but more modest than many abolitionists hoped for. For a discussion of the history and effect of the Act see, Gary B. Nash, *Forging Freedom: The Formation of Philadelphia's Black Community,* 1720–1840 (Cambridge, 1980), 60–65, 91–94.

3. See, generally, Philip D. Morgan, "'To Get Quit of Negroes': George Washington and Slavery," *Journal of American Studies* 39 (December 2005): 403–29.

4. Frankie Hutton, "Economic Considerations in the American Colonization Society's Early Effort to Emigrate Free Blacks to Liberia," *Journal of Negro History* 68 (Autumn 1963): 378; Willis D. Boyd, "The American Colonization Society and the

Slave Recaptives of 1860–1861: An Early Example of United States-African Relations," *Journal of Negro History* 47 (April 1962): 109.

5. Benjamin Banneker to Thomas Jefferson [hereafter, TJ], August 19, 1791, in *The Papers of Thomas Jefferson,* ed. Julian P. Boyd et al., 36 vols. to date (Princeton, NJ, 1950–), 22:49; Annette Gordon-Reed, "Engaging Jefferson: Blacks and the Founding Father," *William and Mary Quarterly,* 3rd ser., 58 (January 2000): 171–82.

6. Annette Gordon-Reed, *The Hemingses of Monticello: An American Family* (New York, 2009), 455–63.

7. Ibid., 463.

8. Davison M. Douglas, "Foreword: The Legacy of St. George Tucker," in "Institute of Bill of Rights Law Symposium: St. George Tucker and His Influence on American Law," special issue, *William & Mary Law Review* 47 (February 2006): 1111–12.

9. Susan Kern, "The Material World of the Jeffersons at Shadwell," *History.com,* http://www.history/cooperative.org/journals/wm/62.2/kern.html (accessed April 2005).

10. Philip Hamilton, *The Making and Unmaking of a Revolutionary Family: The Tuckers of Virginia, 1752–1830* (Charlottesville, VA, 2003), 11, 25–28. Hamilton's book, along with his previous article, "Revolutionary Principles and Family Loyalties: Slavery's Transformation in the St. George Tucker Household of Early National Virginia" (*William and Mary Quarterly,* 3rd ser., 55 [October 1998]: 536–37), stand as necessary correctives to the picture of Tucker as a determined abolitionist.

11. See "George Wythe, June 11, 1806, Last Will and Testament with Codicil," item no. 27971, Library of Congress, Thomas Jefferson Papers, Series 1: General Correspondence, 1651–1827, http://memory.loc.gov/cgi-bin/query/P?mtj:1:./temp/~ammem_RZIy:::; see also Julian Boyd, "The Murder of George Wythe," *William and Mary Quarterly,* 3rd ser., 12 (October 1955): 513. Jefferson considered George Wythe his "second father" who was also his "ancient master, my earliest and best friend" (TJ to John Sanderson, August 31, 1820, item nos. 38932–34, Library of Congress, Thomas Jefferson Papers, Series 1: General Correspondence, 1651–1827; and TJ to William Duval, June 14, 1806, item no. 27898, ibid.; both at http://memory.loc.gov/ammem/collections/jefferson_papers/mtjser1.html). For Lord Dunmore's Proclamation of November 14, 1775, see Dixon's *Virginia Gazette,* November 25, 1775. See, generally, Woody Holton, *Forced Founders: Indians, Debtors, Slaves, and the Making of the American Revolution in Virginia* (Chapel Hill, NC, 1999). On the enslaved people who escaped from Jefferson's plantations and his reaction to their departure, see Catherine Pybus, "Jefferson's Faulty Math: The Question of Slave Defections in the American Revolution," *William and Mary Quarterly,* 3rd ser., 62 (April 2005): 243–64.

12. Hamilton, *The Making and Unmaking of a Revolutionary Family,* 44–45.

13. Ibid., 132–35.

14. *Jefferson's Memorandum Books: Accounts, with Legal Records and Miscellany, 1767–1826,* ed. James A. Bear and Lucia C. Stanton, 2 vols. (Princeton, NJ, 1997).

Much has been written about TJ's early involvement in antislavery efforts: see, e.g., William Cohen, "Thomas Jefferson and the Problem of Slavery," *Journal of American History* 56 (December 1969), 506, outlining TJ's responses to slavery in Virginia and the nation; Annette Gordon-Reed, "Logic and Experience: Thomas Jefferson's Life in the Law," in *Slavery and the American South,* ed. Winthrop Jordan (Oxford, 2003); and Gordon-Reed, *The Hemingses of Monticello,* 347.

15. St. George Tucker, *A Dissertation on Slavery: With a Proposal for the Gradual Abolition of it, in the State of Virginia* (Philadelphia, 1796).

16. Tim Matthewson, "Jefferson and Haiti," *Journal of Southern History* 61 (May 1995): 209–48.

17. For a discussion of reaction to Tucker's plan, see Robert M. Colley, *Slavery in Jeffersonian Virginia,* 2nd ed. (Urbana, IL, 1973), 135; and Hamilton, "Revolutionary Principles and Family Loyalties," 534–35.

18. St. George Tucker to TJ, August 2, 1797, and TJ to St. George Tucker, August 28, 1797, in Boyd et al., eds., *Papers of Thomas Jefferson,* 29:488–89.

19. TJ to St. George Tucker, August 28, 1797, ibid., 29:519.

20. See Hamilton, "Revolutionary Principles and Family Loyalties," 537–38.

21. *Hudgins v. Wright,* 1 Hen. & M. (Va.) 134 (1806). For a discussion of Jefferson and the expansion of slavery in Louisiana, see Peter S. Onuf, *Jefferson's Empire: The Language of American Nationhood* (Charlottesville, VA, 2000).

22. Hamilton, "Revolutionary Principles and Family Loyalties," 545–48.

23. Gordon-Reed, *The Hemingses of Monticello,* 112; Hamilton, *The Making and Unmaking of a Revolutionary Family,* 151–52, 155.

24. Hamilton, *The Making and Unmaking of a Revolutionary Family,* 151–55.

25. TJ to Edward Coles, August 2, 1814, in Thomas Jefferson, *Writings,* ed. Merrill Peterson (New York, 1984), 1345 [hereafter, Peterson, ed., *Thomas Jefferson Writings*].

26. TJ to John Holmes, April 22, 1820, in Peterson, ed., *Thomas Jefferson Writings,* 1433–35; TJ to Jared Sparks, February 4, 1824, in *The Writings of Thomas Jefferson,* ed. Andrew Lipscomb and Albert Ellery Bergh, 20 vols. (Washington, DC, 1903–4), 16:8–14. For a detailed discussion of TJ's post–Missouri Crisis plan for emancipation, see Peter S. Onuf, "'Every Generation in an Independent Nation': Colonization, Miscegenation, and the Fate of Jefferson's Children," in *The Mind of Thomas Jefferson* (Charlottesville, VA, 2007), 213–35.

27. Hamilton, "Revolutionary Principles and Family Loyalties," 555–56.

Domesticating the Captive Nation

Thomas Jefferson and the Problem of Slavery

Peter S. Onuf

In 1782 Thomas Jefferson outlined a bold plan for the eradication of slavery that would vindicate the principles of the American Revolution and help secure its ultimate success. As he reported in his *Notes on the State of Virginia,* Jefferson had prepared an emancipation scheme for consideration as part of the revisal of Virginia's laws that provided that slave children "continue with their parents to a certain age, then be brought up, at the public expence, to tillage, arts or sciences, according to their geniusses, till the females should be eighteen, and the males twenty-one years of age, when they should be colonized to such place as the circumstances of the time should render most proper." Having sent them to their new home "with arms, implements of houshold and of the handicraft arts, feeds, pairs of the useful domestic animals, &c.," Virginia would then "declare them a free and independant people, and extend to them our alliance and protection, till they shall have acquired strength." Recognizing that the loss of their labor would be devastating to the Commonwealth's economy, Jefferson proposed that vessels be sent "to other parts of the world for an equal number of white inhabitants; to induce whom to migrate hither, proper encouragements were to be proposed."[1]

The revisers prudently concluded that Jefferson's emancipation and expatriation scheme would be decisively rejected, and never submitted it to the legislature. Jefferson knew that his fellow Virginians were not yet prepared to grapple with the slavery issue, but he believed they would ultimately come to recognize the compelling logic of a plan that provided for the separation of the two races, thus preempting the "convulsions which will probably never end but in the extermination of the one or the other race," while mitigating damage to the plantation economy by gradually substituting white for black labor.[2] "Change" was "already perceptible" to Jefferson when he drafted his *Notes:* "The spirit of the master is abating, that of the slave rising from the dust, his condition mollifying, the way I hope preparing, under the auspices of heaven, for a total emancipation."[3] It would become chillingly clear to white Virginians that the only alternative to voluntary emancipation was war, "a revolution of the wheel of fortune" that might lead to the violent overthrow of the ruling race. In a world at war, rebellious blacks could forge alliances with America's enemies (just as rebellious colonists had forged alliances with Britain's enemies). It would be much better to liberate the captive nation "and extend to them *our* alliance and protection."

Jefferson was a poor prophet. By the end of his life, the central position of slavery in Southern society and in the national economy was clearly established; with the end of the Napoleonic wars, rebellious slaves could no longer hope to exploit geopolitical instability in the Atlantic world. Jefferson had expected the American Revolution to initiate a "revolution in public opinion" that would lead to emancipation, but now the material interests of slaveholders and the diminishing risk of servile insurrection pointed in the other direction. The prospect for progressive change was no longer "perceptible" and "is not to be expected in a day, or perhaps in an age," he told James Heaton in 1826. "But time, which outlives all things, will outlive this evil also." Jefferson remained committed to his vision of emancipation and expatriation, but he acknowledged its irrelevance. "My sentiments," as published in the *Notes,* "have been forty years before the public." There was no need to repeat them yet once again, for "had I repeated them forty times, they would only have become the more stale and threadbare."[4]

The idea that an aged Jefferson had outlived his time is one that he himself cultivated. "I have overlived the generation with which mutual labors & perils begat mutual confidence and influence," he told Edward Coles in 1814: it was up to the younger generation to carry on the struggle against slavery.[5] But this does not mean that Jefferson ever retreated from or significantly modified his prescriptions, however "stale and threadbare" they might seem to Coles and others who sought Jefferson's support for their own antislavery initiatives, or to modern historians. This essay argues that Jefferson's lifelong commitment to his radical, comprehensive solution to the slavery problem led him to oppose incremental palliatives—for instance, Coles's removal to Illinois and the manumission of his own slaves—that would only strengthen the institution by diminishing the urgency of collective action and postponing, if not subverting, the hoped-for "revolution in public opinion."[6]

It is clear in retrospect that Jefferson's "radical" prescriptions would have profoundly conservative implications for prosperous plantation societies in an increasingly stable and peaceful world: waiting for a transformation of sentiment *within* Virginia effectively meant doing nothing. Meanwhile, the Jeffersonian commitment to republican self-government called into question the good faith of antislavery agitators elsewhere, who threatened to impose solutions on unwilling Virginians jealous of their liberties. And Jefferson's own reformist impulses, reflected both in his pre-Revolutionary legal practice and, most conspicuously, in his early advocacy of private manumissions, were no longer directed *against* the institution of slavery itself after he embraced colonization, but were instead devoted to ameliorating the condition of slaves *within* the institution. In other words, Jefferson's commitment to emancipation and a thoroughgoing "revolution" in race relations in Virginia superseded earlier, much more modest initiatives that came to seem dangerously misguided. Jefferson thus identified himself as the author of a proposed statute that would have liberalized manumissions *before* the Revolution in his letter to Coles, but he did not claim credit for the 1782 Act that it anticipated. Significantly, he told Coles that the failed proposal, introduced by Richard Bland, provided "for certain moderate extensions of the protection of the laws to these people," *not* for manumissions that would have increased the number of free blacks, "pests in society by their idleness, and the depredations to which this leads them."[7]

Jefferson's recollections of his early antislavery initiatives were inevitably colored by his later commitment to emancipation and expatriation. Jefferson did not set himself up as a precocious antislavery crusader, and therefore as a model for Coles, but instead lectured his young neighbor on the need for patience. When Bland offered his proposal, Jefferson recalled, "few minds" then "doubted" that slaves "were as legitimate subjects of property as their horses and cattle." As a result, Bland was "denounced as an enemy of his country," and this is precisely what Jefferson suggested Coles would be if he should abandon his slave "property, and your country with it."[8] David Konig persuasively argues that the young Jefferson's "efforts to ameliorate the conditions of enslaved Virginians, to recognize their entitlement to being considered persons before the law, and even to liberate others must be recognized, if only because as ideals and as actions they represented the 'best' efforts of Virginians taking public action against slavery."[9] The ameliorative impulses did not disappear, but were present after 1776 both in his colonization scheme and, more consequentially, in his efforts to improve slaves' material circumstances and provide for their "happiness."[10] Jefferson might still feel in 1820 that slavery was an institutionalized state of war: "we have the wolf by the ear, and we can neither hold him, nor safely let him go. Justice is in one scale, and self-preservation in the other."[11] But it was also obviously true that the burden and threat were diminishing over time, *not,* as Jefferson's image suggested, growing more onerous. Because the "wolf" was being domesticated, emancipation was no longer so urgent. Indeed, it only seemed so in the midst of the Missouri Crisis, when the increasing likelihood of disunion threatened the kind of geopolitical instability that had made servile insurrections seem so dangerous.

Domestication

Emancipation and expatriation remained compelling for Jefferson as long as he imagined masters and slaves to be in a state of war. He never renounced this understanding of slavery, or of the injustice perpetrated against the enslaved. Yet just as the cessation of war in the wider world made slave revolts less likely, and booming markets for slave-grown staples made slavery more profitable, planters like Jefferson came to terms with the institution. Paradoxically, the idea that slaves collectively constituted a hostile captive nation encouraged masters to make exceptions for the loyal and loving slaves in their own "families." As the Floridian Richard Keith Call made clear on the eve of the Civil War, Jefferson was by no means unusual in embracing this profoundly incoherent conception of slavery. "Though divided into families, and domesticated with white families," Call wrote, the slaves of the South constituted "a distinct nation of near 4,000,000 of people, and constitute a part of the American people."[12]

Call's use of the term "nation" instead of "race" evokes Jefferson's geopolitical conception of slavery, betraying lingering fears of servile insurrection. But for Call, as for Jefferson in his later years, the insurrectionary threat was mitigated, if not altogether eliminated, by the division of the enslaved "nation" into families and their simultaneous incorporation into white families. Through this double domestication, enslaved blacks' family loyalties subverted their racial solidarity—or black "national" identity—even while, through their white families, they became "part of the American people." This was a complete reversal and negation of Jefferson's original understanding of slavery: the latent enmity of the captive nation, he had famously predicted, would erupt into "convulsions" and a genocidal race war whenever the balance of power, locally or in the larger world, permitted. Proceeding from Jeffersonian premises about racial (national) difference, antebellum Southerners reached the opposite conclusion: slavery not only sustained interracial peace, but underwrote the prosperity and power of their section and the nation. Slavery "has become a power of itself, inherent, massive and moving," according to a writer in the *Southern Quarterly Review*. "Full of life, vigour, and pliability," it is "capable of self-creating power and preservation."[13] Under the aegis of domestication, "nation" was transmuted into "race," enmity into complementarity, war into peace. For his heirs, Jefferson's principled opposition to slavery pointed first toward accommodation with the institution and ultimately toward proslavery, its principled defense. Domestication was the pivot.

Jefferson was obsessed with domesticity. His famous ambivalence about public service, Jan Lewis demonstrates, led him imaginatively to construct an idealized private, domestic sphere as the site and source of morality and contentment.[14] The distinction between private and public was psychologically compelling to Jefferson because it was so often transgressed, or, perhaps more accurately, because there was no natural, self-evident boundary between "spheres" of life that had been seamlessly integrated under the "old regime."[15] For Jefferson, domesticity was the sacred domain of the self, fulfilled in the bosom of family: privacy and mastery were co-constitutive. The crucial point here is that domesticity for Jefferson was a protean and inclusive construction—embracing everything and everyone, including his slaves, that he surveyed from his mountaintop—which at the same time valorized an absolute, clearly marked boundary between his world and the rest of the world.

If Jefferson's sense of self was precociously "modern," with its emphasis on privacy, self-control, the cultivation of sensibility, and family values, the circumstances of plantation society could give it an archaic, aristocratic coloration. Jefferson's bitter animosity toward aristocracy—and his projection of "aristocratic" motives onto his opponents—was undoubtedly a case of protesting too much, reflecting his compelling need to define himself and his family against the privileged, politically powerful, and prosperous families who traditionally ruled Virginia. Hypersensitive about his status, Jefferson rarely let his guard down, though he did portray himself as a "patriarch" in a playful letter to Angelica Schuyler Church (sister-in-law of Jefferson's "aristocratic" nemesis, Alexander Hamilton) on the eve of his retirement as George Washington's secretary of state in 1793. When he returned to his beloved Monticello, he would "be liberated from the hated occupations of politics," Jefferson told Church, and thereafter "remain in the bosom of my family, my farm, and my books." "In due process of time," when his second daughter, Maria, was as well-married as his first, Martha, and both were situated nearby, "I shall imagine myself as blessed as the most blessed of the patriarchs." Until then, "I have my house to build, my fields to farm, and to watch for the happiness of those who labor for mine."[16] Jefferson's patriarchal fantasy included not only his extended white family but his slaves. He even imagined—notwithstanding his dire warning in his *Notes* that vengeful blacks would never forget "the injuries they have sustained"—that he could make his slaves "happy." Blacks could never be "incorporate[d] into the state" as freed people, but they could be made happy—lulled into a state of benign forgetfulness?—under the ministrations of benevolent masters.[17]

Mastery over the domestic sphere, however modest its extent, was the prerogative of all household heads. Jefferson's democratic theory was predicated on a "gradation of authorities," "dividing and subdividing these republics from the great national one down through all its subordinations, until it ends in the administration of every man's farm by himself; by placing under every one what his own eye may superintend, that all will be done for the best."[18] The foundational principle of equality guaranteed the "sovereignty" of constituents at each ascending level of authority, protecting citizen freeholders from each other as well as from encroachments on their rights from higher levels. Jefferson thus did not envision anything like a "general will" of an undifferentiated "people." To the contrary, his federal theory authorized the proliferation of rights claims within and among different levels of government, an elaborate set of boundaries that secured the mastery of Jefferson and other "blessed patriarchs" over their domestic domains. "The true foundation of republican government," Jefferson concluded, "is the equal right of every citizen, in his person and property, and in their management." Paradoxically, the strength of government was predicated on strict limitations on authority enforced by vigilant citizens. "Making every citizen an acting member of the government" would reinforce his identification with the regime, attaching "him by his strongest feelings to the independence of his country, and its republican constitution."[19] In other words, the devolution of authority would lead to its reconstitution; the separation of private and public that the libertarian emphasis on rights promoted would be the threshold for a more perfect union that would transcend that separation, conflating "home" and "nation" and domesticating power.

The protean concept of domesticity defined value and drew boundaries. Jefferson was legendarily sensitive about the transgression of boundaries by outsiders and the threats they posed to states' rights and slaveholders' mastery. However unjust their enslavement, Jefferson's slaves were part of his household and therefore subject to his paternal discipline. Interference in that relationship compounded the original sin of slavery, as Jefferson wrote in his draft of the Declaration of Independence: George III stirred up "domestic insurrection among us," encouraging slaves "to purchase that liberty of which he has deprived them, by murdering the people on whom he also obtruded them: thus paying off former crimes committed against the LIBERTIES of one people, with crimes which he urges them to commit against the LIVES of another."[20] Decades later, Jefferson leveled the same charge against "restrictionists" who sought to ban the spread of slavery into the new state of Missouri and thus concentrate a growing and therefore increasingly dangerous slave population in the old slave states. "Are our slaves to be presented with freedom and a dagger?" Jefferson asked John Adams. "For if Congress has the power to regulate the conditions of the inhabitants of the States, within the States, it will be but another exercise of that power, to declare that all shall be free."[21] Interference in the domestic affairs of the slave states was an incitement to "murder," an assault on slave owners that would diminish rather than advance slaves' prospects for freedom. Only when slave owners were secure against outside threats to their domestic tranquility—and to their property rights—would they institute measures that would bring an end to the institution. The deprivation of slaves' "liberties" was a terrible injustice, but letting go of the wolf's ear—unleashing the dogs of war—would be a still greater crime, for it would preempt the moral renovation of Jefferson's cherished Commonwealth. Emancipation must begin at home.

The Commonwealth was a great household, a family of families, absolutely independent of other Commonwealths. Paradoxically, the separation of private and public spheres, household and state, made their analogical conflation irresistible for liberal republicans who sought to demolish the hierarchical order of the old regime. Domesticity provided the high moral ground for resisting encroachments by "foreigners," shielding both familial and civic affairs from any outside interference. This freedom from interference, Jefferson lectured Republican John Holmes of the Maine District of Massachusetts, was the foundational premise of self-government, "the exclusive right of every State, which nothing in the [federal] constitution has taken from them and given to the General Government." It was no business of any state or any combination of states to challenge the peculiar civic arrangements of any other state, including the enslavement of a part of the population. "Could Congress, for example, say that the non-freemen of Connecticut shall be freemen, or that they shall not emigrate into any other State?"[22]

As Jefferson in his retirement years became increasingly anxious about the encroaching power of the federal government, and particularly the judiciary, he routinely invoked the distinction between "domestic" (the sacred and inviolable sphere of state authority) and "federal" ("whatever concerns foreigners, or the citizens of other States").[23] His tendency was to think of federal authority as delegated (and therefore remote from its original source, in the "people" of the respective states) and strictly limited, particularly as external threats to the union as a whole seemed to diminish. As a result, "federal" and "foreign" converged: the federal government exercised jurisdiction over foreign affairs and its jurisdiction was foreign.[24]

The question of jurisdiction was particularly important to Jefferson when he broached emancipation. The only authority that could legitimately interfere in this peculiarly domestic institution was that of the state government. The problem was that only the nation as a whole had sufficient resources to compensate the state's slave owners for their property rights in slaves—perhaps, as he estimated in an extraordinary letter to Jared Sparks in 1824, a staggering $900,000,000. But Jefferson suggested an ingenious solution that would ease economic disruption, diminish costs, and preempt the interference in Virginia's domestic affairs that a massive, federally financed emancipation scheme seemed to entail. Recurring to the plan he offered in his *Notes,* Jefferson urged that newborn children be purchased by the state, "leaving them, on due compensation, with their mothers, until their services are worth their maintenance, and then putting them to industrious occupations, until a proper age for deportation." Instead of costing $200, the average value of all slaves at the time, "the estimated value of the new-born infant is so low, (say twelve dollars and fifty cents,) that it would probably be yielded by the owner gratis." The "deportation" and colonization of freedpeople would still entail a formidable financial burden (a third of Jefferson's original estimate), but it would be amortized over a quarter-century (as slave children reached maturity) and could be paid for from the sale of public lands—lands that had been ceded by Virginia and other landed states, "on no consideration, for the most part, but that of the general good of the whole." With the existing land office generating sufficient income, the federal government could not invoke emancipation as a pretext for aggrandizing its power, a leading concern of Jefferson and other "Old Republicans." Instead, the retrocession of land-sales revenue would simply return what was originally Virginia's, thus achieving an object of the highest importance not only "to the slave States" but to the union as a whole. In effect, Virginian benevolence would underwrite the great philanthropic project of emancipation.[25]

The crucial point for Jefferson was that emancipation proceed from *within* the domestic sphere and that property rights—the foundation of household independence—be fully secured. Under such a scheme, enlightened slave owners could afford to act on their better impulses, voluntarily "yielding" their property interests in young slaves. After all, as Jefferson insisted to Holmes, "the cession of that kind of property, for so it is misnamed, is a bagatelle which would not cost me a second thought, if, in that way, a general emancipation and expatriation could be effected."[26] Jefferson would even acknowledge that his property in slaves was no property at all—as long as no outsider challenged his rights and threatened to interfere in his domestic affairs. The connection between domesticity (the domain of self) and familial governance, and property (the sacred and legally enforced boundary between "meum and teum," "mine and yours"), was foundational for Jefferson. Yet if his rights as a "patriarch" were absolute with respect to other patriarchs, they entailed fundamental moral obligations to his dependents, family members white and black, and even, in his stewardship of the land, to unborn generations. The Jeffersonian patriarch was no despot at home, but his neighbors must act as if he were one in their respect for the inviolability of his domestic domain.[27]

Geopolitics

Jefferson's commitment to emancipation was thus qualified by his solicitude for the domestic security and property rights of slave owners. When the nation as a whole was threatened by a foreign power, for instance, he was less concerned about states' rights, and his awareness of the urgency of emancipation increased. The alliance between British invaders and rebellious slaves during the Revolution and yet again in the War of 1812 demanded a united response to a common danger. In the 1790s, instability in the Caribbean, culminating in the Haitian Revolution, threatened to unleash the insurrectionary contagion on the mainland, generating a new wave of interest in emancipation in Virginia. "From the present state of things in Europe & America," Jefferson wrote St. George Tucker in 1797, "the day which begins our combustion must be near at hand; and only a single spark is wanting to make that day to-morrow." In proposing an emancipation scheme that would have left former slaves in place, but as second-class citizens with minimal rights, Tucker had rejected Jefferson's colonization plan. But Jefferson recognized the urgency of addressing the slavery problem: "If something is not done, & soon done, we shall be the murderers of our own children."[28]

The unstable and unpredictable geopolitical situation resulting from the undeclared naval war with France (the "Quasi-War") made servile revolts seem more likely, and more ominous in their implications. Gabriel's abortive rebellion in 1800 precipitated a swift and vicious response by embattled slave owners fearful of assaults on multiple fronts.[29] When Jefferson became president in 1801, he took the first (and only) practical steps to implement his colonization scheme, exploring with the British government the possibility of deporting rebels to Sierra Leone as he discussed strategic options with Governor James Monroe and the Virginia legislature. The urgency of Jefferson's commitment to emancipation depended on the likelihood of war: geopolitical instability provided a dangerous opening to domestic insurgents. Jefferson also understood that self-preservation demanded that Virginia take all necessary measures to suppress insurgencies, including, of course, the execution of leading rebels. The challenge was to calculate an appropriate response, recognizing that the rebels were not "common male-factors" guilty of "ordinary crimes." If they were guilty of "conspiracy, in-surgency, treason, [or] rebellion," American patriots had merited the same charges in their revolutionary resistance to British tyranny in 1776.[30]

William Merkel suggests that Jefferson sought to strike a prudent bal-ance in responding to Gabriel's Rebellion that would sustain the rule of law and render justice to the captive nation.[31] Yet if deportation was clearly a humane alternative to execution—and might even, if it led to widespread colonization, produce the just outcome Jefferson had long advocated—it was at the same time a punitive sanction that was routinely deployed against recalcitrant slaves. Death and deportation—justice and punishment—were inextricably linked in moments of crisis, and Jefferson's search for a "re-ceptacle" for banished blacks suggests his own difficulty in sustaining the distinction between them. What is clear, however, is that for Jefferson a just solution to the slavery problem entailed the complete erasure of the black presence from the American landscape. Furthermore, the blacks' new home, or "receptacle," must be located at a safe distance from the United States: not on its frontiers, where it might strengthen America's counter-revolutionary imperial neighbors, nor anywhere else in the world where the blacks might present a security threat. If the Sierra Leone project failed, Jef-ferson told Monroe, "we should prefer placing them with whatever power is least likely to become an enemy, and to use the knowledge of these exiles in predatory expeditions against us."[32] Perhaps the most practicable out-come would be to deport slaves to "the island of St. Domingo, where the blacks are established into a sovereignty de facto"—but not, significantly, de jure—"& have organized themselves under regular laws & government." Jefferson jettisoned the notion that the United States would establish a benign protectorate over the new black nation: he had no illusions about the vengefulness of the deportees. But as long as the "receptacle" was iso-lated and unrecognized—and therefore incapable of forming alliances with America's enemies—the resulting imbalance of power guaranteed Ameri-can security. "The possibility that these exiles might stimulate & conduct vindicative or predatory descents on our coasts, & facilitate concert with their brethren remaining here," he reassured Monroe, "looks to a state of things between that island & us not probable on a contemplation of our relative strength, and of the disproportion daily growing." Any resulting risks were "overweighed by the humanity" of finding a home for the black exiles and "the advantages of disembarrassing ourselves of such dangerous characters."[33]

Jefferson's opposition to slavery, forged in the Revolution and focused on colonization, was inextricably linked with war. Expatriation would eliminate the possibility of servile insurrection, strengthen the union, and discourage future assaults by foreign powers. As a preemptive military policy, Jefferson's emancipation scheme did not betray the benevolent impulses characteristic of the early antislavery movement. Intent on preserving the new nation from security threats at home and abroad, Jefferson's goal was to do justice to the captive nation, *not* to relieve the suffering of particular slaves. (His own slaves were happy enough, or could be made so.) Indeed, colonization was a brutally unsentimental project that would remove young African Virginians from the only homeland they knew and destroy their families; in a social and familial sense, deportation was a kind of death—customarily the most severe punishment, short of death, for a recalcitrant slave. "The separation of infants from their mothers," Jefferson acknowledged to Sparks, "would produce some scruples of humanity," but it was only by such a radical generational break that the institution could be uprooted, to the benefit of blacks as well as whites. To take these "scruples" too seriously "would be straining at a gnat, and swallowing a camel": the ultimate achievement of black nationhood far outweighed any imaginable damage to particular slaves, even mothers.[34]

Jefferson's prescriptions for enslaved blacks represented the utter negation of his idealized conception of the family as the source and site of moral value in the white republic. For expatriated blacks, their nation—"declared free and independant" for them by their former masters—came first, and the formation of new families would follow. Jefferson periodically wondered if blacks, given the nature of their "faculties of reason and imagination," would be willing to sacrifice the security, welfare—and even "happiness"— they enjoyed under slavery for the elusive and uncertain goal of national independence.[35] Manumissions in Virginia, he told Edward Bancroft in 1789, suggest that "to give liberty to or rather abandon persons whose habits have been formed in slavery is like abandoning children."[36] Bancroft reminded Jefferson of an earlier conversation, in which the Virginian had reported a failed experiment to make slaves into wage laborers. "After a tryal of some time it was found that Slavery had rendered them incapable of Self Government," Bancroft recalled Jefferson saying, that, with "no regard for futurity," the former slaves could not be induced to work, even to feed and clothe themselves. "The most sensible of them desired to be returned to their former state."[37] Jefferson knew that such evidence of slaves' supposed happiness with their condition should not be exaggerated, for when wartime conditions were propitious slaves proved all too willing to enlist under the enemy's banners in their bid for freedom. If the numbers of slaves grew to a critical, disproportionate mass, rebels would no longer have to depend on foreign assistance. In the next generation, Jefferson told Sparks in 1824, the present slave population of "a million and a half" would quadruple to six million, "and one million of these fighting men, will say, 'we will not go.'"[38]

Jefferson's personal experiences and observations minimized the security threat presented by an enslaved population; his geopolitical "realism," based on calculations about the relative disposition of forces in a world always at war or on its brink, exaggerated that threat. It was as if Jefferson lived in two totally distinct worlds: one, an expansive, interdependent, domestic domain, tied together by bonds of interest and fellow-feeling—a domain that *included* "happy" slaves; the other, the domain of foreign relations, a "mad contest of the lions and tigers" in which might demolished right and discontented slaves stood ready to reclaim their freedom by force.[39] But if Jefferson could keep his "domestic" and "foreign" worlds apart—a separation strongly reinforced by his understandings of both domesticity and federalism—his fellow Virginians were more inclined to think holistically. Planters' calculations about security risks entailed by slavery were incorporated in the price of slaves: clearly, over time, they worried less and less about servile insurrections and foreign intervention. For their part, slaves calculated that conditions were sufficiently stable to justify family-formation, and their population multiplied at a rate that alarmed Jefferson. And finally, white Virginians with scruples about slavery manumitted significant numbers of slaves after the liberalization of manumission in 1782, thus leading to the extraordinary growth of the free-black population.[40]

All of these developments—rising slave prices and the increasing numbers of slaves and free blacks—defied Jefferson's fearful prognostications and undercut his emancipation and expatriation scheme. Long before 1824, when Jefferson assessed population trends in his letter to Sparks, compensated emancipation had become prohibitively expensive. It was understandable that material interests would shape public opinion (though Jefferson liked to think this was not true of his own, Revolutionary generation), but it was more profoundly distressing that the misdirected philanthropic impulses of Edward Coles and other enlightened Virginians should simply exacerbate the underlying problem and postpone, if not altogether preempt, its ultimate solution.

Justice could only be rendered to the captive nation through colonization; in the meantime, he told Coles, "we should endeavor, with those whom fortune has thrown on our hands, to feed and clothe them well, protect them from all ill usage, require such reasonable labor only as is performed voluntarily by freemen, & be led by no repugnancies to abdicate them, and our duties to them." In other words, it was the "duty" of slave owners to treat their slaves well, not to "abandon" them, as Coles proposed, or "to commute them for other property" and thus "to commit them to those whose usage of them we cannot control." There was ample scope for planters' benevolence in working toward the amelioration of their slaves' condition within slavery. Jefferson reassured Coles that the "hour of emancipation is advancing, in the march of time." But it would come either through "the bloody process of St Domingo, excited and conducted by the power of our present enemy"—the British, who were then, in 1814, infesting the Chesapeake—or through Jefferson's colonization scheme. It would not come through the benevolence of misguided masters who liberated their own slaves.[41]

As the slave population grew, the prospects for implementing Jefferson's emancipation scheme diminished. By the time of the Missouri Crisis (1819–21), slave owners were committed not only to the perpetuation of slavery but to its expansion. No longer fearful of foreign intervention, and therefore of large-scale slave revolts, the "slave power" began to push aggressively into the Spanish borderlands. The only serious threat came from within the union. As professed opponents of slavery sought to capture the federal government and block the institution's expansion, Old Republican anxieties about the dangerous "consolidation" of power in the central government took on a new urgency. If the federal government interfered in the new state of Missouri's domestic affairs, it would have a plausible precedent—and a congressional majority—for attacking slavery in the old states.

Southern anti-restrictionists drew their inspiration from Jefferson's strict-constructionist constitutionalism and shared his deep suspicions about the motives of antislavery agitators. Restrictionists merely pretended sympathy for slaves in order to justify their power grab. As Jefferson wrote Charles Pinckney, neo-Federalist "partisans to the principle of monarchism" exploited "the virtuous feelings of the people to effect a division of parties by a geographical line." But Jefferson insisted that his opposition to slavery remained undiminished. If they were sincere, restrictionists would forgo their "Jeremiads on the miseries of slavery" and "unite their counsels with ours in devising some reasonable and practicable plan of getting rid of it." Far from promoting their ostensible goal of improving the lot of the slaves, restriction would rivet the shackles of bondage more tightly. The only "reasonable" plan was Jefferson's colonization scheme: anyone who failed to see this obviously had ulterior motives.[42] Other Southerners might advance more-forthright defenses of slavery, divining threats to their peculiar institution in every exercise of federal authority, for they were convinced that "consolidation"—the concentration of authority in the federal government—would lead to assaults on slavery. But because Jefferson fashioned himself a genuine opponent of slavery, his response to the Missouri Crisis reversed this sequence: all the restrictionists' talk about slavery was a cover for a consolidationist assault on states' rights, a Northern bid for sectional domination. Restrictionists did not care about the welfare of slaves; Jefferson did.

In retrospect, it is difficult, perhaps not even possible, to take Jefferson's "antislavery" commitments in the Missouri Crisis very seriously. Given recent demographic and economic developments, Jefferson's "reasonable" plan for eradicating slavery was increasingly implausible. His insistence that emancipation must come from the voluntary, uncoerced initiatives of enlightened slave owners themselves meant that the institution would be guaranteed against all external threats, whether from foreign powers, rebellious blacks, or other parts of the union: the most unabashed proponent of a "slaveholders' republic" could ask for little more. Nor would Jefferson be outdone in his solicitude for the "property" rights of slave owners, not only in their own states but in new states formed out of the federal domain. Perversely, it was Jefferson's conviction that he was acting in good faith as a genuine opponent of slavery that justified these positions, which were as a practical matter proslavery. When—and only when—Jefferson and his fellow slave owners were absolutely secure against all outside threats, they would emancipate their slaves. How, in the meantime, could the false philanthropists of the North imagine that "we were advocates for" an "evil" and unjust institution, or for "property" that derived from man-stealing?

Jefferson may have remained faithful to his colonization scheme, but the circumstances that might have generated support for it no longer existed after the War of 1812. As a result, his thinking about the future of slavery took a critical turn: it was geopolitical *insecurity* of a Revolutionary age initiated by the Americans, and spreading to France, across Europe, and back to the Americas, that first made emancipation seem urgent to Jefferson; now, he insisted, American slave owners would only rid themselves of slavery under conditions of absolute *security*. In other words, Jefferson was counting on an altruistic and enlightened "public opinion" to promote emancipation in the absence of security threats and despite slave owners' interest in their increasingly valuable property. "The mind of the master is to be apprised by reflection," Jefferson wrote in 1815, "and strengthened by the energies of conscience, against the obstacles of self-interest to an acquiescence in the rights of others."[43] No wonder emancipation was "not to be expected in a day, or perhaps in an age."[44]

Changing geopolitical circumstances postponed into the indefinite future implementation of any practical effort to end slavery. They also gave fuller scope to Jefferson's benevolent impulses to ameliorate the condition of slaves while they remained in bondage in Virginia and other slave states. This recessive strain in Jefferson's thinking, long kept in check by his commitment to colonization, came to the fore in his advocacy of "diffusion" during the Missouri Crisis. The argument that opening up new territory for slavery would enhance slaves' productivity and welfare—and lead to a distribution of the black population that would make servile insurrections less likely and, therefore, emancipation more likely—seems breathtakingly cynical, a mere sop to genuine opponents of the institution. "The passage of slaves from one State to another, would not make a slave of a single human being who would not be so without it," Jefferson thus assured John Holme. And "their diffusion over a greater surface would make them individually happier, and proportionally facilitate the accomplishment of their emancipation, by dividing the burthen on a greater number of coadjutors."[45] On the face of it, diffusion was the antithesis of colonization, the concentration and removal of the slave population. But Jefferson was not as cynical as he seems. He was convinced that the alleviation of security threats, the security of property in slaves, and the vindication of states' rights were all necessary preconditions for any ultimately successful emancipation scheme. By promoting those conditions, the expansion of slavery would hasten slavery's demise. In the meantime, diffusion would enhance slaves' welfare and happiness, preparing them for the freedom they would finally claim, at some distant day.[46]

Amelioration

Jefferson's tendency to think in starkly dichotomous terms—to juxtapose slavery and freedom, war and peace, Old World and New—made colonization seem like the only possible, lasting solution to the problem of slavery. By the same logic, he was convinced that incremental steps toward dismantling the institution would only exacerbate the problem. For Jefferson the transformation of slaves into semi-free peasants, bound to the land and circumscribed in their civil rights, would have marked the complete failure of the American experiment in republican self-government. The growth of a class of free blacks under the liberalized manumission statute of 1782 pointed to the recrudescence of a European-style old regime in Virginia: if this was the only way to dismantle the institution, the cure was worse than the disease. Jefferson's young protégé, William Short, writing from France in 1798, did not seem to understand this when he looked forward to the emergence of a racially mixed peasantry, taking gradual steps away from slavery by protecting slaves' families, "by attaching them to the glebe" and assimilating them to the condition of "the serfs of Europe."[47] The only way to guarantee Virginia's republican future, Jefferson responded, was to get rid of the slaves as well as slavery. Slaves should be well-treated while they remained in bondage, but the palliative measures Short and other temporizing reformers promoted did not mark the way toward freedom in America: they would simply make the new nation a crude and barbarous replica of Europe, with its aristocrats and peasants.

The colonization scheme Jefferson sketched out in his *Notes on the State of Virginia* did not allow for intermediate statuses between slavery and freedom. Nor did Jefferson see any role for slaves themselves in securing their own freedom. After declaring their own independence, white Virginians would then take the initiative in declaring their former slaves "a free and independant people." Of course, this was the whole point for Jefferson: to preempt a bloody race war by radically separating and pacifying the two hostile "nations." But if emancipation was the only means of achieving permanent peace, its success was predicated on the passive acquiescence in the colonization process of the slaves themselves. Blacks must be prevented from assuming the prerogatives of a self-governing nation until they were safely deported from Virginia. The existence of a class of free blacks *in Virginia* was particularly troubling to Jefferson because these masterless and ungovernable "pests" exercised a potentially dangerous degree of agency. Better to maintain a clear boundary between slavery and freedom than to allow the emergence of a hierarchy of civil statuses—and a promiscuous mixing of the races—that would compromise and subvert republicanism. And better for blacks to submit to the superior wisdom of their masters in providing both for their present welfare and for their ultimate freedom.

The paradoxical premise of Jefferson's emancipation scheme was that masters would be able to govern their slaves peacefully and productively while, over the course of a generation, the state deported their children. But if slavery could function effectively under such conditions, it could function effectively under *any* conditions and, therefore, survive indefinitely. In other words, the means Jefferson prescribed for achieving the great end of emancipation demonstrated that emancipation was not necessary, or at least not urgently compelling, to securing interracial peace. In practice, the binary opposition of war and peace did not map neatly onto the binary of slavery and freedom. If slavery institutionalized a state of war, making possible the despotic rule of one race over the other, it also enforced a kind of "peace" that could benefit blacks as well as whites. Under the regime of a benevolent master like Jefferson, slaves would enjoy security, stability, material well-being, and even a measure of "happiness." Such conditions could reconcile slaves to the deprivation of liberty while they patiently awaited their masters' enlightenment and the implementation of an emancipation plan that would finally achieve their children's—or their children's children's—freedom.

Jefferson remained convinced to his dying day that slavery was an unjust institution and that it must be destroyed before Virginia could fulfill its republican promise. But until that wondrous day arrived, Jefferson and his fellow slaveholders should dedicate themselves to improving the living conditions of slaves, for prudent reasons—to preserve the peace—and for the fulfillment of their domestic responsibilities to their black and white families. Jefferson's fealty to colonization thus enabled him both to advance arguments for the institution as it actually existed in the Southern states, which anticipated the "positive good" proslavery ideology of a later generation, and to question the good faith of professed enemies of slavery who sought to restrict its expansion: colonization was the only plausible solution to the slavery problem, and therefore the measure of authentic antislavery commitments.

Under the peculiarly benign conditions of American slavery, Jefferson wrote in his *Notes*, "the slaves multiply as fast as the free inhabitants. Their situation and manners place the commerce between the two sexes almost without restraint." Jefferson even argued that their civil disabilities *benefited* American slaves, who were not allowed to testify in court. "With the Romans, the regular method of taking the evidence of their slaves was under torture," Jefferson reported. "When a master was murdered, all his slaves, in the same house, or within hearing, were condemned to death." By contrast, only a guilty American slave was subject to punishment, "and as precise proof is required against him as against a freeman." Plantation governance protected American slaves *from* the state, enabling them to enjoy conditions of security and material well-being that Roman slaves would have envied. Yet, despite "deplorable" conditions in Rome, "their slaves were often the rarest artists," and "excelled too in science."[48]

American slavery compared favorably with ancient slavery, though American slaves did not take advantage of their relatively benign circumstances. Mild treatment and material abundance mitigated the theoretical horrors of the institution, as did Jefferson's "suspicions" about blacks' "inferiority."[49] Lacking in foresight and deficient in reason, blacks might not in any case be fit for freedom. "It may perhaps be doubted whether many of these people would voluntarily consent to such an exchange of situation," Jefferson wrote in 1811, "and very certain that few of those advanced to a certain age in habits of slavery, would be capable of self-government."[50]

When Jefferson considered the brutal treatment of the European laboring classes, American slavery looked even better. Slaves "are better fed in these States, warmer clothed, and labor less than the journeymen or day-laborers of England," he wrote the English refugee Thomas Cooper in 1814. "They have the comfort, too, of numerous families, in the midst of whom they live without want, or fear of it; a solace which few of the laborers of England possess." Jefferson acknowledged that slaves were "condemned . . . to a subjection to the will of others," but the same could be said for "hundreds of thousands of British soldiers and seamen subject to the same, without seeing, at the end of their career, when age and accident shall have rendered them unequal to labor, the certainty, which the other has, that he will never want." For Jefferson, the moral and material contrast between Old World and New grew progressively more conspicuous in the early decades of the nineteenth century, *despite* the persistence and expansion of racial slavery in America. A generation of war had drenched Europe in "rivers of blood," but its peoples remained in virtual bondage to oppressive ruling classes. "Can any condition of society be more desirable [than America's?]" Jefferson asked Cooper.[51]

Jefferson recognized that his invidious comparisons between Europe and America could be misconstrued, particularly when he contrasted American freedom and happiness to the benighted condition of "the whole enslaved world."[52] "I am not advocating slavery," he assured Cooper (and perhaps himself). "I am not justifying the wrongs we have committed on a foreign people, by the example of another nation committing equal wrongs on their own subjects. On the contrary, there is nothing I would not sacrifice to a practicable plan of abolishing every vestige of this moral and political depravity." Given the increasingly obvious impracticability of his colonization scheme—the only plan that would eliminate "every vestige" of the institution—Jefferson knew no such "sacrifice" would be required in the foreseeable future. In the meantime, he could not resist pursuing crossnational comparisons that inevitably cast slavery in a more favorable light. Invoking classic Utilitarian calculations, Jefferson invited Cooper to compare the "condition and degree of suffering" of slaves and oppressed workers and then "compute by numbers the sum of happiness of the two countries." Only aristocrats were "happy" in England, Jefferson asserted, and estimating "the proportion they bear to the laborers and paupers" at "four in every hundred, then the happiness of the nation would be to its misery as one in twenty-five." By comparison, the American ratio of happiness to suffering was "as eight millions to zero, or as all to none."[53]

Jefferson made two important moves in his letter to Cooper. First, as the comparison seemed to require, he included approximately one and a half million enslaved African Americans *within* the total American population, denying their separate nationality and thus "domesticating" them by statistical means. Second, and more significantly, he defined "happiness" for purposes of this comparison solely in terms of material welfare. This was not to say that slavery was a benign institution, for Jefferson continued to embrace the Declaration's more familiar definition of happiness, as an end to be chosen and pursued by free citizens as a matter of right. Precisely because slaves *as slaves* could never be happy in this sense, Jefferson saw no contradiction in talking about their "happiness" in the merely material and sensual terms appropriate to their condition. James Oakes suggests that Jefferson's apparently conflicting conceptions of happiness were in practice inextricably linked. "Personal freedom" might be valuable in its own right, but it was also valuable for the conditions it produced, the "ease and comfort" and "the material well-being, that made for human happiness."[54] By this standard, it was clear to Jefferson that slaves could be made "happy."

The diffusion of slaves across the American continent would improve their material conditions and therefore increase their "happiness." Yet colonization remained Jefferson's lodestar, or so he claimed, because it promised even more happiness: increasing our own "happiness and safety" by eliminating the dangerous and demoralizing presence of the captive nation and securing the future happiness of expatriated blacks as "a separate, free and independent people, in some country and climate friendly to human life and happiness."[55] Yet given the unpredictable contingencies of geopolitics—and the consolidation and expansion of racial slavery in the United States—the prospects for colonization looked increasingly dim in Jefferson's later years, more plausibly the subject of "prayers" than planning. There was apparently nothing slave owners could do to hasten that day, beyond waiting patiently for the long-postponed "revolution in public opinion" that would make emancipation possible. In the meantime, however, the master should keep in mind the "moral duties which he owes to the slave, in return for the benefits of his service, that is to say, of food, clothing, care in sickness, and maintenance under age and disability, so as to make him in fact as comfortable and more secure than the laboring man in most parts of the world."[56] The slave owner should work to ameliorate the condition of his slaves, thus redeeming the institution from the ignorant and unjust aspersions of antislavery critics in Europe and the free states of the North.

Conclusion

William Short challenged Jefferson on the slavery issue as the end of his mentor's life approached. The argument for diffusion was based on a faulty

premise, that there was a meaningful distinction between the foreign slave trade—which Jefferson and all right-thinking slave owners condemned—and the domestic slave trade. "In their present movable state," slaves could be "carried from Virginia to Louisiana as from Africa to the West Indies," Short wrote, regardless of their happiness and however happiness was defined. The benevolent rule of kind masters could not protect slaves, as property, from market forces. Reviving an idea he had first broached decades earlier, "of converting our slaves into serfs," Short asked Jefferson if the creation of such a neo-feudal regime might not be more humane—a better means to secure slaves' welfare and happiness—than the market-driven labor system that now flourished across the antebellum South.[57]

Short once had believed that Virginia should follow the lead of Northern states, gradually incorporating ex-slaves into the larger population. But he now conceded that "the greatest difficulty only begins where I thought it would end; that is, with these people in their new state of freedom." Jefferson had been right to insist that the growth of a free-black "population amongst us is an evil without a remedy." But Short also saw, as Jefferson would not, that "all the plans of expopulating the State of them are fraught with more cruelty than humanity, although I know that the motives of these who are aiming at it flow from benevolence."[58] Short acknowledged Jefferson's "preference for the plan of expatriation," but he wondered whether his old friend might instead opt for serfdom if, "on experiment," colonization "should be found impracticable."[59]

The logic of amelioration pointed toward humane modifications of the institution. Jefferson was well aware of previous proposals to split the difference between slavery and freedom and extend limited civil rights to former slaves. He had himself proposed importing Germans to meet Virginia's labor needs, thus reviving an older form of temporary white indentured servitude.[60] On the eve of his departure from France in 1789, Jefferson had even imagined mixing German immigrants with former slaves in a sharecropping arrangement that would give them a "comfortable subsistence," while "their children shall be brought up, as others are, in habits of property & foresight, & I have no doubt that they will be good citizens."[61] But Jefferson could not pursue any such proposal without abandoning his great panacea of colonization. Improving the conditions of slaves *in* slavery was entirely compatible with his long-term commitment to emancipation and expatriation; creating a hierarchy of civil statuses *outside of* slavery was unthinkable. From Jefferson's perspective, blurring the boundary between slavery and freedom—and between black and white—would fatally jeopardize the republican experiment.

Jefferson finally responded to Short's letters in January 1826, a few months before his death. Yes, he agreed, "the plan of converting the blacks into Serfs would certainly be better than keeping them in their present condition." Yet even at this late date Jefferson was not prepared to give up on his cherished emancipation scheme. Though large-scale colonization in West Africa might be prohibitively expensive, "I consider that of expatriation to the governments of the W[est] I[ndies] of their own colour as entirely practicable" and much "preferable to the mixture of colour here," the inevitable consequence of leaving former slaves in place. Jefferson's "great aversion" to race-mixing was a concomitant of his dedication to equal rights in the white republic. But the octogenarian found the topic tiring. "On the subject of emancipation I have ceased to think," he told Short, because it is "not to be a work of my day."[62]

Notes

1. Thomas Jefferson [hereafter, TJ], *Notes on Virginia,* Query XIV ("Laws"), in Thomas Jefferson, *Writings,* ed. Merrill Peterson (New York, 1984) [hereafter, Peterson, ed., *Thomas Jefferson Writings*], 264. For further discussion of TJ and slavery, with citations to the extensive literature on this controversial theme, see my *Jefferson's Empire: The Language of American Nationhood* (Charlottesville, VA, 2000), 147–91.

2. TJ, *Notes on Virginia,* Query XIV ("Laws"), in Peterson, ed., *Thomas Jefferson Writings,* 264.

3. Ibid., Query XVIII ("Manners"), 289.

4. TJ to James Heaton, May 20, 1826, in Peterson, ed., *Thomas Jefferson Writings,* 1516.

5. TJ to Edward Coles, August 25, 1814, ibid., 1345.

6. For further discussion of the centrality of enlightened public sentiment in TJ's thinking about slavery, see Ari Helo and Peter Onuf, "Jefferson, Morality, and the Problem of Slavery," *William and Mary Quarterly,* 3rd ser., 60 (July 2003): 583–614.

7. TJ to Edward Coles, Monticello, August 25, 1814, in Peterson, ed., *Thomas Jefferson Writings,* 1344. In his *Autobiography* (January 6, 1821), TJ recalled that he had "made one effort . . . for the permission of the emancipation of slaves, which was rejected: and indeed, during the regal government, nothing liberal could expect success" (ibid., 5). See the scathing commentary in Paul Finkelman, "Jefferson and Slavery: 'Treason Against the Hopes of the World,' " in *Jeffersonian Legacies,* ed. Peter S. Onuf (Charlottesville, VA, 1993), 188–89.

8. TJ to Edward Coles, Monticello, August 25, 1814, in Peterson, ed., *Thomas Jefferson Writings*, 1345–46.

9. See David Thomas Konig, "Antislavery in Jefferson's Virginia: The Incremental Attack on an Entrenched Institution," unpublished manuscript in author's possession.

10. My understanding of Jefferson's ameliorative impulses is heavily indebted, as is the broader conception of this paper, to Christa Dierksheide's important dissertation, "The Amelioration of Slavery in the Anglo-American Imagination, 1780–1840" (University of Virginia, 2009). A poignant casualty of Jefferson's global solution to the slavery problem was his failure to honor his commitment to Thaddeus Kosciusko to devote the proceeds of the Polish patriot's American estate to the emancipation cause, even if only by compensating himself for freeing his own slaves. The story of Kosciusko's will and of Jefferson's failure to discharge his trust to his old friend is carefully reconstructed and powerfully told in Gary B. Nash and Graham Hodges, *Friends of Liberty: Tadeuz Kosciuszko, Thomas Jefferson, and Agrippa Hull; A Tale of Three Patriots, Two Revolutions, and a Tragic Betrayal of Freedom in the Nation* (New York, 2008).

11. TJ to John Holmes, Monticello, April 22, 1820, in Peterson, ed., *Thomas Jefferson Writings*, 1434.

12. Richard Keith Call, *Letter to John S. Littell* (Philadelphia, 1861), in Jon L. Wakelyn, ed., *Southern Pamphlets on Secession, November 1860-April 1861* (Chapel Hill, NC, 1996), 187. On the family idea, see Eugene Genovese, *Roll, Jordan, Roll: The World the Slaves Made* (New York, 1974), 133–49.

13. "Destinies of the South," *Southern Quarterly Review* 7 (January 1853): 203, 191. For further discussion of this point, see Nicholas Onuf and Peter Onuf, *Nations, Markets, and War: Modern History and the American Civil War* (Charlottesville, VA, 2006), 333–41.

14. I am indebted to the important work of Jan Lewis on this theme. See, particularly, Lewis, "'The Blessings of Domestic Society': Thomas Jefferson's Family and the Transformation of American Politics," in *Jeffersonian Legacies*, ed. Peter S. Onuf (Charlottesville, VA, 1993), 109–46; and Lewis, *The Pursuit of Happiness: Family and Values in Jefferson's Virginia* (New York, 1983). On Jefferson and "self-fashioning," see Jay Fliegelman, *Declaring Independence: Jefferson, Natural Language, and the Culture of Performance* (Stanford, CA, 1993).

15. For a brilliant and comprehensive study of the origins of modern conceptions of privacy and "interiority" in Britain, see Michael McKeon, *The Secret History of Domesticity: Public, Private, and the Division of Knowledge* (Baltimore, 2005).

16. TJ to Angelica Schuyler Church, Germantown, November 27, 1793, in Peterson, ed., *Thomas Jefferson Writings*, 1013.

17. TJ, *Notes on Virginia*, Query XIV ("Laws"), in Peterson, ed., *Thomas Jefferson Writings*, 264.

18. TJ to Joseph C. Cabell, February 2, 1816, *in Peterson, ed., Thomas Jefferson Writings*, 1380.

19. TJ to Samuel Kercheval, July 12, 1816, ibid., 1399. For further discussion of

TJ's federal theory, see Onuf, *Jefferson's Empire*, 117–21. On "levels," see Nicholas Greenwood Onuf, *The Republican Legacy in International Thought* (Cambridge, 1998), chap. 8. On "devolution," see McKeon, *Secret History of Domesticity,* 3–48.

20. TJ's draft, Declaration of Independence, in Peterson, ed., *Thomas Jefferson Writings,* 22.

21. TJ to John Adams, January 22, 1821, in *The Writings of Thomas Jefferson,* ed. Andrew A. Lipscomb and Albert Ellery Bergh, 20 vols. (Washington, DC, 1903–4), 15:308–9. On TJ and Missouri, see Onuf, *Jefferson's Empire,* 109–21 and passim.

22. TJ to John Holmes, April 22, 1820, in Peterson, ed., *Thomas Jefferson Writings,* 1434.

23. TJ to Major John Cartwright, June 5, 1824, ibid., 1493.

24. *Cohens v. Virginia* "was between a citizen and his own State, and under a law of his State. It was a domestic case, therefore, and not a foreign one" (TJ to Justice William Johnson, June 12, 1823, in Peterson, ed., *Thomas Jefferson Writings,* 1475; and see also TJ to William Branch Giles, December 26, 1825, ibid., 1509–10).

25. TJ to Jared Sparks, February 4, 1824, ibid., 1485–86. For further commentary on this letter, see my "Every Generation is an 'Independant Nation': Colonization, Miscegenation, and the Fate of Jefferson's Children," *William and Mary Quarterly,* 3rd ser., 57 (January 2000): 155–72.

26. TJ to John Holmes, April 22, 1820, in Peterson, ed., *Thomas Jefferson Writings,* 1434.

27. See the illuminating discussion in Jan Lewis, "The Problem of Slavery in Southern Discourse," in *Devising Liberty: Preserving and Creating Freedom in the New American Republic,* ed. David T. Konig (Stanford, CA, 1995), 265–97.

28. TJ to St. George Tucker, August 28, 1797, in *The Works of Thomas Jefferson,* ed. Paul Leicester Ford, 12 vols. (New York, 1904–5); a digitized transcription is available from the American Memory Collection, Library of Congress, Washington, DC [hereafter, DLC]). For Tucker's plan, see *A Dissertation on Slavery: With a Proposal for the Gradual Abolition of It, in the State of Virginia* (Philadelphia, 1796).

29. Douglas R. Egerton, *Gabriel's Rebellion: The Virginia Slave Conspiracies of 1800 and 1802* (Chapel Hill, NC, 1993).

30. TJ to James Monroe, November 24, 1801, in Peterson, ed., *Thomas Jefferson Writings,* 1096.

31. William G. Merkel, "To See Oneself as a Target of a Justified Revolution: Thomas Jefferson and Gabriel's Uprising," *American Nineteenth Century History* 4 (Summer 2003): 1–31.

32. TJ to James Monroe, June 2, 1802, in Ford, ed., *Works of Thomas Jefferson* (American Memory transcription, DLC).

33. TJ to James Monroe, November 24, 1801, in Peterson, ed., *Thomas Jefferson Writings,* 1097–98. For further discussion of this point, see Onuf, *Jefferson's Empire,* 177–82.

34. TJ to Jared Sparks, February 4, 1824, in Peterson, ed., *Thomas Jefferson Writings,* 1487.

35. TJ, *Notes on Virginia*, Query XIV ("Laws"), in Peterson, ed., *Thomas Jefferson Writings*, 266.

36. TJ to Edward Bancroft, January 26, 1789, Paris, in *The Papers of Thomas Jefferson*, ed. Julian P. Boyd et al., 36 vols. to date (Princeton, NJ, 1950–), 14:492–93.

37. Edward Bancroft to TJ, September 16, 1789, London, ibid., 13:606–8.

38. TJ to Jared Sparks, February 4, 1824, in Peterson, ed., *Thomas Jefferson Writings*, 1487.

39. TJ to Clement Caine, September 16, 1811, in Lipscomb and Bergh, eds., *Writings of Thomas Jefferson*, 13:89–90.

40. The best study is still Robert McColley, *Slavery and Jeffersonian Virginia*, 2nd ed. (Champaign, IL, 1973). For a more general survey, see Adam Rothman, *Slave Country: American Expansion and the Origins of the Deep South* (Cambridge, MA, 2005).

41. TJ to Edward Coles, Monticello, August 25, 1814, in Peterson, ed., *Thomas Jefferson Writings*, 1345–46.

42. TJ to Charles Pinckney, September 30, 1820, in Lipscomb and Bergh, eds., *Writings of Thomas Jefferson*, 15:280. See also TJ to Albert Gallatin, December 26, 1820, in Peterson, ed., *Thomas Jefferson Writings*, 1448–49. On Jefferson's interpretation of the restrictionists, see Glover Moore, *The Missouri Controversy, 1819–1821* (Lexington, KY, 1953).

43. TJ to David Barrow, May 1, 1815, in Lipscomb and Bergh, eds., *Writings of Thomas Jefferson*, 14:296.

44. TJ to James Heaton, May 20, 1826, in Peterson, ed., *Thomas Jefferson Writings*, 1516.

45. TJ to John Holmes, April 22, 1820, ibid., 1434. For similar language, see TJ to Albert Gallatin, Monticello, December 26, 1820, ibid., 1448–49; and TJ to Lafayette, December 26, 1820, in Lipscomb and Bergh, eds., *Writings of Thomas Jefferson*, 15:300–301. For an earlier expression of the diffusion idea, focusing on security, see TJ to John Dickinson, January 13, 1807, in which Jefferson writes that opening up the Louisiana Territory to the importation of slaves from other states would "divid[e] that evil" and "lessen its danger" (in Ford, ed., *Works of Thomas Jefferson* [American Memory transcription, DLC]).

46. For an excellent discussion of diffusion, see Rothman, *Slave Country*. Rothman suggests that diffusion constituted the deep source of later positive good arguments: emphasis on gradual emancipation gave way to "amelioration of slaves' condition," yoking "the new proslavery humanitarianism to the expansion of slavery" (213).

47. William Short to TJ, Phila., February 27, 1798, in Thomas Jefferson and William Short Correspondence, transcribed and edited by Gerard W. Gawalt, Manuscript Division, Library of Congress, Washington, DC (American Memory transcription, DLC).

48. TJ, *Notes on Virginia*, Query XIV ("Laws"), in Peterson, ed., *Thomas Jefferson Writings*, 268.

49. Ibid., 270.

50. TJ to John Lynch, Monticello, January 21, 1811, in Peterson, ed., *Thomas Jefferson Writings*, 1241.

51. TJ to Thomas Cooper, September 10, 1814, in Lipscomb and Bergh, eds., *Writings of Thomas Jefferson*, 14:183. TJ often invoked the "rivers of blood" trope: see, for examples, TJ to Benjamin Austin, January 9, 1816, ibid., 14:389; and TJ to John Adams, September 4, 1823, in *The Adams-Jefferson Letters: The Complete Correspondence between Thomas Jefferson and Abigail and John Adams*, ed. Lester J. Cappon, 2 vols. (Chapel Hill, NC, 1959), 2:596.

52. TJ to Richard Rush, October 20, 1820, in Lipscomb and Bergh, eds., *Writings of Thomas Jefferson*, 15:283–84.

53. TJ to Thomas Cooper, September 10, 1814, ibid., 14:184. For the "felicific calculus," see Jeremy Bentham, *An Introduction to the Principles of Morals and Legislation* (1823 ed.; Oxford, 1907), chap. IV ("Value of a Lot of Pleasure or Pain, how to be Measured"), available online at http://www.la.utexas.edu/research/poltheory/bentham/ipml/index.html (accessed July 18, 2006).

54. James Oakes, "'Whom Have I Oppressed?': The Pursuit of Happiness and the Happy Slave," in *The Revolution of 1800: Democracy, Race, and the New Republic,* ed. James Horn, Jan Ellen Lewis, and Peter S. Onuf (Charlottesville, VA, 2002), 220–39.

55. TJ to Jared Sparks, February 4, 1824, in Peterson, ed., *Thomas Jefferson Writings*, 1484. It would also be a "happy event," as William Short told Jefferson, if a colony could be successfully established "on the coast of Africa" and "aid towards civilizing & ameliorating the state of that unhappy region" (Short to TJ, Phila., July 4, 1817, Phila., in Thomas Jefferson and William Short Correspondence, transcribed and edited by Gerard W. Gawalt, Manuscript Division, Library of Congress, Washington, DC [American Memory transcription, DLC]).

56. TJ to Clement Caine, September 16, 1811, in Lipscomb and Bergh, eds., *Writings of Thomas Jefferson*, 13:89.

57. Short to TJ, Phila., January 11, 1826, in Thomas Jefferson and William Short Correspondence, transcribed and edited by Gerard W. Gawalt, Manuscript Division, Library of Congress, Washington, DC (American Memory transcription, DLC).

58. Short to TJ, Phila., December 14, 1825, ibid.

59. Short to TJ, Phila., January 11, 1826, ibid.

60. TJ to Rufus King, July 13, 1802, in Ford, ed., *Works of Thomas Jefferson* (American Memory transcription, DLC); and TJ to J. Philip Reibelt, December 21, 1805, ibid.

61. TJ to Edward Bancroft, January 26, 1789, Paris, in Boyd et al., eds., *Papers of Thomas Jefferson*, 14:492–93.

62. TJ to William Short, January 18, 1826, in Ford, ed., *Works of Thomas Jefferson* (American Memory transcription, DLC).

Perfecting Slavery

Rational Plantation Management at Monticello

✦   ✦   ✦   Lucia Stanton

On January 5, 1794, Thomas Jefferson boarded the stagecoach in Philadelphia. Weary of political conflict, he was returning to Virginia and a retirement he expected to be permanent. Six weeks earlier he had written that soon he was "to be liberated from the hated occupations of politics, and to sink into the bosom of my family, my farm, and my books. I have my house to build, my feilds to form, and to watch for the happiness of those who labor for mine." Those who labored for his happiness were the one hundred enslaved men, women, and children who lived and worked on his Albemarle County plantation.[1] Jefferson was laying aside his battle against tyranny and barbarism at the cosmic level. On the smaller stage of Monticello, however, he still was a zealous reformer, driven by the Enlightenment beliefs that inspired his private as well as public actions. Postponing the grand project of enlarging his house, he devoted himself to perfecting the operations of his plantation in accordance with laws of physical and human nature that he considered—like any good Newtonian—universal in their application. They governed the motions of the celestial bodies as well as his treble-geared threshing machine. They applied as much to blacksmiths and carpenters as to nations.

In his three years of retirement at Monticello, Jefferson, armed with timepieces, decimalized scales, and surveying instruments, used geometry and mathematics to improve the functioning of his plantation and make the work processes in his fields and shops more economic and efficient. At the same time, in conformity with his belief in the natural law that made self-interest and moral duties inseparable, he sought ways to "watch for the happiness" of his enslaved laborers. Freedom formed no part of this plan. As Peter Onuf has written in this volume, Jefferson had ceased battling against slavery itself and instead devoted himself to "ameliorating the condition of slaves *within* the institution."[2] If he could not abolish slavery, then he could use his retirement to reform it at home by applying humanitarian principles to labor management. He could experiment with new "modes of government" compatible with new ways of exercising power that were being implemented all over the transatlantic world, in governments, schools, factories, and prisons. His own plantation, and a nail shop on Mulberry Row, could be run according to "the principles of reason and honesty" that he believed were central to enlightened government.[3]

Jefferson spent the first two years of his retirement in daily contact with the Monticello plantation, crisscrossing its five thousand acres to survey new field boundaries, direct the wheat harvests, measure crops of rye, and test new agricultural machinery. This was a new era at Monticello and a new role for its proprietor. For the very first time, Jefferson was continuously and personally involved in the plantation's day-to-day operations. Previously, he had paid so little attention to the production of his staple crop that, after more than thirty years as a tobacco planter, he admitted, "I never saw a leaf of my tobo. packed in my life."[4] In the mid-1790s, however, he was, in his own words, "the most ardent and active farmer in the state," possibly even "the most industrious farmer in the world."[5] After leaving Monticello to "the unprincipled ravages of overseers" for decades, he was now dedicated to improving his plantation operations on every level, from riverside field to mountaintop workshop.[6]

Scaling down his efforts to dispel the global "cloud of barbarism and despotism," Jefferson lowered his sights to his immediate surroundings and began to tackle a host of barbarisms that were entirely agricultural.[7] His closer examination revealed a land devastated by the extractive rotation of corn and tobacco. As he wrote his friend Eliza Trist, "Never had reformer greater obstacles to surmount from the barbarous mode of culture and management which had been carried on."[8]

On the culture side, the reforms Jefferson had in mind were the elimination of "the slovenly business of tobacco making," and the restoration of the fertility of the soil through approved practices like crop rotation and the planting of soil-improving crops like red clover.[9] On the management side, he strove to eliminate waste—particularly of time and labor—from every aspect of his plantation. Although he lived in a region that had long been locked into an economic system based on the waste of both land and labor, the Enlightenment quest for economy and efficiency was second nature to him, and, for the next few years, he managed to remain undaunted by the challenges he faced. He reorganized the Monticello plantation, dividing it into independent quarter farms identical in size, each "cultivated by four negroes, four negresses, four oxen, and four horses," as one French visitor recorded. Each farm had seven fields of forty acres, with the fields of the home farm laid out in an actual grid over the angular upland landscape of Monticello. Jefferson's "system," as the same Frenchman observed, "is entirely confined to himself."[10]

One of the more arresting records of Jefferson's application of rational and mechanistic approaches to plantation practices was his plan for the wheat harvest of 1796.[11] He had begun preparing for this climactic event a year earlier, after the 1795 crop had been cut and stacked. "Were the harvest to go over again with the same force," he wrote in his Farm Book, "the following arrangement should take place." His first prescription revealed problems that must have beset that harvest. It called for laying down the treading floors in advance and laying in a supply of spare scythe blades and wooden "fingers" for the grain cradles. Then he proceeded to the division of labor. To each category of worker—mowers, binders, gatherers, loaders, stackers, carters, and cooks—he assigned appropriate individuals: fifty-eight men, women, and children from the age of nine to sixty-nine.

Jefferson's "Diary of harvest" for 1796 indicates that his more-efficient plan was carried out almost exactly as he designed it.[12] Its central component was an ever sharp scythe. In the planning, he may have recalled the words of his hero Sir Francis Bacon, who had likened the "unlearned man," unable to amend his faults, to "an ill mower, that mows on still, and never whets his scythe."[13] Jefferson made the sharpening process—and thus the mowing—perpetual, by assigning to "Great George" Granger the task of advancing alongside the mowers in a mule cart, "with tools & a grindstone . . . constantly employed in mending cradles & grinding scythes." Because of Granger's continuous repairs, the "18. cradlers should work constantly." Jefferson's scheme thus did away with traditional short breaks, when scythemen stopped mowing at the signal of their leader, pulled out their whetstones, sharpened their scythes, and caught their breaths.

Jefferson's aims were clear: the elimination of idle moments, an ordered succession of interlocking tasks, and the efficiency and dependability of precision engineering. In other words, he sought to achieve the clockwork regularity of a machine. And a machine is what he called this combination of tools, carts and wagons, mules and oxen, and almost sixty human beings. At the bottom of the plan, he concluded with a flourish of Enlightenment confidence: "In this way, the whole machine would move in exact equilibrio, no part of the force could be lessened without retarding the whole, nor increased without a waste of force."[14]

Even his final stipulation—an allowance of four gallons of whiskey each day—could not fuel the "machine" fast enough to achieve the speed Jefferson had predicted. The 1796 harvest of 320 acres took twelve days, instead of the estimated six, and its machinery evidently broke down at almost every step. Despite the twenty-seven scythes, the grindstone, and the repairs of George Granger, the men cut the grain at a slower rate than the year before (two acres a day instead of three). As Jefferson explained, "The wheat was so heavy for the most part that we had not more than 13. or 14. mowers cutting on an average." Even with the reduced mowing team, midway through the harvest the "pickers up" were unable to keep up with the cutters, so that eight women Jefferson had hoped could continue to drive their weeding plows through the corn fields had to be brought to the wheat field to help out.[15]

Whiskey no doubt contributed to some of the disarray. Ten years later, Jefferson called the regular allotment of ardent spirits to the laborers "an injurious & demoralising practice. They do more for a day or two but less afterwards as we see where a harvest is lengthy."[16] But liquor and the bountiful crop could not have been wholly responsible for the breakdown of the system at so many points. Two hundred years down the line, we inevitably look to the laborers, not so easy to predict and control as the laws of motion. It was common for enslaved men and women to regulate their mowing or binding speed to relieve their friends and family members. As one former Virginia slave recalled, "One could help the other when they got behind. . . . The Man what was doing the cradling would always go no faster than the woman, who was most times his wife, could keep up."[17] An inevitable conclusion is that everyone, from George Granger to the cradlers to the women and boys binding and gathering the sheaves, was engaged in collective resistance to Jefferson's all-controlling harvest machinery, which was intended to be labor-saving. They found ways to save their *own* labor.

And the mowing rate continued to decline over the years, despite Jefferson's use of what later agricultural writers called an "ambulatory shop."[18]

While it is a rather striking expression of how eighteenth-century gentlemen viewed people and processes in mechanistic terms, Jefferson's harvest plan was far from unique in its approach. Seventy years earlier, in a well-known letter to the Earl of Orrery, William Byrd II, of Westover, had written: "I must take care to keep all my people to their duty, to see all the springs in motion, and to make every one draw his equal share to carry the machine forward."[19] What distinguishes Jefferson from Southern slaveholders of previous generations is that he considered the humanity of his slaves while reducing them to cogs in a many-wheeled machine. His return to Monticello coincided with a new mode of management that addressed his concern to "watch for the happiness" of his enslaved laborers. In an unusual experiment, he began to employ overseers from another state.

In Jefferson's view, the typical free white overseer in Virginia not only "barbarously managed" the land, but was notably severe in his management of labor.[20] Family members, overseers, and former slaves recalled Jefferson as a "kind" and "indulgent" master, and referred to his efforts to minimize harsh physical punishment at Monticello.[21] "I love industry and abhor severity," Jefferson wrote in 1805. In 1792 he was delighted to hear from his son-in-law that the new Monticello overseer, Manoah Clarkson, had "a valuable art of governing the slaves which sets aside the necessity of punishment allmost entirely" (a virtue that turned out too good to be true). Jefferson responded: "My first wish is that the labourers may be well treated, the second that they may enable me to have that treatment continued by making as much as will admit it. The man who can effect both objects is rarely to be found."[22]

Jefferson made one concerted effort to find men who could unite both productivity and humanity. On his regular journeys between Monticello and Philadelphia, he was impressed with the farms in Cecil County, Maryland, which had benefited from the latest approved agricultural practices. In 1792 he wrote to Jacob Hollingsworth, of Elkton, about his search for overseers: "I am anxious to provide myself from your neighborhood because the degree of farming there practised is exactly that which I think would be adopted in my possessions, and because the labour with you being chiefly by Negroes, your people of course understand the method of managing that kind of laborer."[23] Farmers in this borderland between freedom and slavery not only practiced the diversified husbandry Jefferson wished to pursue at Monticello, but, "because the labour there being performed by slaves with some mixture of free labourers," they also understood "the management of negroes on a rational and humane plan."[24]

The new regime began in late 1793 and early 1794 when Eli Alexander and Samuel Biddle moved from Elkton, Maryland, to Monticello to take up their responsibilities, Alexander on the north side of the Rivanna River and Biddle on the south, or Monticello mountain, side. This agricultural and humanitarian experiment was short-lived and never repeated. After just a few months, Jefferson described Biddle as "a poor acquisition."[25] He lasted only a year, while Alexander served for two years.[26] Jefferson's papers reveal neither what went wrong nor what, if any, were the effects of the new mode of management. At the end of 1796, Jefferson was drawn into another stretch of public service and began to lease out the quarter farms in his Monticello plantation, along with the enslaved families that lived on them. He turned his back on agriculture for the next ten years.

Consoling Jefferson through his struggle with seemingly incompatible goals was his energetic belief in the "law of nature which makes a virtuous conduct produce benefit, & vice loss to the agent, in the long run."[27] In the age-old debate over the relationship between self-interest and moral duty, Jefferson was emphatically certain: "So invariably do the laws of nature create our duties and interests, that when they seem to be at variance, we ought to suspect some fallacy in our reasonings." His confidence in this "law of nature" and its broad application is also revealed in his Second Inaugural, where he stated, "We are firmly convinced, and we act on that conviction, that with nations as with individuals, our interests soundly calculated will ever be found inseparable from our moral duties."[28]

The person of a slave, both as human and as property, was a singular embodiment of this "inseparable" combination. It is no surprise to find Jefferson harking back to the laws of nature in his role of slaveholder and plantation manager. In 1819 he wrote his steward that the high infant mortality at Poplar Forest involved "moral as well as interested considerations," and urged him to provide better treatment to the enslaved women and to "inculcate upon the overseers that it is not their labor, but their increase which is the first consideration with us." "In this, as in all other cases," he wrote, "providence has made our interests & our duties coincide perfectly."[29] For Jefferson, maximizing the efficiency of his plantation must go hand in hand with watching "for the happiness of those who labor for mine." A "happy" labor force would be the most productive and profitable.

Of course, it was no simple task to keep the mechanism of interest and duty in perfect equilibrium, and there must have been countless occasions when he had to close his mind entirely to the conflict inherent in the combination of "moral as well as interested considerations." The qualifying clause in Jefferson's letter about overseers—that his slaves might "enable" him to continue their good treatment by "making as much as will admit it"—is just one example of the mental maneuvers he had to engage in. Every decision to buy, sell, lease, or give away a slave, to punish misbehavior, or to relocate individuals tested the equation. In 1797, when his younger daughter Maria married, Jefferson wished to make her marriage settlement equal in value to her older sister's. A surviving document (obviously a fair copy made after long spells of computation) has two columns of names, thirty-one on each side, divided into males and females and listed according to their ages, and thus value. Family integrity inevitably came second in this effort to calibrate human fates to make a perfect match. In this case, four children, from ten to fourteen, were separated from their families.[30]

Two of the boys made motherless by this marriage settlement worked in a shop on Mulberry Row, the site of Jefferson's most significant venture in pursuit of both his interest and his duty. For more than a year before his retirement he had been planning to add a non-agricultural activity to his Monticello operations, to provide an income "subsidiary to the farm."[31] Late in 1793, his first idea, potash production, was suddenly superseded by nail-making, a process that required no skilled workers and would thus minimize the drain on labor needed in his fields. A nailery would employ only "a parcel of boys who would otherwise be idle."[32] Yet, more than the efficient use of labor seems to have been at the root of Jefferson's change of mind. In Philadelphia, on December 17, 1793, he met with Quaker merchant Caleb Lownes. The next day, he placed an order with Lownes for a ton of nail rod, the imported iron product from which nails were made.[33]

Lownes was far more than an ironmonger. He is generally given credit for being the "principal agent" of penal reform in the federal city, having played a leading role in the transformation of state laws and prison management that made Philadelphia a focus of international attention for decades.[34] Philadelphia's new system of penal management was established during the years that Jefferson spent there as secretary of state. Criminals were brought in from the city streets, where they had worked encumbered by ball and chain, to a reformed Walnut Street jail that incorporated what has been called "the first penitentiary in the world."[35] There, the most hardened criminals were placed in solitary confinement, while the other inmates of the jail pursued an active regime of work from dawn to dusk—weaving and spinning, tailoring and shoemaking, stone-polishing and plaster-grinding, tending cabbages in the prison garden, and—by 1795—making nails. Bells sounded to mark their mealtimes and their arrival and departure from the daytime work spaces, and rang every hour through the night.[36]

According to the duc de La Rochefoucauld-Liancourt, it was Caleb Lownes who initiated the change of discipline, proposing to "substitute a mild and rational, but firm treatment, in the room of irons and stripes."[37] Lownes, an indefatigable member of the prison's Board of Inspectors for a decade, wrote that "some seem to forget that the prisoner is a rational being, of like feelings and passions with themselves. Some think that he is placed there to be perpetually tormented and punished."[38]

Jefferson, like Lownes, had already absorbed the works of Beccaria and John Howard, and had even engaged in prison design: the prison plan he sent home to Virginia from France in 1786 was based on a design that favored solitary confinement over public works and "unites in the most perfect manner the objects of security and health."[39] He almost certainly knew Lownes before they discussed the price of nail rod in December 1793, as the Quaker had been the dedicated right-hand man of Mayor Matthew Clarkson during the recent yellow fever crisis. Jefferson moved in the circles of Philadelphians, such as Benjamin Rush, who were involved in the Philadelphia Society for Alleviating the Miseries of Public Prisons. He cannot have missed what was going on at the prison just a few blocks from his Market Street residence. The elimination of corporal punishment and the importance of work, for which the prisoners were compensated, was noted by all commentators. Robert Turnbull likened the prison to a beehive when he wrote: "Such a spirit of industry [was] visible on every side and such contentment pervaded the countenances of all."[40]

Nail-making apparently did not join the panoply of occupations at the prison until 1795, but Lownes, as a purveyor of nail rod, may have considered adding this trade—soon to be a staple in American penitentiaries—when he met with Jefferson at the end of 1793.[41] Whether or not the Monticello nailery was directly inspired by Lownes and the Walnut Street prison, Jefferson's methods of managing his nailmakers were certainly influenced by the ideas that sustained penal reform at this time. From the 1770s, writers like Jeremy Bentham had begun to apply the principle of the junction of interest and duty to institutions of superintendence. Rational modes of management were applicable to all forms of "government," not just the purely political, and especially to institutions that involved discipline and control—prisons, poorhouses, hospitals, asylums, schools, and factories.[42] The reformed Walnut Street jail, in the eyes of its observers, incorporated elements of these other institutions. In 1798 one writer described it as "more resembling a College than a prison," remarking that it gave "the pleasing idea of a great manufactory combining in its appearance taste with utility."[43]

From its beginning in the spring of 1794, the Monticello nailery combined the attributes of a school and a prison, as well as a factory. For Jefferson, it was not just an adventure of industrial entrepreneurship. It was an experimental laboratory for working out new ideas about exercising power, a place to try to manage enslaved labor in harmony with current ideas of humanitarian reform. Stopping short of utopian fantasy, he had joined the search for perfected social systems. While Jefferson never explicitly described or promoted his enterprise in humanitarian terms, there are many indications that it was conceived and carried out in the same paternal spirit as reformed institutions in the new republic, where prisons and factories, not just academies, were being touted as "nurseries of virtue."[44]

"I now employ a dozen little boys from 10. to 16. years of age, overlooking all the details of their business myself," Jefferson wrote in the second year of the nailery's operation.[45] This supervision included daily visits to the shop to weigh iron and constant monitoring of the youthful labor force. Critical to the enterprise—as for the Walnut Street prison—was the removal of violence from the system of discipline. In 1801, Jefferson warned a new nailery manager to refrain from using the whip, which "must not be resorted to but in extremities."[46] How, then, were a dozen teenagers, cooped up in a smoky shop, to be kept at a boring and repetitive task for ten to fourteen hours a day according to the season? The duc de La Rochefoucauld-Liancourt, who was intensely interested in prison reform, spent a week at Monticello and must have talked with Jefferson about the nailery and its management. His published account of his visit is disappointingly laconic: "the children [Jefferson] employs in a nail-manufactory, which yields already a considerable profit." But he did acknowledge the new disciplinary regime: "He animates them by rewards and distinctions."[47]

Isaac Granger, an enslaved youth who worked in the nailery as well as the blacksmith shop, later remembered that the nailers received special meat and fish rations and that Jefferson gave "them that wukked the best a suit of red or blue; encouraged them mightily."[48] In keeping with the late eighteenth-century enthusiasm for the motivating power of emulation, Jefferson improved the performance of the nailers through competition, and built esprit de corps through distinctions. The incredibly painstaking accounts that he transcribed after his daily visits to the shop include columns of the weights of both nail rod and nails, so that he could calculate efficiency as well as productivity. Thus he could write in 1794, "Jamey wastes 29.83 lb. in the [hundredweight]." Sporadic computations in the accounts reveal that as soon as a boy achieved a certain rate of "waste," Jefferson set him a new efficiency goal. This policy seems to have been successful in steadily improving performance. Jamey (i.e., James Hubbard), from being one of the most wasteful nailmakers when he began at the age of eleven, had by age thirteen decreased his loss to 10 percent. As a group the young nailers even surpassed what was considered the "common" iron loss in the trade of 14 percent.[49]

In the case of the adult workers on the plantation, Jefferson encouraged industry through actual financial incentives. Up to the 1790s he had occasionally given his enslaved workmen what he called "gratuities," that is, gratuitous payments made without expectation or prior arrangement.[50] Henceforth, however, he began to distribute small sums of money by agreement, and with the specific aim of animating work that went beyond the ordinary. To fuel the newly established nailery, Jefferson hired a free white man, Jacob Silknitter, to produce charcoal and to train slaves in the charcoal-burning process.[51] After Silknitter left, an enslaved man, Frank, carried on the periodic charcoal-burning according to terms Jefferson penned into his memorandum book: "I am always to give Frank a half dime for every bushel to the cord of wood which his coal kilns yield. His last yielded 30 bushels to the cord: therefore paid 1.5 D."[52] In his pursuit of half-dimes, Frank was producing 39 bushels to the cord by the time of his third kiln. Jefferson's agreement with his charcoal-burner reveals a prime objective in his ongoing battle against waste. He paid Frank not according to the quantity of charcoal he produced but according to the efficiency with which he burned it. This is an understandable goal given the staggering amounts of wood required for the charcoal kilns—as many as two hundred cords a year at the height of nailery operations.[53]

It is also another indication of the Jeffersonian blend of system and sympathy, interest and duty. In Jefferson's view, Nature had drawn "indelible lines of distinction" between whites and blacks, who were inferior in "the endowments both of body and mind."[54] Those distinctions did not, however, exile blacks from the human family. They behaved according to the same laws of human nature as whites. They had the same desire to excel, and thus their labor could be encouraged by similar appeals to reason. Jefferson made clear his expectations in a letter of 1797 to his son-in-law John Wayles Eppes. Since Eppes did not yet have a fully equipped shop, Jefferson advised him to find alternative occupations for his enslaved blacksmith: "You would do well to employ Isaac in the mean time in preparing coal for his year's work. He should have about 2000. bushels laid in. Nor will it be amiss to cord his wood in order to excite him to an emulation in burning it well."[55]

Measurement dogged every step of the enslaved men associated with the nailery, whether they were stacking wood for charcoal kilns or swinging a hammer to make tenpenny nails. Jefferson continued to keep precise records of charcoal-burning—dimensions of kilns, numbers of bushels, and payments by the original formula. They show that David Hern, Monticello's charcoal-burner in the years of Jefferson's final retirement, achieved a very respectable average of 35 bushels of charcoal to the cord of wood. And, in 1819, Jefferson began to use a new term to describe his payments to Hern: "Davy has burnt a kiln yeilding 1016. bushels which is 33.86 bushels to the cord, & makes his premium 1.70 D."[56] The word "premium" had been used for some time in the education field as well as in learned societies (Jefferson himself had earned a gold medal as a "premium" in 1806 for his moldboard of least resistance).[57] It became more common in the first decades of the nineteenth century, when the rhetoric of emulation had intensified along with the rise of agricultural societies and their attendant competitions and fairs. Agricultural journals were full of references to the need to "excite" a "spirit of emulation," and many writers voiced the opinion that premiums were the key to agricultural improvement.[58] Excellence was measurable in the charcoal-burning and nail-making operations. In trades where it was not, Jefferson focused on production rather than efficiency. He allowed his enslaved coopers to keep one of every thirty-one flour barrels they made for their own benefit, and referred to their incentives as "allowances" rather than premiums.[59]

With the enslaved manager of the nailery, Jefferson entered into an almost contractual profit-sharing agreement, similar to his contracts with the free men who at times directed his textile and blacksmith shops. From 1794, head blacksmith George Granger, the son of "Great George" Granger the scythe sharpener, was in charge, combining his supervision of the nailers with his own work at the forge. Jefferson "allowed" him 3 percent of the total sales of nails. As the nailery became more productive, Granger's percentage of gross sales was reduced to 2 percent. Still, he earned about forty dollars in 1796, and again in 1797, a considerable sum for an enslaved man.[60] When Jefferson returned to public life in 1797, Granger was Jefferson's understudy as quality-control manager. The effectiveness of his management was made manifest by the state of affairs after he fell ill in 1798: the business went on "poorly," with a significant decrease in both the volume and quality of nails, and at one point nail-making almost ceased altogether.[61] The nailery showed a striking profit in its first years, when George Granger was in good health, even in Jefferson's absence.[62]

Yet, Jefferson's daily presence, from 1794 to 1797, was also undoubtedly a significant factor in its success. For reasons beyond economy, it was important that he carry on his works with "little boys." Even when he wished to significantly expand the nailery's operations in 1796, Jefferson did not turn to older farm laborers. He brought three eleven-year-old boys from his Bedford County plantation, Poplar Forest, ninety miles away, and, in a rare step, purchased two others.[63] That Jefferson was conducting a kind of academy on the mountaintop is also suggested by the fact that the nail boys seem to have been housed together, not with their families.[64] His corps of youthful nailers was, as Jefferson said of prospective University of Virginia students, "at that age of aptness, docility, and emulation of the practices of manhood" when lessons were "soonest learnt and longest remembered."[65] Young African Americans were rational beings, their characters as susceptible of improvement as the Pennsylvania criminals transferred from labor on the "high roads" to the confines of the reformed Walnut Street prison. Exhibiting these prisoners "as a public spectacle," Jefferson wrote, "with shaved heads and mean clothing, . . . produced in the criminals such a prostration of character, such an abandonment of self-respect, as, instead of reforming, plunged them into the most desperate and hardened depravity of morals and character."[66]

As manager, schoolmaster, and warden, Jefferson focused on the characters of the enslaved teenagers in his nailery. He could harness the universal human desire to excel to turn tons of nail rod into thousands of nails. In early 1801, soon to return to Monticello for a spring break, Jefferson wrote home to enjoin mild treatment of the nailers. As they "will be again under my government, I would chuse they should retain the stimulus of character."[67] His explicit references to the molding of slave character are scarce, but there are echoes of his ideas in the words, some years later, of his son-in-law Thomas Mann Randolph, whose plantation adjoining Monticello was another laboratory for new methods of management. After hearing of the suicide of a slave on a nearby plantation, Randolph wrote a friend that he no longer needed "the old mode of government" and had long ago "dismissed the man-whip" from his own property: "I find however that the cane of a Corporal must be tolerated yet. But I allways scrupulously distinguish, and exempt, manly and moral character, when it shews itself with any steadiness of ray in the sooty atmosphere of our slave discipline." In Randolph's view, the overseer at the other plantation "could not understand the value of character in a slave, and concluded that fear would be safer security for good conduct than any determination to do right."[68]

The duc de La Rochefoucauld-Liancourt highlighted the changing attitudes toward management and discipline in this period of transition at the end of the eighteenth century, noting how a young judge of the Pennsylvania supreme court, one of the leading lights of the penal reform movement, was "less inclined" than his older colleagues "to despair of the melioration of the human character."[69] Jefferson applied similar principles to education. He described "the best mode of government for youth" in one of the founding documents of the University of Virginia: "Pride of character, laudable ambition, and moral dispositions . . . have a happier effect on future character than the degrading motive of fear." He recommended instead the "affectionate deportment between father and son" as the "best example" for tutor and pupil. This system, "founded in reason and comity, will be more likely to nourish, in the minds of our youth, the combined spirit of order and self respect, so congenial with our political institutions, and so important to be woven into the American character."[70]

Although Jefferson tried to make his plantation more politically "congenial" through the introduction of "reason and comity" into the government of his slaves, the qualities he was trying to encourage were not intended to be woven into the fabric of the American character. Reformed prisons and enlightened educational institutions restored or prepared individuals as useful citizens in a free society. The Monticello nailery, however, was a prison for life, a school for slavery, training up useful members of Jefferson's economic enterprise. Both he and his son-in-law were most concerned with the "*value* of character" in their slaves. In his letter urging restraint in corporal punishment of the nailers, Jefferson wrote that "it would destroy their value, in my estimation, to degrade them in their own eyes by the whip."[71]

Jefferson tried to minimize the "degrading motive of fear" and to instill character traits that were no different from those he—and most employers—sought in free workmen: industry and honesty. Sobriety, the third trait he sought, in vain, in free workmen was less of an issue in the case of his enslaved workers, who had little access to alcohol.[72] The inspectors of the Walnut Street prison had similar aims, according to rules drawn up in 1792: "The prisoners who distinguish themselves by their attention to cleanliness, sobriety, industry and orderly conduct, shall . . . meet with such rewards as is in their power to grant or procure for them."[73] While exciting emulation helped to achieve industry, Jefferson pursued honesty by methods that were quite unusual for the time and place. He allowed his enslaved smiths and carpenters a surprising freedom from supervision. Thomas Mann Randolph wrote his father-in-law in 1798 referring to "the thorough confidence you place in the companies of tradesmen" and expressing his fear that "being under no command whatever they will become idle and dissipated." He acknowledged the management goal he shared with Jefferson when he concluded, "Tho' I am clear that it confirms them in honesty."[74] Both Jefferson and Randolph understood "honesty" in its broad, eighteenth-century sense, as signifying virtue, integrity, and morality, not just veracity. According to Jefferson's "creed on the foundation of morality in man," it could be demonstrated "by sound calculation that honesty promotes interest in the long run."[75]

The enslaved men's greater degree of autonomy was not just a result of Jefferson's labor reforms. It was also a function of the transition, made at Monticello in the 1790s, from tobacco culture to a more diversified operation with wheat as the staple crop. Since wheat cultivation required about one-fifth the amount of labor as tobacco, more attention could be given to raising subsidiary crops and livestock. This more complex enterprise required more vehicles and draft animals, more complicated machinery, and workers with a greater variety of skills. Multiple activities that spread themselves across the entire plantation landscape were beyond the range of a single overseer. The master or overseer now had to focus on the products of his workers rather than on the labor process. Archaeological excavations at Monticello have shown that there was increased autonomy in the slave quarters as well as in the fields. On Mulberry Row, single-family dwellings replaced the larger multi-family structures of the 1770s. On the plantation, cabins that had once been clustered near the overseer's house were, by the turn of the century, moved to the fringes of the greatly expanded plowlands and scattered about on their own.[76]

It is interesting that this greater autonomy on the plantation occurred at a time when Jefferson's own vigilance was dramatically increased by his full-time presence at Monticello, from 1794 to 1797. These were the years when Jefferson monitored the performance of the nailers on a daily—even twice-daily—basis. Considered in the context of surveillance, his small Virginia mountain begins to take on the shape of a panopticon, with Jefferson, elevated above the surrounding landscape and its inhabitants, inspecting the workings of his world. Monticello thus echoes Jeremy Bentham's panopticon, an ideal prison that incorporated both the principle of the junction of interest and duty, and the more infamous "inspection principle" with its "invisible eye."

At the center of Bentham's panopticon design, the warden, shielded by venetian blinds, was able to see into every cell but was invisible to the prisoners. Jefferson, in 1797, included such blinds (which, he wrote, "exclude the sight" while admitting air) in his plan for a Virginia penitentiary, and he had them added to every house he lived in. At Monticello, he had built what he called "Venetian porches," or "porticles," with louvered blinds, that adjoined his private apartments, and thus, from inside, he could see without being seen.[77]

In the preface to *Panopticon,* Bentham described his "simple idea in Architecture" as "a new mode of obtaining power of mind over mind."[78] There is no question that the African Americans within the Sage of Monticello's extensive panorama were acutely conscious of an all-seeing Jefferson and his Enlightenment optical equipment. In his recollections late in life, Peter Fossett, who was a child of eleven when Jefferson died, combined the telescope he could see every day on Monticello's North Terrace with Revolutionary War events he had heard about from older family members: "One day while Mr. Jefferson was looking through his telescope to see how the work was progressing over at Pan Top, one of his plantations, he saw 500 soldiers, headed by Col. Tarleton, . . . coming up the north side of the mountain to capture him." It is curious that Fossett chose Pantops, which means "all-seeing," as the quarter farm Jefferson was inspecting. Similarly, a black man who had worked on the construction of the University of Virginia, three miles distant from Monticello, recalled Jefferson standing in the yard, watching "we alls at work through his spyglass."[79] Jefferson's perpetual attention was also conveyed through sound as well as sight: he acquired a Chinese gong to broadcast the measurement of time "all over my farm."[80]

When Jefferson was called back into public service in 1797, his reforming experiments at Monticello came to a standstill. He leased out his quarter farms and their laborers, while the pursuit of agriculture on the home farm was so minimal that its fields grew up in broomsedge.[81] Jefferson was "overshadowed . . . with despair" because of his inability to pursue a systematic reformation of his farm and the treatment of its laborers. He admitted to a sense of defeat in his dual pursuit of profit and humanity, when he wrote in 1799, "I am not fit to be a farmer with the kind of labour that we have."[82] While president, Jefferson poured his resources into rebuilding his house and pressing on with several monumental earthmoving projects: clearing roads, digging a canal for his mills, and leveling a 1,000-foot vegetable garden terrace. Enslaved men hired from other owners bore the brunt of this work, while the African American men who remained on the Monticello mountaintop carried on with their gardening, wagoning, woodworking, and blacksmithing tasks.

Work in the nailery continued but in a much-altered form. The nail boys had grown up, and it was mainly a crew of young men in their twenties who carried on the work on a reduced scale. Dependable management had ended with the death of George Granger in 1799. In 1801, Jefferson hired a free white blacksmith from Philadelphia to supervise the nailers as well as work at the forge. The highly talented, but often inebriated William Stewart was unable to cope with them: "They require a rigour of discipline to make them do reasonable work, to which he cannot bring himself."[83] A shifting set of overseers, some known to be quick to use the whip, took charge, and there were episodes of violence and misbehavior.

James Hubbard, the nailer whose efficiency had risen so swiftly in the early days, became a chronic runaway, was flogged in the presence of his fellow workers, and was sold—in keeping with Jefferson's policy of removing disruptive elements from the plantation.[84] In 1803, when Jefferson was in Washington, eighteen-year-old Cary violently struck a fellow nailer, Brown Colbert, with his hammer, nearly killing him. Jefferson ordered swift plantation justice: "Should Brown recover so that the law shall inflict no punishment on Cary, it will be necessary for me to make an example of him in terrorem to others, in order to maintain the police so rigorously necessary among the nailboys." Cary's fate was that most feared by enslaved people—sale to the Deep South. If no Georgia slave trader happened to pass by, wrote Jefferson, "if he could be sold in any other quarter so distant as never more to be heard of among us, it would to the others be as if he were put out of the way by death."[85] This was the Monticello equivalent to sending a prisoner to solitary confinement, which Caleb Lownes had described as "an object of *real terror*" to all in the Walnut Street prison.[86] One incident in 1807 indicates the persistence of Jefferson's "power of mind" and the motivating force of character. Monticello overseer Edmund Bacon discovered the hiding place of several hundred pounds of nails, worth fifty dollars or more, stolen by one of the nailers. He caught the thief, who was brought before Jefferson: "I never saw any person, white or black, feel as badly as he did when he saw his master. He was mortified and distressed beyond measure. He had been brought up in the shop, and we all had confidence in him. Now his character was gone. The tears streamed down his face, and he begged pardon over and over again."[87]

On the whole, Jefferson succeeded in producing a set of enslaved artisans who were highly skilled, productive, and dependable. Several of the first occupants of the nailery became blacksmiths, carpenters, or wagoners. Others occupied the positions of butler, cooper, gardener, and shoemaker. Former nailers had charge of Jefferson's house, stables, garden, and shops. One of them, Wormley Hughes, when he was the thirty-year-old head gardener and head stableman at Monticello, was, in Jefferson's eyes, "one of the most trusty servants I have."[88]

No matter how honest and industrious they were, the Monticello tradesmen could never achieve instant liberty through good behavior, as could inmates of the Walnut Street jail, where pardons were granted to prisoners who were considered rehabilitated. Jefferson had no intention of freeing his slaves so long as slavery was the law in Virginia. He does, however, seem to have been thinking of their ultimate future in freedom, however remote. He was beginning to carry out, within the confines of Monticello, part of his plan of gradual emancipation, which included expatriation beyond the boundaries of the United States. The attributes he was trying to develop in his enslaved tradesmen are like those described in his emancipation scheme as a preparation for freedom and citizenship, even if in a distant land. The slaves were entitled, eventually, to the blessings of democracy, a word Jefferson rarely used, and never in the way we do today.[89] As he wrote in 1815, "The mind . . . of the slave is to be prepared by instruction and habit for self-government, and for the honest pursuits of industry and social duty."[90]

Whether or not he was intentionally preparing them for freedom, his pursuit of the "happiness" of his slaves in conjunction with his own gave them tools to pursue their own ideas of happiness. The development of skills as well as "character" provided some of the prerequisites for freedom, a measure of personal autonomy, and the capacity for self-government. This is not to suggest that the enslaved men needed Jefferson's training to acquire such traits. But under his humanitarian management they had a broader and safer space in which to "soundly calculate" their own best interests than did many of their fellow slaves. Most of them concluded that productivity and trustworthiness were of greatest benefit to themselves and their families. And in several cases, the end result was freedom.

Jefferson apparently had considered bequeathing freedom to three of the original corps of nailers for some time. He freed butler Burwell Colbert and blacksmith Joseph Fossett in his will, and recommended unofficial freedom for gardener Wormley Hughes. His granddaughter Ellen Coolidge, who had left Monticello a year before Jefferson's death, recalled that several of the slaves "knew that at his death they were to become free—he had promised it to those among them who, possessing a trade by which they could support themselves, ran no risk of falling burthens on the community, or of being reduced to unlawful means of living."[91]

In the absence of any Emancipation Acts on the state or national level, Jefferson's recipe for dealing with slavery depended, as he told Isaac Briggs in 1820, on "improving the condition of this poor, afflicted, degraded race," which would eventually end in their "equal liberty and the enjoyment of equal rights."[92] Yet the rational and moral society Jefferson imagined for Monticello remained unperfected, and it never served as a shining example to help achieve a revolution in public opinion, much less a general emancipation. Despite their humanitarian reforms, he and other more enlightened slaveholders failed to convince a skeptical world of any improvement in Southern society. Two British women were among those who made this point. In 1818, Frances Wright, while acknowledging the humanity of Virginia slaveholders in their efforts to ameliorate the conditions of their slaves, considered that they were merely "gilding" rather than breaking the chains of slavery. Seventeen years later, Harriet Martineau lamented the "blunting of the moral sense of the most conscientious" of the Southerners she met.[93] Soon, the humanitarian rhetoric of the ameliorators would be co-opted by Southerners extolling the benefits of their way of life. The cherished axiom that had consoled Jefferson in his efforts to humanize the institution of slavery was perverted to defend it. Virginia-born William H. Holcombe invoked the deity in 1860: "As the calls for the abolition of slavery became world-wide, eventually just about all Southerners would come to believe they not only had a right to own slaves, but were serving a God-given duty in owning slaves in order to improve them. . . . God has lightened our task and secured its execution by making our interests happily coincide with our duty."[94]

While Dr. Holcombe and other proslavery writers were making their cases, the flame of genuine Jeffersonian ideals was maintained largely by African Americans, plus a small band of white abolitionists. Descendants of Monticello's enslaved men and women were among those who worked steadily through the nineteenth and early twentieth centuries to make the nation live up to the ideals of its founding document, Jefferson's Declaration. The family of one of Monticello's original nailers is exemplary. Joseph Fossett had worked in the nailery from the age of fourteen. After training as a blacksmith, he was in charge of the Monticello shop for twenty years. While Fossett was freed in Jefferson's will, his wife and eight children were not, and all were put on the auction block six months after Jefferson's death. Joe Fossett availed himself of his money-earning skills as a blacksmith and his character as a man who could be trusted: he was able to persuade local white merchants to purchase some of his children until he could repay them. By mid-century, Fossett, his wife, Edith, and all but one of their children had left the world of slavery and were living in Cincinnati, where they owned a house and blacksmith shop.

It is clear that Joseph Fossett had high ambitions for his children. The importance of education, as well as social status, is indicated by his gift of a writing-book and a silver watch to his still-enslaved son, Peter. Peter Fossett and his brothers became dynamic leaders in Cincinnati's political, religious, and educational life and its leading caterers after the Civil War. And the entire family was incessantly active in opposing the institution of slavery—through the forging of free passes, the sheltering of fugitives on the Underground Railroad, the integration of streetcars, and through putting civil rights laws to the test.[95] Joseph and Edith Fossett's character emerged most strongly in their great-grandson William Monroe Trotter, the famously dedicated and uncompromising warrior on behalf of liberty and equality, who raised the ire of Woodrow Wilson in one of many spirited encounters with American presidents. In W. E. B. Du Bois's words, Trotter was "a man of heroic proportions, and probably one of the most selfless of Negro leaders during all our American history."[96] The *Philadelphia Tribune* saluted Trotter on his sixtieth birthday: "For 30 years he has been foremost among those who have borne the 'toil and heat of the day' battling unceasingly, unrelentingly for those rights guaranteed colored Americans by the Declaration of Independence."[97]

Notes

1. Thomas Jefferson [hereafter, TJ] to Angelica Church, November 27, 1793, in *The Papers of Thomas Jefferson*, ed. Julian P. Boyd et al., 36 vols. to date (Princeton, NJ, 1950–), 27:449. Until the publication of volume 27 of the *Papers*, "my feilds to farm" was the usual rendering of the phrase. Whether or not Jefferson intended it, he certainly wrote "to form."

2. Peter S. Onuf, "Domesticating the Captive Nation: Thomas Jefferson and the Problem of Slavery," this volume.

3. TJ to John Adams, February 28, 1796, in Boyd et al., eds., *Papers of Thomas Jefferson*, 28:618.

4. TJ to Thomas Leiper, February 23, 1801, in *Thomas Jefferson's Farm Book*, ed. Edwin M. Betts (Princeton, NJ, 1953), 280.

5. TJ to Philip Mazzei, May 30, 1795, in Boyd et al., eds., *Papers of Thomas Jefferson*, 20:270; TJ to Elizabeth House Trist, September 23, 1795, ibid., 28:478.

6. TJ to George Washington, May 14, 1794, ibid., 28:75.

7. TJ to John Adams, September 12, 1821, in *The Adams-Jefferson Letters: The Complete Correspondence between Thomas Jefferson and Abigail and John Adams*, ed. Lester J. Cappon, 2 vols. (Chapel Hill, NC, 1959), 2:575; TJ to William Ludlow, September 6, 1824, in *The Writings of Thomas Jefferson*, ed. Andrew A. Lipscomb and Albert Ellery Bergh, 20 vols. (Washington, DC, 1903–4), 16:75.

8. TJ to Elizabeth House Trist, September 23, 1795, in Boyd et al., eds., *Papers of Thomas Jefferson*, 28:478. For further references to "barbarous" agricultural practices, see TJ to John Taylor, December 29, 1794, ibid., 28:233; TJ to George Washington, September 12, 1795, ibid., 28:494; and TJ to Francis Willis, July 15 1796, ibid., 29:153.

9. TJ to Francis Willis, July 15, 1796, ibid., 29:153.

10. François-Alexandre-Frédéric de La Rochefoucauld-Liancourt, *Travels through the United States of North America*, 4 vols. (London, 1799), 2:75.

11. Betts, ed., *Thomas Jefferson's Farm Book*, 46F ("F" denotes facsimile page numbers).

12. For instance, the plan called for eighteen cradlers and twenty-four scythes, and in June 1796, "the 18. mowers had been fixed on & furnished with 27. scythes" (Betts, ed., *Thomas Jefferson's Farm Book*, 46F, 54F).

13. Francis Bacon, *The Advancement of Learning* (New York, 2001), 58.

14. Betts, ed., *Thomas Jefferson's Farm Book*, 46F.

15. Ibid., 54F.

16. TJ to John Holmes Freeman, December 21, 1805, ibid., 417.

17. *Weevils in the Wheat: Interviews with Virginia Ex-Slaves*, ed. Charles L. Perdue Jr., Thomas E. Barden, and Robert K. Phillips (Charlottesville, VA, 1976), 26 [indications of pronunciation removed].

18. Betts, ed., *Thomas Jefferson's Farm Book*, 58F. Squire was the man with the grindstone in a cart in the 1799 harvest. No such role is listed in the harvest plan for 1800. For "ambulatory shop," see, e.g., the letter from "Agricultor," in the *Farmer's Register* (vol. 1, no. 1, [June 1833], 48). In the two subsequent harvests for which calculations are possible (1799 and 1812), the average for each cutter was only 1½ acres per day (Betts, ed., *Thomas Jefferson's Farm Book*, 58F, 143).

19. *The Correspondence of the Three William Byrds of Westover, Virginia, 1684–1776*, ed. Marion Tinling, 2 vols. (Charlottesville, VA, 1977), 1:355.

20. TJ to David B. Warden, January 12, 1811, in *Thomas Jefferson's Garden Book*, ed. Edwin Morris Betts (Philadelphia, 1944), 451. Of more than thirty overseers employed at Monticello in Jefferson's lifetime, only one, George Granger, was an enslaved man.

21. Ellen Randolph Coolidge to Joseph Coolidge, October 24, 1858, box 3 (Coolidge Letterbook, p. 98), Correspondence of Ellen Wayles Randolph Coolidge, 1810–1861, accession no. 38–584, 9090, 9090-c, Albert and Shirley Small Special Collections Library, University of Virginia, Charlottesville, VA [hereafter, UVA]; Thomas Jefferson Randolph recollections, ca. 1873, Papers of the Randolph Family of Edgehill, accession no. 1397, UVA; recollections of Edmund Bacon and Isaac (Granger) Jefferson, in James A. Bear Jr., ed., *Jefferson at Monticello* (Charlottesville, VA, 1967), 23, 97; and recollections of Peter Fossett, in *New York World*, January 30, 1898.

22. TJ to John Strode, June 5, 1805, in Betts, ed. *Thomas Jefferson's Garden Book*, 302–3; Thomas Mann Randolph to TJ, March 27, 1792, in Boyd et al., eds., *Papers of Thomas Jefferson*, 23:347; TJ to Thomas Mann Randolph, April 19, 1792, ibid., 23:435–36; and TJ to Thomas Mann Randolph, June 24, 1793, ibid., 26:356.

23. TJ to Jacob Hollingsworth, November 22, 1792, in Boyd et al., eds., *Papers of Thomas Jefferson*, 24:656.

24. TJ to Thomas Mann Randolph, February 18, 1793, ibid., 25:230. This statement was made in connection with Jefferson's effort to find tenants as well as overseers in Cecil County; he was unsuccessful in luring any tenants from Maryland to Monticello.

25. TJ to James Madison, February 15, 1794, ibid., 28:22.

26. Biddle vanished from the local scene, while Alexander became a permanent Albemarle County resident, at one point leasing from Jefferson the lands he had previously managed (for the lease [dated July 21, 1805], see Betts, ed., *Thomas Jefferson's Farm Book*, 171–72).

27. TJ to Sir John Sinclair, March 23, 1798, in Boyd et al., eds., *Papers of Thomas Jefferson*, 30:206.

28. TJ to Jean Baptiste Say, February 1, 1804, in Thomas Jefferson, *Writings*, ed. Merrill Peterson (New York, 1984), 1144; Second Inaugural Address, March 4, 1805, ibid., 518.

29. TJ to Joel Yancey, January 17, 1819, in Betts, ed., *Thomas Jefferson's Farm Book*, 43.

30. TJ comparison of marriage settlements [1797], Thomas Jefferson Papers, Massachusetts Historical Society, Boston. The four children were Judy Hix's sons Ben and Kit, Mary Hemings's daughter Betsy, and Betty Brown's daughter Melinda Colbert.

31. TJ to Thomas Mann Randolph, May 19, 1793, in Boyd et al., eds., *Papers of Thomas Jefferson*, 26:65.

32. TJ to William Short, April 13, 1800, ibid., 31:502. On Jefferson's nailery, see David Howard Shayt, "The Nailery of Thomas Jefferson: Ironworking in Arcadia," May 8, 1983, unpublished manuscript in the Jefferson Library at Monticello. Shayt provides excellent background information on nail-making at the time; some of his conclusions about nail-making at Monticello are incorrect.

33. TJ to Caleb Lownes, December 18, 1793, in Boyd et al., eds., *Papers of Thomas Jefferson*, 27:586.

34. See François-Alexandre-Frédéric de La Rochefoucauld-Liancourt, *On the Prisons of Philadelphia* (Philadelphia, 1796), 22; La Rochefoucauld-Liancourt, *Travels through the United States of North America*, 2:345–46; Negley K. Teeters, *The Cradle of the Penitentiary: The Walnut Street Jail at Philadelphia, 1773–1835* (Philadelphia, 1955), 36–38.

35. Teeters, *Cradle of the Penitentiary*, 39.

36. Teeters, *Cradle of the Penitentiary*, 36–62; LeRoy B. DePuy, "The Walnut Street Prison: Pennsylvania's First Penitentiary," *Pennsylvania History* 18 (April 1951): 130–44.

37. La Rochefoucauld-Liancourt, *On the Prisons of Philadelphia*, 22.

38. Caleb Lownes, *An Account of the Gaol and Penitentiary House of Philadelphia* (Philadelphia, 1793), cited in Teeters, *Cradle of the Penitentiary*, 42.

39. TJ to James Buchanan and William Hay, August 13, 1785, in Boyd et al., eds., *Papers of Thomas Jefferson*, 8:368; TJ to James Buchanan and William Hay, 26 January 1786, ibid., 9:222; Howard C. Rice Jr., "A French Source of Jefferson's Plan for the Prison at Richmond," *Journal of the Society of Architectural Historians* 12 (December 1953): 28–30.

40. Robert Turnbull, *A Visit to the Philadelphia Prison* (Philadelphia, 1796), cited in Teeters, *Cradle of the Penitentiary*, 45.

41. La Rochefoucauld-Liancourt's account suggests that nail-making was present in the first half of 1795. The first advertisement found for nails supplied from the prison, "on an extensive plan," is dated July 30, 1795 (*Pennsylvania Gazette*, September 12, 1795). It is possible nails were made on a smaller scale before that.

42. As Bentham stated on the title page to his *Panopticon; or, The Inspection House*, the principles of the Panopticon were applicable "to any sort of establishment, in which persons of any description are to be kept under inspection; and in particular to Penitentiary-Houses, Prisons, Poor-Houses, Lazarettos, Houses of Industry, Manufactories, Hospitals, Work-Houses, Mad-Houses, and Schools."

43. Thomas Condie, "Plan, Construction and etc. of the Jail and Penitentiary House of Philadelphia," *Philadelphia Monthly Magazine*, February 1798, printed in Teeters, *Cradle of the Penitentiary*, 129–32 (quotations, 129–30).

44. Benjamin Rush was one of the reformers who particularly mentioned the virtue-promoting properties of prisons. For a typical view of factories, see the letter to the editors of New Haven's *Connecticut Herald* for January 9, 1811; written by officials of Humphreysville, Connecticut, it describes the Humphreysville Manufacturing Co. and expresses the view that manufacturing establishments, "instead of being productive of drunkenness, debauchery and vice, may become nurseries of sobriety, diligence and virtue" (*The Papers of James Madison: Presidential Series*, ed. J. C. A. Stagg et al. [Charlottesville, VA, 1999], 4:148–49).

45. TJ to Jean Nicolas Démeunier, April 29, 1795, in Boyd et al., eds., *Papers of Thomas Jefferson*, 28:341.

46. TJ to Thomas Mann Randolph, January 23, 1801, ibid., 32:500.

47. La Rochefoucauld-Liancourt, *Travels through the United States of North America*, 2:80.

48. Bear, *Jefferson at Monticello*, 23. Called "Jefferson" by the Reverend Charles Campbell, who recorded his recollections, it is now known that Isaac's family name was Granger (see Monticello's "Getting Word" oral history project, www.monticello. org/gettingword/). His statement about special rations is validated by Farm Book entries.

49. Betts, ed., *Thomas Jefferson's Farm Book*, 110–11F; Thomas Jefferson, *Nail Book* (1796–1826) [rare book], at William A. Clark Memorial Library, University of California, Los Angeles. Jefferson, who had no success in decimalizing the nation's weights and measures, made sure that Monticello's scales were decimalized.

50. In the 1770s, the enslaved blacksmiths customarily received a "gratuity"; in later years, John Hemmings, joiner, and Burwell Colbert, butler, were given an "an-

nual gratuity" (James A. Bear Jr. and Lucia C. Stanton, eds., *Jefferson's Memorandum Books: Accounts, with Legal Records and Miscellany, 1767–1826* [Princeton, NJ, 1997], 459, 1265, 1275, and passim).

51. Bear and Stanton, *Jefferson's Memorandum Books,* 925 (January 28, 1795). No explicit reference to training has been found; it is assumed that subsequent charcoal-burners at Monticello—all enslaved—learned first from Silknitter and then from each other.

52. Ibid., 1001 (May 14, 1799).

53. "Statement of Nailery Profits," 1794–97, in Boyd et al., eds., *Papers of Thomas Jefferson,* 29:540–41; Memorandum to Richard Richardson, ca. December 21, 1799, in Boyd et al., eds., *Papers of Thomas Jefferson,* 31:271.

54. Jefferson, *Autobiography* (1821), in Peterson, ed., *Thomas Jefferson Writings,* 44; Thomas Jefferson, *Notes on the State of Virginia,* ed. William Peden (Chapel Hill, NC, 1958), 143.

55. TJ to John Wayles Eppes, December 21, 1797, in Boyd et al., eds., *Papers of Thomas Jefferson,* 29:586. The blacksmith was Isaac Granger, apparently one of Jacob Silknitter's pupils in charcoal-burning; Jefferson had given Granger to Eppes.

56. Bear and Stanton, *Jefferson's Memorandum Books,* 2:1354 (May 5, 1819), 1361 (February 15, 1820).

57. TJ to Philip Tabb, June 1, 1809, in Betts, ed., *Thomas Jefferson's Garden Book,* 412.

58. From its beginning in 1819, John S. Skinner's agricultural weekly, *The American Farmer,* evidences a rising tide of such references (see, as a sampling, 1:265, 329–30; 2:150, 165; 3:164; 4:90, 273–74).

59. Bear and Stanton, *Jefferson's Memorandum Books,* 2:1287 (March 17, 1813), 1329 (December 21, 1816), 1376 (June 26, 1821).

60. "Statement of Nailery Profits," 1794–97, in Boyd et al., eds., *Papers of Thomas Jefferson,* 29:540–41. In 1795, Granger's brother Isaac received a percentage as well.

61. TJ to John McDowell, October 22, 1798, in Boyd et al., eds., *Papers of Thomas Jefferson,* 30: 563; TJ to John McDowell, March 21, 1799, ibid., 31:83; TJ to Archibald Stuart, 14 May 1799, ibid., 31:110.

62. "Statement of Nailery Profits," 1794–97, ibid., 29:540–41.

63. Jefferson purchased Ben and Cary from his brother Randolph Jefferson, and Philip Hubbard, John, and Davy were brought from Poplar Forest; all were born in 1785 or 1786 (see Bear and Stanton, *Jefferson's Memorandum Books,* 945 [September 3, 1796], 952 [February 9, 1797]; Betts, ed., *Thomas Jefferson's Farm Book,* 56F; and Jefferson, *Nail Book*).

64. See Betts, ed., *Thomas Jefferson's Farm Book,* 50F–52F (for bread list), 53F.

65. Reports of the Commissioners for the University of Virginia, August 4, 1818, in Peterson, ed., *Thomas Jefferson Writings,* 468.

66. Jefferson, *Autobiography* (1821), ibid., 41.

67. TJ to Thomas Mann Randolph, January 23, 1801, in Boyd et al., eds., *Papers of Thomas Jefferson,* 32:500.

68. Thomas Mann Randolph to Nicholas P. Trist, November 22, 1818, Papers of

the Trist, Randolph, and Burke Families, 1721–1969, accession no. 10487, UVA. The suicide took place at Morven, the property of David Higginbotham.

69. La Rochefoucauld-Liancourt, *On the Prisons of Philadelphia*, 22. The judge was William Bradford.

70. Report to the Commissioners, in Peterson, ed., *Thomas Jefferson Writings*, 469.

71. TJ to Thomas Mann Randolph, January 23, 1801, in Boyd et al., eds., *Papers of Thomas Jefferson*, 32:499–500.

72. Those seeking workers in this period invariably used some variation of the phrase "honesty, industry, and sobriety" in their advertisements (see, e.g., New York's *Columbian Gazetteer* for March 24, 1794, and Charleston, South Carolina's *City Gazette* for May 10, 1794). For examples of Jefferson's appreciation of the same qualities in his employees, see TJ to John Harvie, September 27, 1804, Thomas Jefferson Papers, Massachusetts Historical Society; and TJ to Samuel H. Smith, August 15, 1813, in *The Papers of Thomas Jefferson: Retirement Series,* ed. J. Jefferson Looney et al., 6 vols. to date (Princeton, NJ, 2004–), 6:399.

73. Teeters, *Cradle of the Penitentiary,* 134.

74. Thomas Mann Randolph to TJ, February 3, 1798, in Boyd et al., eds., *Papers of Thomas Jefferson,* 30:79.

75. TJ to Thomas Law, June 13, 1814, in Peterson, ed., *Thomas Jefferson Writings,* 1335–38.

76. Fraser D. Neiman, "Changing Landscapes: Slave Housing at Monticello" (2003), available online at http://www.pbs.org/saf/1301/features/archeology.htm (accessed October 8, 2009). I am indebted to Dr. Fraser D. Neiman, Monticello's director of archeology, for expanding my understanding of the late eighteenth-century transitional period at Monticello. For a full account of the effects of the transition, from tobacco to wheat, see his "The Lost World of Monticello: An Evolutionary Perspective," *Journal of Anthropological Research* 64 (Summer 2008): 161–93.

77. "Notes on Plan of a Prison," enclosure in TJ to James Wood, March 31, 1797, in Boyd et al., eds., *Papers of Thomas Jefferson,* 29:337. Jefferson received a copy of Bentham's *Panopticon* from England in 1792 (Thomas Pinckney to TJ, August 29, 1792, in Boyd et al., eds., *Papers of Thomas Jefferson,* 24:331; see also E. Millicent Sowerby, *Catalogue of the Library of Thomas Jefferson,* 5 vols. [Washington, DC, 1952–59], 3:28–29). For Jefferson's venetian blinds, see Bear and Stanton, *Jefferson's Memorandum Books,* 2 (under index entry for "Furnishings and Furniture"); William L. Beiswanger, "Thomas Jefferson's Essay in Architecture," *Thomas Jefferson's Monticello* (Charlottesville, VA, 2002), 20–22; and Jack McLaughlin, "The Blind Side of Jefferson," *Early American Life* 20 (April 1989), 30–33.

78. Jeremy Bentham, *Panopticon; or, the Inspection-House* (London, 1812), 1.

79. Interview with Peter Fossett, *New York World,* January 30, 1898; Orra Langhorne, "Southern Sketches," *Southern Workman and Hampton School Record* 17 (September 1888), 71.

80. TJ to Henry Remsen, November 13, 1792, in Boyd et al., eds., *Papers of Thomas Jefferson,* 24:617.

81. Thomas Mann Randolph to TJ, June 16, 1805, Edgehill-Randolph Papers, 1749 (1790–1850), 1886, accession no. 1397, UVA.

82. TJ to William Strickland, March 23, 1798, in Boyd et al., eds., *Papers of Thomas Jefferson*, 30:212; TJ to Stevens Thomson Mason, October 27, 1799, ibid., 31:222.

83. TJ to James Dinsmore, December 1, 1802, accession no. 6540, UVA.

84. Lucia Stanton, *Free Some Day: The African-American Families of Monticello* (Charlottesville, VA, 2000), 75–82.

85. TJ to Thomas Mann Randolph, June 8, 1803, in Betts, ed., *Thomas Jefferson's Farm Book*, 19.

86. Lownes, *An Account of the Gaol and Penitentiary House of Philadelphia*, 19.

87. Bear, *Jefferson at Monticello*, 98. The identity of the thief remains uncertain. Bacon named James Hubbard but described the man as a repentant who turned to religion and was "always a good servant afterwards," something that does not fit the rebellious Hubbard (ibid., 97–99).

88. TJ to John Wayles Eppes, May 10, 1810, in Looney et al., eds., *Papers of Thomas Jefferson: Retirement Series*, 2:378; see also Bear and Stanton, *Jefferson's Memorandum Books*, 2:1257 (May 11, 1810).

89. For Jefferson, democracy was pure democracy—that is, a government in which every citizen participated directly in the business of governing (see TJ to Isaac H. Tiffany, August 26, 1816, in Lipscomb and Bergh, eds., *Writings of Thomas Jefferson*, 15:65–66; and TJ to Samuel Kercheval, September 5, 1816, ibid., 15:71–72).

90. TJ to David Barrow, May 1, 1815, ibid., 14:296.

91. Ellen Wayles Coolidge to Mr. Maümur, 1845 (Coolidge Letterbook, p. 24), Correspondence of Ellen Wayles Randolph Coolidge, 1810–1861, accession no. 38–584, 9090, 9090-c, UVA. Wormley Hughes was given "his time" by Jefferson's daughter Martha Randolph, a kind of unofficial freedom that allowed him to avoid the stipulations of the 1806 law that dictated that freed slaves had to leave Virginia within a year.

92. TJ, in conversation with Isaac Briggs, November 1820, in *Visitors to Monticello*, ed. Merrill D. Peterson (Charlottesville, VA, 1989), 90.

93. Frances Wright, *Views of Society and Manners in America* (London, 1821), 518; Harriet Martineau, *Society in America*, 2 vols. (New York, 1837), 2:120.

94. William H. Holcombe, *The Alternative: A Separate Nationality, or the Africanization of the South* (New Orleans, 1860), 6. I thank Charles A. Miller for alerting me to this quotation.

95. For more on the Fossett family, see Stanton, *Free Some Day*, 131–33, 149–55; and Monticello's "Getting Word" oral history project, www.monticello.org/gettingword/.

96. *The Crisis*, May 1934, in *W. E. B. DuBois: Writings* (New York, 1986), 1248–49.

97. *Philadelphia Tribune*, April 7, 1932, 9, 15.

II LINCOLN

Personal Encounters

Abraham Lincoln and African Americans

★ ★ ★   Jean H. Baker

My subject in this essay is Abraham Lincoln and his personal encounters with African Americans. My premise is that Lincoln's various contacts with African American groups and individuals—from childhood, through his two decades in Springfield, and continuing with his later interactions with African Americans in Washington—continually and diversely helped to shape our sixteenth president's changing attitudes about the relations of blacks and whites in a democratic society. My contention is that many of Lincoln's ideas about black slavery and, later, freedom came from firsthand acquaintance, not from idealized, abstract notions discovered through his reading or discussions with colleagues. Moreover, Lincoln's solution to his philosophical dilemma that a system of government based on equality rightfully denied political and social equality to blacks defined as inferior beings rested in his personal relationships with talented blacks. While it is hardly a new idea that Lincoln's political ideas were constantly evolving, the degree to which his various experiences shaped his views has been little appreciated.

As a political philosopher, Lincoln held to democracy and a limited version of equality, one based mostly on merit and opportunity, throughout his life. But his fervent and continuing belief in white supremacy contradicted his views on democracy and equality, and this created a conspicuous dilemma for a man of logic and reason. It is often asserted that our sixteenth president had no political theories and that he instead was representative of that well-known species, the American pragmatist. Lincoln scholar Mark Neely has argued that we should neither over-intellectualize Lincoln's views nor try to systematize his political theories.[1] Still, Lincoln did develop memorable, ever-so-quotable formulations about democracy, and he did grapple with the contradictions that his claims for a republic based on the people's consent represented for blacks.

Clearly, Lincoln believed in a republic grounded in the consent of the governed. Voting was the critical mechanism in achieving the representation of a majority view, and he encouraged "peaceful ballots," enabling every "right-thinking man to go to the polls and without fear or prejudice vote as he thinks."[2] His premise for a democratic government rested on Jefferson's famous first paragraph in the Declaration of Independence, that all men were created free and equal and had certain inalienable rights.

In a speech delivered in Springfield, Illinois, in 1857 that decried the *Dred Scott* decision, Lincoln took issue with Chief Justice Taney's denial of *all* rights for *all* black Americans. Instead, Lincoln expressed his own views on the centrality of the Declaration's founding principles, which "contemplated the progressive improvement in the condition of men everywhere." According to Lincoln, the ideals of the Declaration represented American aspirations, and he cautiously pointed to those constraints on equality, based on the public interest, that necessarily existed in any stable government. There were some violations of freedom that public opinion would permit, he said. For example, the institution of slavery in the southern and border states was guaranteed by the U.S. Constitution and thus could not be assailed; only in the new territories could slavery's expansion be prevented. And of course, to Lincoln, slavery was the ultimate denial of the notion of equality, because all humans possessed moral dignity and must be given some level of freedom of opportunity: "All are human and must be treated accordingly." Yet even the Declaration of Independence, that linchpin of national democracy, did not guarantee total equality. "I think," said Lincoln in June of 1857, "the authors of that notable instrument intended to include *all* men, but they did not intend to declare all men equal *in all respects*. They did not mean to say all were equal in color, size, intellect, moral developments or social capacity. They defined with tolerance distinctness, in what respect they did consider all men created equal—equal in certain inalienable rights, among which are life, liberty and the pursuit of happiness."[3]

In his famous Peoria speech in 1854, Lincoln acknowledged that slavery must end, but when it did, he said, "his own feelings" would not acknowledge blacks as political and social equals. Nor did society at large accept any false abstraction that rendered all humans the same. What would happen if all slaves were freed? "Is it quite certain that this betters their condition? I think I would not hold one in slavery, at any rate. . . . What next? Free them and make them politically our equal? My own feelings will not admit of this, and if mine would we well know that those of the great mass of white people will not. Whether this feeling accords with justice and sound judgment is not the question, if indeed, it is any part of it. A universal feeling, whether well or ill-founded, cannot be solely disregarded."[4]

By 1858, partisan politics compelled Lincoln to be even more blunt. At the fourth debate with Stephen Douglas, in Charleston, Illinois, in the eastern part of the state, Lincoln was quite explicit: "I am not now nor never have been in favor of bringing about in any way the social and political equality of the white and black races (applause)—I am not nor ever have been in favor of making voters or jurors of negroes, nor of qualifying them to hold office nor to intermarry with white people; and I will say in addition to this that there is a physical difference between the white and black races which I believe will for ever forbid the two races living together on terms of social and political equality."[5] Lincoln never went so far with this statement of inequality as to support the popular pseudo-religious and pseudo-scientific view of the origin of blacks in a separate creation—the so-called polygenetic theory. Never did he deny a single creation for all humans. But his later views on the colonization of blacks did develop from his views on racial inequality.

Yet Lincoln continued to believe that blacks were equal in their need to work and to benefit from their labor, just as he himself was equal to better-educated and richer white men. During his debates with Senator Douglas, he once again asserted the right of even "inferior races" to life, liberty, and the pursuit of happiness—the last meaning, to Lincoln, the right to earn a living. Lincoln was a great believer in the importance of achieving equality through economic endeavors; this was, in fact, what he identified as the story of his own life.[6] In time, his personal encounters with successful blacks would hammer away at his views of the social and political prohibitions that should be placed on black citizenship.

Besides allowing for a better understanding of Lincoln's views on democracy and equality, any investigation into the effect his racial experiences may have had in reshaping his philosophical dilemma of race and democracy requires the familiar historical techniques of evidence-gathering and use of empirical data. But it also requires the development of a conceptual framework. My theoretical underpinnings rest with the sociologist's insight that personal contacts with members of minority groups operate as stimulus and response. In the case of Lincoln, such contact made him more aware of his whiteness and, as well, more or less sympathetic, depending on circumstances, to members of marginalized groups. Perceptions based on actual experiences inform our attitudes, just as preconceived societal notions do, and, in turn, our contacts with others elicit characteristics of personality that range across a wide spectrum, from tolerance to authoritarianism.[7]

Of course, Lincoln's reactions were filtered through his own particular personality and temperament, themselves the result of his early relationship with his parents. For example, traveling by steamboat from a visit to his friend Joshua Speed in Louisville in 1841, Lincoln observed the slaves, chained together, being shipped down the Ohio River to a miserable future on a cotton plantation—"separated," as he wrote to Speed's mother, "forever from the scenes of their childhood." Yet, to his astonishment, they appeared cheerful and happy. Lincoln's reflective predisposition took over as he mused on the uncertain effect of "condition upon happiness": "God tempers the wind to the shorn lamb." Here was an encounter that most Americans in the antebellum period would have used to confirm their implanted view of blacks as too stupid and dull to realize their fate—another instance of "Sambo's," to use the familiar nineteenth-century slur, racial inferiority. Lincoln, however, saw African Americans, as George Frederickson has written, "behaving in a way that could be understood in terms of a common humanity and not as the result of peculiar racial characteristics."[8] When Lincoln became president, such encounters, and his reactions to them, made up the building blocks for policies that affected not just four million slaves but half a million free blacks and, ultimately, all white Americans, North and South.

It has long been the conventional wisdom that Lincoln did not have much contact with blacks, either in his youth or in Springfield, and that he came as a personal naïf to Washington's large community of slaves and freed blacks. William Herndon, so often and so mischievously wrong about so many things relating to Lincoln, began this misperception when he wrote that there were only fifty slaves in the whole of Hardin County, Kentucky, where Lincoln was born, outside of Elizabethtown, in 1809. In fact, there were over 1,000 slaves as well as 58 free blacks in the county, out of a total white male population of 1,600.[9] This diversity became an important factor in Lincoln's racial education. Lincoln's father, Thomas—inaccurately characterized by Lincoln's biographer Albert Beveridge as unconscious about slavery, due to his intellectual dullness and "pallid mind"—bought and sold lumber from a man who owned twenty slaves.

When the Lincolns moved to Knob Creek, outside of Elizabethtown, they lived just a mile from the Old Cumberland Road, the popular route for sending slaves from the slave markets of Louisville south to Nashville, and from there, farther west and south. Indeed, the creek faced the road. Doubtless, Lincoln's first personal encounter with African Americans involved his observations of black slaves being herded to the cotton lands of the Deep South. He also saw slave drivers and dealers, who made such an impression that he singled them out years later for condemnation. In Peoria, in 1854, Lincoln identified one of these slave traders: "You have amongst you a sneaking individual of the class of native tyrants, known as the slave dealer. He watches your necessities and crawls up to buy slaves at a speculating price."[10]

As a child, Lincoln not only *saw* slavery, he also heard its sounds—the sighs and moans and baleful singing of the bondsmen.[11] And, as is the case with all children, he necessarily absorbed his parents' attitudes toward slavery. The Lincolns were Baptists in a community in which discussions of slavery and its fate in the border state of Kentucky were in the air everywhere. A bitter controversy over slavery had developed among the Baptists and, to a lesser extent, the Methodists. Some congregations, refusing to worship with slaveholders, had gone so far as to abandon their churches over the issue. In the Lincolns' South Fork church, two miles from the family's log cabin, such a split over the "peculiar institution" had recently occurred, and a self-styled "Emancipator Pastor" had formed a new parish. Thomas and Nancy Lincoln made their convictions known when they affiliated with this Little Mount Church, which was well known in the community as an antislavery congregation and which was farther away from their home.

Later, Lincoln would say that he could not remember when he was not against slavery, which suggests the childhood origins of his antislavery attitude. And he always said that his family had moved to Indiana in 1816, "partly on account of slavery in order to live in a free state," along with the rather more practical reason that Thomas Lincoln wanted more secure land titles.[12] In Lincoln's isolated new home on Pigeon Creek, in Spencer

County, Indiana, where he lived from the age of seven until he was twenty-one, he came in contact with few blacks (there were only fourteen in the entire county) or, for that matter, whites. Unlike some other settlements, the Pigeon Creek area never developed a town, and Lincoln remembered the animals (including bears) and wild vegetation more than the humans.

Louis Warren has calculated that only forty families lived within a five-mile radius, and it is doubtful that a young boy working the seven acres of what he called his father's "big field" had time to visit. What is significant about this period of Lincoln's life—a period when he said he grew up—is that he had few contacts beyond his family, all of whom were antislavery. He went to school, four-and-a-half miles away, at odd times and for only a few months during two winters in Indiana. Although his new home was in a free state, bound by the terms of the Northwest Ordinance of 1787, as was the case in Illinois, there was considerable support at the time for weakening the article of the ordinance that prohibited slavery and involuntary servitude. In any case, the young Lincoln was not subjected to the influence of any schoolmates who might have been infected with the popular proslavery, anti-black attitudes of southern Indiana.

In fact, Lincoln was an unusual student—an autodidact, a self-taught learner who learned from observation. As C. A. Tripp has argued, the ability to think for himself and not accept prevailing ideas without examination was an important part of Lincoln's personality. He thought differently than others; he was less influenced by conventions and, given his circumstances, he was not affected by his peers, because he did not have many. Only his family's antislavery opinions and his own reading influenced him.[13]

Sometime during the fourteen years he lived in Indiana, Lincoln read an extraordinary book by James Riley titled *Narrative of the Loss of the American Brig with an Account of the Sufferings of Her Surviving Officers and Crew*. Reversing the African American experience in the United States, Riley told the story of shipwrecked white sailors captured off the coast of Africa, brutally enslaved by blacks, and eventually emancipated through the payment of compensation to their owners.[14] Years later, in 1854, Lincoln made the point he had absorbed from this book, "that if you have the right to enslave another—very well. And if he can make it his interest, he has the right to enslave you."[15] Such a position denied popular notions that slavery benefited uncivilized Africans, as many Americans then insisted.

There were two unusual circumstances during this period that placed

Lincoln in touch with blacks. In 1828, Lincoln traveled to New Orleans on Dennis Offutt's flatboat, and on this trip, and a subsequent voyage in 1831, as he floated down the Ohio and Mississippi Rivers, he had numerous documented encounters with African Americans. One night, outside of Baton Rouge, Louisiana, he and his companion, Allen Gentry, were attacked by a group of presumably free blacks intent on stealing the boat's cargo. Lincoln suffered a facial laceration in the ensuing fight that left a tiny permanent scar above his eye. Yet he rarely referred to this episode. Instead, what Lincoln remembered most from this trip were the scenes of slavery—the advertisements in New Orleans for runaway slaves and the miserable slave auctions that, according to Gentry's later account, made Lincoln "angry."[16]

Three years later, Lincoln, now twenty-one years old, undertook another flatboat trip to New Orleans, and once again he found the slave auctions repugnant. Years later, his disgust with the institution was manifested in a letter he sent to his friend Joshua Speed. In the letter, he recalled yet another trip, taken in 1841—a "tedious low-water trip on a Steam boat"—and remembered the "continual torment that the ten or a dozen slaves shackled together in irons" had caused him. "I confess I hate to see the poor creatures hunted down and caught and carried back to their stripes, and unrewarded toils but I bite my lip and keep quiet."[17]

By the time Lincoln moved to Springfield, in 1837, he no longer kept quiet about his views on slavery or the political rights of blacks. As a state legislator, he went on record opposing the institution that he had encountered in its rawest form in New Orleans and on the Mississippi and Ohio Rivers. His lifelong antagonism, reinforced by his family's views, was expressed in a resolution he and a legislative colleague introduced that year into the Illinois legislature; it opposed slavery as founded on "both injustice and bad policy." In the same resolution, Lincoln, with characteristic caution, also disavowed abolitionism, as tending to increase "rather than abate its evils."[18] On the other hand, Lincoln also spoke in the legislature against black suffrage, arguing that "the vote must be kept pure from the contamination of colored voters."[19]

Through his observance of slavery, Lincoln had come to understand its maximal contradiction—democracy. Slavery denied human beings the fruits of their labor and thereby violated the notion so palpably obvious in Lincoln's personal ambitions—of the American dream of upward mobility that he saw as crucial to economic democracy. Slavery—this "monstrous unjustice"—denied the right of blacks to govern themselves and to do for themselves individually what the government did not. "If the Negro is a man, is it not to that extent a total destruction of self-government to say that he too shall not govern himself? . . . If the negro is a man, why then my ancient faith teaches men that 'all men are created equal.'"[20]

Additionally, slavery, as he said in his 1854 Peoria speech, "deprives our republican example of its just influence in the world—enables the enemies of free institutions with plausibility to taunt us as hypocrites, causes the real friends of freedom to doubt our sincerity." His famous maxim, "As I would not be a slave, so I would not be a master," described the essence of his conviction that slavery violated the equality implicit in democracy.[21] Lincoln's bedrock opposition to the extension of slavery developed naturally from his experience as a child of the border states, as one cognizant of the difference between the slave state of Kentucky and the free states of his adolescence and manhood, Indiana and Illinois. But his personal experiences with blacks had done nothing to counter his denial of political and social freedom to blacks.

In 1837, Lincoln rode into Springfield with two saddlebags holding all his possessions, unable even to afford a mattress. The capital of Illinois, where he lived from 1837 to 1861, provided him with more contact with African Americans than he had experienced in his earlier years. His chosen state was technically free territory, but on several occasions the legislature seemed poised to return the state to slavery by rewriting its constitution. And, in the late 1840s, the extent of anti-black prejudice was revealed in the community's response to a referendum restricting black migration. Seventy percent of the white males voting in this referendum wanted to exclude blacks from the state; in Springfield, even more—84 percent—voted in favor of exclusion.

The postures and procedures of white supremacy flourished in the growing city, reflected in a number of legal arrangements that made some of Springfield's blacks less than free. For example, the state fostered a system of legalized indentured servitude, and during the 1830s and 1840s it was possible to import slaves under the age of fifteen and register them as indentured servants whose contracts for involuntary service could be bought and sold. Thus, a quasi-legal arrangement of involuntary registered peonage flourished in Illinois.

In his early days in Springfield, Lincoln took the case of one such indentured servant named Nance, who had been sold to another master. In this contract dispute between two white masters, Lincoln argued the position that Nance was not an indentured servant. She had a wage-paying job, an income, and credit. Moreover, said Lincoln, the promissory note that was the nexus of the case was void, because it involved the illegal sale of a human being in a free state.[22] The brief was classic Lincoln, in that he rested his winning case on the economic grounds of Nance's financial success. On the other hand, in 1847, Lincoln supported the claims of Robert Matson, a Kentucky planter, to retain slaves who worked seasonally in Illinois, on the grounds that these slaves were not residents of the free state of Illinois but rather were residents of Kentucky, where slavery was the law of the land. Lincoln lost the Matson case, but his two legal positions are indicative of his views of an American system of slavery that was sustained by legal and constitutional arrangements, and of the potential for free blacks within a democratic system.[23]

Besides the potential for these kinds of judicial violations of black freedom, there were also restrictions in Springfield on those African Americans who were considered free people of color. Free blacks were required to have certificates of freedom, and they could not vote or serve on juries, nor testify in court cases, nor run for office. In an effort to keep Illinois white, blacks were required to post bonds to enter the state, and they could be expelled by a town's commissioners.[24] The result was a black population under duress, whose population did not increase as quickly as the white population. What is significant here is the diversity of the black experience in Springfield as well as the arrangements that circumscribed black freedom, all observed by Lincoln in a community in which such issues were constantly under discussion.

To be sure, there were never many blacks in Lincoln's Springfield—some 234 in a town of 9,000 in 1860. And given blacks' invisibility, historians have noted that most of Lincoln's encounters were with servants who worked in menial positions in his friends' homes and, later, after he married Mary Todd, in his own household. Lincoln's contact with African Americans seemed to end in the dining rooms, kitchens, cellars, and laundry rooms where inferiors like Mariah Vance and Jane Jenkins cooked and cleaned.

But there were exceptions, the best-known case being that of Billy the Barber, the Haitian-born William Fleurville, who cut Lincoln's often disheveled locks and who consulted with Lincoln over problems with his real estate holdings. Fleurville was a prosperous real estate investor whose economic status was above that of most whites. Still, the general view has been the one promulgated by the historian David Herbert Donald, who dismissed any personal contact Lincoln might have experienced with Springfield's blacks in this way: "These were not people who could speak out boldly to say they were as American as whites, that they had no African roots and that, in relation to the colonization efforts, that they did not want to leave the United States."[25]

Yet, as we are beginning to appreciate, such a view of Springfield's previously invisible black community distorts the activities of those free blacks who owned property, lived independently, and had opinions, especially about colonization—the movement that sought to send America's blacks to Liberia.[26] In meetings of local black Americans held in the 1850s, resolutions were passed decrying the efforts "by ignorant and ill-disposed persons to take measures for our expulsion from the land of our nativity, from our country and our homes." Some blacks were active participants in the Underground Railroad in nearby Farmingdale, eight miles west of Springfield, which operated as a station for fugitive slaves throughout Lincoln's years in Illinois.[27]

Springfield's blacks were activists: they celebrated the anniversary of the emancipation of slaves in the British West Indies by marching to one of the many groves outside of town and, after their picnics, listening to speeches. This annual event was faithfully reported in the *Illinois State Journal*. On August 1, 1859, when Lincoln was in Springfield working on a murder case, P. L. Donnigan spoke to this group about West Indian emancipation, and another black property-holder gave a lecture on the evils of American slavery. This particular meeting ended with hearty cheers for Frederick Douglass.[28] Certainly, Lincoln, who was a member of the local colonization society, knew about the public activities of blacks who rejected any plan to send blacks overseas as a solution to the dilemma of a biracial society comprised of superior whites and inferior blacks.

Just as crucial to Lincoln's contacts with and understanding of blacks was his proximity to them. The Lincoln home on Eighth and Jackson was part of an integrated neighborhood within a walking city. The U.S. Census reveals as much. In 1860, writes Richard Hart, "at least 21 African American families—approximately 10 percent of Springfield's African American population—lived within a three block radius of the Lincoln home."[29] Many of the contacts Lincoln must have had with blacks in the everyday routines of neighborly concourse have been lost, but other interactions took place in his office, where free blacks, like Fleurville, consulted him on legal matters. Not surprisingly, Lincoln had substantial acquaintance with several talented African Americans, including the Reverend Henry Brown and the blacksmith Aaron Dyer.

Another Springfield resident, William Johnson, would accompany Lincoln to Washington, where the new president would intervene to find him a job in the Treasury Department after the lighter-skinned blacks on the White House staff refused to accept him. Johnson was with Lincoln at Gettysburg. He died from an infection of the same smallpox-like virus, varioloid, that Lincoln also suffered from. It was Abraham Lincoln who arranged to have Johnson—a man he invariably characterized as honest and worthy—buried in Arlington Cemetery, in January of 1864. Johnson's headstone bears his name and the single evocative epitaph chosen by Lincoln— "citizen."[30] But citizenship was a category that Lincoln had denied blacks earlier, and that he still denied them as a group.

Still, Lincoln had begun to make some exceptions based on his experiences with intelligent, hardworking blacks. He no longer classified all African Americans as being part of an inferior group, and he now recognized that some had the capacity to become members of the political community. His accumulation of personal experiences with free blacks led the president to believe, as he said during the Civil War, that there was a difference between slaves, whose minds had been "clouded" by slavery, and free blacks like Brown and Johnson, who were "capable of thinking like white men."[31]

Lincoln's twenty-five years in Illinois also introduced him not only to the diversity of the position of blacks in society, but also to their variation in aptitudes, just as was the case with whites. Some blacks were independent taxpayers and property-holders, struggling to support their families just as he was, though with far greater odds set against them. Richard Hart counts twenty-three such free and independent families in Springfield—evidently not enough to move Lincoln away from his position, argued in Springfield in 1837, that only in some "trifling particulars" had the condition of blacks in the United States improved: "Their ultimate destiny has never appeared so hopeless."[32]

Gradually, Lincoln's contacts with blacks changed his opinions. Yet these encounters, in the 1850s, certainly did not erase Lincoln's belief that whites were superior to blacks in every way except—and it is a big exception in nineteenth-century America—their humanity and their individual potential. "Blacks have the right to eat their bread, without leave of anybody, which his own hand earns."[33] But overall, as a lawyer and emerging politician, Lincoln had little to say about the relations between free blacks and whites. He said almost nothing about race, in part because he was concerned with only slavery during the decades in which its extension into new territories emerged as the critical political issue. As George Frederickson has written, "Race itself was not then the critical issue it has become for us. It would only become such for Lincoln after emancipation."[34] Only when forced to answer Stephen Douglas's charge, during the Lincoln-Douglas debates, that because he was against slavery he was for racial equality, and therefore supported that greatest heresy of white America, intermarriage, did Lincoln respond with his adroit statement—and to this generation, the ultimate *reductio ad absurdum*—that because he did not want a black woman for a slave did not mean he wanted her for a wife.

He accepted the ruling wisdom—North and South—that whites, by virtue of their color, were superior to blacks. "I am not, nor ever have been in favor of bringing about in any way the social and political equality of the white and black races," he said, in different ways and in many venues. And such sentiments, in the 1850s, were more than political pragmatism to be delivered in the southern, race-baiting part of the state.[35] Certainly, in this view, Lincoln was behind some of his fellow Republicans, as well as black and white abolitionists, who were challenging the notions of white supremacy.[36] On the other hand, Lincoln was not a believer in the innate, and therefore uncorrectable, inferiority of African Americans.

Lincoln's experience in Springfield sustained his denial of the central lever of democracy—the vote—to blacks. His was a democracy of white males. He paid little heed to the black opposition in Springfield to colonization and came to his presidency with the idea that the racial contradiction to democracy could be solved only by the removal of blacks from the United States—albeit voluntarily through colonization. But Springfield also had contributed a racial context in which Lincoln had experienced warm personal relations with the blacks who were his neighbors.

By 1862, these personal encounters had made a difference in Lincoln's attitudes. In his annual message delivered to Congress in December 1862, the president acknowledged his preference for colonization. Still, he believed the grounds on which the objections were made to "free colored persons remaining in the country" were imaginary, "if not malicious." Blacks would not displace white laborers. "It is dreaded the freed people will swarm forth and cover the whole land. Will liberation make them any more numerous? Equally distributed among the whites of the whole country there would be one colored to seven whites. Could the one, in any way greatly disturb the seven? There are many communities now, having more than one freed colored person to seven whites, and this without any apparent consciousness of evil from it."[37]

In Washington, the range of Lincoln's experience with blacks expanded exponentially. With a total population of 75,000 in 1860, the city was home to 14,000 blacks, 3,000 of them enslaved and 11,000 free. Soon there would be a third category—contrabands, the not-officially-freed blacks who, before the Emancipation Proclamation, had left slavery and who flooded into Washington only to live in miserable conditions, having neither work nor housing. Lincoln promptly noticed the difference from the predominately white Midwest of his earlier years, commenting that the District of Columbia and the states of Maryland and Delaware "had more Negroes than he had ever seen and yet the whites never [petitioned] against the presence of free persons as one of its grievances."[38]

At least the slave markets had disappeared since his days as a congressman in 1847–48, outlawed by the Compromise of 1850. In the White House, in that strange judgmental American calculus of colors, the president was served by light-skinned blacks, and his wife's seamstress and friend Elizabeth Keckly exemplified talented African Americans. A former slave, Keckly had managed, through her own diligence, talent, and hard work, to buy her freedom and that of her son, and while in Washington she organized a Contraband Relief Society to which Abraham and Mary Lincoln contributed.

To all those African Americans with whom he came in contact, the president was hospitable and kind. To two visitors in 1863—C. H. Putnam and Martin Delany—he provided letters of introduction to Edwin Stanton, the secretary of war, in which he characterized Dulany, the famous author and exponent of black power, as "a most extraordinary and intelligent black man."[39] With others, including an 1864 delegation from New Orleans who promised they were neither "amalgamationists nor social levellers," he merely listened and promised nothing—giving his regrets that they were not given their rights to free public schools, or the vote, or an end to the

Black Codes. After her meeting with the president, the black suffragist Sojourner Truth commented that she "never was treated by anyone with more kindness and cordiality."[40] Indeed, the president had signed the autobiography that she had brought with her. Two black women who preceded Truth into Lincoln's office were delighted with the pass through the military lines he had given them.

Certainly the diversity of the condition of blacks was even more apparent in Washington than it had been in Springfield, and that variation provided Lincoln with a solution to his race dilemma. In opening the White House to more blacks than ever before, Lincoln received lessons in the possibilities for blacks after their emancipation. Among the visitors was Bishop Daniel Paine of the African Methodist Church, who came to urge Lincoln to sign a resolution emancipating slaves in the District, which in fact he did after the passage of congressional legislation in 1862. Joseph Roberts, a commissioner of emigration, came to report on the possibility of colonization in Liberia, a concept that Lincoln was abandoning in the face of black potential. More famously, a delegation of five African Americans, three of whom were former slaves, arrived on August 14, 1862—the first time blacks as a group with a political purpose had ever met with an American president to discuss a public issue.

It was hardly a give-and-take session. Uncharacteristically, Lincoln launched into a monologue supporting colonization, on the basis that racial differences made any equitable future for blacks impossible in the United States. And he delivered the results of his personal experience: nowhere in America were blacks treated as equals of whites. "Your race are suffering the greatest wrong inflicted on any people. But even when you cease to be slaves you are yet far removed from being placed on an equality with the white race. You are cut off from many of the advantages which the other race enjoys." (Note the use of the plural verb following the word "race," for Lincoln thought of blacks as individuals, not a group.) And then, more harshly, "Not a single man of your race is made the equal of a single man of ours." And finally, Lincoln noted the evil effects "of your present condition on the white man," and this included blame for the Civil War. In this interview, Lincoln promoted his pet solution of colonization, but this at the same time that (ever an enigma) he was developing—indeed, had already done—an entirely different plan: emancipation.[41]

The most famous meetings of Lincoln with African Americans were those that took place with Frederick Douglass, who came to the White House in August 1864 to discuss Lincoln's proposal that the government set up an agency to persuade slaves in the South to come into Union lines. Douglass had been to the White House earlier, having sought an audience to protest the differences between the treatment of whites and blacks in the army. On that occasion, Douglass had been impressed. He had not waited long, despite the crowd of those hoping to talk to the president. Lincoln had risen when he came in the room, and Douglass had felt "as though I could put my hand on his shoulder." Later, Douglass had been invited to tea at the Old Soldiers Home, Lincoln's summer sanctuary.[42]

This meeting, on August 19, 1864, had been on Lincoln's invitation, suggesting that the president was ready to consider blacks as policy consultants, at least on slave matters. In an unhurried conversation, the president expressed his fears that the war might end with Southern slaves still in the possession of their masters. Lincoln wanted to establish an agency, "a band of scouts composed of colored men . . . to carry the news of emancipation" behind the lines. An uncertain Douglass replied that he would consult with other black leaders. But as Sherman's army sliced through Georgia, the issue became moot. Its significance lies in Douglass's reaction to his encounter with Lincoln. In Douglass's words, "In all my interviews with Mr. Lincoln I was impressed with his entire freedom from popular prejudice against the colored race." To a friend, Douglass, who also understood that Lincoln was "the white man's president," nonetheless enthused that he had been treated as a man. "He did not for a moment let me feel there was any difference in the color of our skins. . . . I was never in any way reminded of my humble origin or of my unpopular color."[43] The president treated blacks on a personal level, concluded historian Benjamin Quarles, "as human beings."[44]

From his perspective, believing Douglass to be "one of the most meritorious men in America," Lincoln took a different message from his encounters with blacks. His conclusion was apparent in a letter he wrote in March 1864 to Michael Hahn, the governor of the newly reclaimed state of Louisiana. In this letter, Lincoln encouraged the vote for the "very intelligent"—men like Frederick Douglass and William Johnson and a few of those whom he had known in Springfield. In Washington he often referred to such men in conversations with his secretaries as "intelligent colored men." And although the president had been slow to endorse the recruitment of blacks into the army, he concluded that "those who have fought gallantly" should also be enfranchised—to keep, as he put it, "the jewel of liberty within the family of freedom."[45]

Who knows what Lincoln would have done during Reconstruction? Certainly, the racial dilemmas of that era would have provided a clearer test of his views on race and democracy. His lifelong experiences with blacks had hardly transformed him into a supporter of civil rights. His target had persistently been the eradication of slavery, and so, to shore up his wartime proclamation on emancipation, Lincoln vigorously advocated a proposed Thirteenth Amendment, which would forever end slavery throughout the United States. He called it "a king's cure for all the evils of slavery." Of course, we know—and Radical Republicans, like Charles Sumner, knew at the time—that it was not. But Lincoln also signed the Freedman's Bureau Act, and he surely would have supported its extension.

But the president's last comments on the future, uttered shortly before his assassination, dealt not with the freedmen, but with the process of returning the seceded states to the Union—as "the egg is to the fowl." And it was this aspect of Reconstruction that Lincoln focused on, even as he had promised, in his Second Inaugural, "malice toward none and charity for all" in the uncertain context of "firmness in the right." How he would have protected newly freed blacks from white Southerners remains uncertain.

Surely had he lived he would have thought of what he was—an individual who had risen from a log cabin to be the president of the United States through hard work, a unique case that showed, as he liked to say, that anyone's son could become president. Lincoln was ready to see not just the color, but the individual behind it. He was willing to open white society to meritorious blacks as individuals in a democratic society, even as he remained what Frederick Douglass called him in 1876, "the white man's president." His racial understandings did not extend to blacks as a category. They ended with those who were, in the manner of Lincoln himself, exceptional.

Notes

1. Mark Neely, "Lincoln and the Constitution," *Lincoln Lore* (March–April, 1987): 1–2.

2. *The Collected Works of Abraham Lincoln,* ed. Roy Basler, 9 vols. (New Brunswick, NJ, 1953–55), 2:454 [hereafter, Basler, ed., *Lincoln Works*].

3. Ibid., 2:405, 406.

4. Ibid., 2:256.

5. Ibid., 3:145.

6. Ibid., 3:222.

7. See T. W. Adorno et al., *The Authoritarian Personality* (New York, 1950); Adorno also defines a "democratic personality." See also Gordon Allport, *The Nature of Prejudice,* (Cambridge, MA, 1954), 425–42; and Beverly Daniel Tatum, "*Why Are All the Black Kids Sitting Together in the Cafeteria?*": And Other Conversations about Race (New York, 1997), 96.

8. George Frederickson, "A Man but Not a Brother: Abraham Lincoln and Racial Equality," *Journal of Southern History* 41 (February 1975): 44. See also Basler, ed., *Lincoln Works,* 1:260.

9. Louis Warren, *The Slavery Atmosphere of Lincoln's Youth* (Fort Wayne, IN, 1933); Albert Beveridge, *Abraham Lincoln, 1809–1858* (Cambridge, MA, 1928), 33.

10. Basler, ed., *Lincoln Works,* 2:264.

11. See Shane White and Graham White, *The Sounds of Slavery: Discovering African American History through Songs, Sermons, and Speech* (Boston, 2005).

12. Basler, ed., *Lincoln Works,* 4:61.

13. C. A. Tripp, *The Intimate World Of Abraham Lincoln* (New York, 2003), 33n15.

14. Louis Warren, *Lincoln's Youth—Indiana Years, 1816–1830* (Indianapolis, 1959) 109–11.

15. Basler, ed., *Lincoln Works,* 2:320.

16. Warren, *Lincoln's Youth—Indiana Years,* 185.

17. Basler, ed., *Lincoln Works,* 2:222–23.

18. Ibid., 1:75.

19. Kenneth J. Winkle, *The Young Eagle: The Rise of Abraham Lincoln* (Dallas, 2001), 253.

20. Basler, ed., *Lincoln Works,* 2:266.

21. Ibid., 2:255.

22. Benjamin Quarles, *Lincoln and The Negro* (New York, 1962), 21; the case is *Bailey v. Cromwell,* 4 Ill. 71 (1841).

23. Winkle, *The Young Eagle,* 262.

24. Ibid.

25. David Herbert Donald, *Lincoln* (New York, 1995), 167.

26. Richard Hart, "Springfield's African Americans as a Part of the Lincoln Community," *Journal of the Abraham Lincoln Association* 20 (Winter 1999): 35–55. Richard Hart, a resident of Springfield, is responsible for much of the historical work being done on the black community in Springfield.

27. Richard Hart, "Lincoln's Springfield: The Underground Railroad," unpublished paper in author's possession. See also Hart, "Springfield's African Americans as a Part of the Lincoln Community," 53.

28. Lincoln Sesquicentennial Commission, *Lincoln Day by Day: A Chronology, 1809–1865,* ed. Earl Miers Schenck (Washington, DC, 1960), 257.

29. Hart, "Springfield's African Americans as a Part of the Lincoln Community," 47.

30. I am grateful to Gabor Boritt for the information about Johnson, which appears in his recently published book *The Gettysburg Gospel* (New York, 2006), at pages 53, 54, 122, 128, and 170.

31. Basler, ed., *Lincoln Works,* 5:372–73; 3:16; 4:156; Frederickson, "A Man but Not a Brother," 304.

32. Basler, ed., *Lincoln Works,* 3:145–46.

33. Ibid., 3:16.

34. Frederickson, "A Man but Not a Brother," 44–45.

35. Basler, ed., *Lincoln Works,* 3:145–46.

36. James Bilotta, *Race and the Rise of the Republican Party* (New York, 1992), 316–17.

37. Basler, ed., *Lincoln Works,* 5:534–35.

38. Quoted in Mark Neely, *The Abraham Lincoln Encyclopedia* (New York, 1982), 219.

39. Quarles, *Lincoln and The Negro,* 206, 233.

40. Ibid., 205.

41. Basler, ed., *Lincoln Works,* 5:372.

42. Albert Thorndike Rice, ed., *Reminiscences of Abraham Lincoln by Distinguished Men of His Time* (New York, 1886), 18–195, 325; Frederick Douglass, *The Life and Writings of Frederick Douglass,* by Philip S. Foner, 5 vols. (New York, 1952–), 3:36–37, 45–46.

43. Frederick Douglass, draft of a speech, Douglass Papers, Library of Congress, cited in Richard Striner, *Father Abraham: Lincoln's Relentless Struggle to End Slavery* (New York, 2006), 63.

44. Quoted in Doris Kearns Goodwin, *Team of Rivals: The Political Genius of Abraham Lincoln* (New York, 2005), 650. See also Quarles, *Lincoln and The Negro,* 204; and Rice, *Reminiscences of Abraham Lincoln by Distinguished Men of His Time,* 193.

45. Basler, ed., *Lincoln Works,* 7:243; Quarles, *Lincoln and The Negro,* 204.

Lincoln and Colonization

Eric Foner

Abraham Lincoln produced only one book during his lifetime—a collection of excerpts from his speeches of the 1850s dealing with the question of "negro equality." During the 1858 campaign in Illinois, when Lincoln was running for the Senate against Stephen A. Douglas, Democrats persistently represented Lincoln as an abolitionist who favored "the equality of the races, politically and socially." William Brown, like Lincoln a native of Kentucky who had served as a Whig in the Illinois legislature, was running as the Republican candidate for Lincoln's old seat. In October 1858, he asked Lincoln for material he could use to fend off Democratic appeals to racism. Lincoln put together a series of passages that, he wrote, "contain the substance of all I have ever said about 'negro equality,'" beginning with excerpts from his celebrated Peoria speech of 1854 and ending with passages from the Lincoln-Douglas debates. Brown used the collection to reply to Democratic charges against Lincoln, but both he and Lincoln lost their races. The scrapbook remained in Brown's family until 1900, when a collector purchased it. It appeared in print in 1903 with the engaging title *Abraham Lincoln: His Book.*[1]

In the excerpts he chose, Lincoln's position on racial equality was, as he claimed, clear and consistent. As he explained to Brown, "I think the negro is included in the word 'men' used in the Declaration of Independence," and slavery, which violated this "great fundamental principle" of equal entitlement to the natural rights of mankind, was therefore wrong. But natural rights were one thing, political and social rights quite another. As Lincoln explained, "I have expressly disclaimed all intention to bring about social and political equality between the white and black races." His position differentiated Lincoln from the abolitionists, who advocated not only an end to slavery but the incorporation of blacks as equal members of American society, and from Douglas and the Democrats, who insisted that the natural rights enumerated in the Declaration applied only to whites. And what did Lincoln believe should be blacks' fate if and when slavery ended? He included in his book a passage from his Peoria speech, in which he envisioned their being colonized to Africa, which he called "their own native land," even though by the mid-nineteenth century Africa was no more the native land of most black Americans than England, the home of his ancestors, was Lincoln's.[2]

Lincoln's embrace of colonization was no passing fancy. He had advocated the policy a number of times during the 1850s, and pursued it avidly during the first two years of the Civil War. In his annual message to Congress in December 1862, Lincoln stated bluntly, "I cannot make it better known than it already is, that I strongly favor colonization." Indeed, while Lincoln almost always maintained that colonization must be voluntary, in this speech he three times used the ominous word "deportation."[3]

For writers, like Lerone Bennett, who see Lincoln as an inveterate racist, colonization serves as "Exhibit A." For Lincoln's admirers, no aspect of his life has proved more puzzling. Don Fehrenbacher calls Lincoln's zeal in promoting colonization the "strangest feature" of his career.[4] Many members of the Lincoln industry (of which I count myself an interested observer rather than a member) find it impossible to reconcile colonization with Lincoln's strong moral dislike of slavery. They either ignore the question or fall back on the explanation that Lincoln did not really mean what he said.

David Donald insists that until "well into his presidency," Lincoln really did believe in colonization. But Donald is one of the few scholars to do Lincoln the courtesy of taking him at his word. Peter Parish contends that Lincoln could not have been serious about colonizing African Americans outside the country. Stephen B. Oates writes that Lincoln did not really believe in the plan, but promoted it to fend off racist attacks on his administration. Richard Striner says that Lincoln promoted colonization as a strategic device, "to appease white supremacist Democrats" and "defuse . . . resistance to emancipation." In William Lee Miller's study of Lincoln's moral leadership, colonization receives a brief mention three-quarters of the way through the book. In her recent eight-hundred-page work on Lincoln as a political leader, Doris Goodwin says almost nothing about the colonization plan. Frequently, Lincoln scholars fall into what Bennett calls the "fallacy of the isolated quotation." They cite his powerful condemnation at Peoria of the "monstrous injustice of slavery," while ignoring the passage in the same speech embracing colonization. They quote his eloquent words, in his message to Congress in December 1862, about the "fiery trial" through which the nation was passing, but fail to note that much of that speech was devoted to advocacy of three proposed constitutional amendments, one of which offered federal funding for colonizing freed slaves outside the country.[5]

A new look at Lincoln and colonization must begin by taking colonization seriously as a political movement, an ideology, and a practical program. Absurd as the plan may appear in retrospect, it seemed quite realistic to its advocates. Many large groups have been expelled from their homelands in modern times—for example, Spanish Muslims and Jews after 1492, and Acadians during the Seven Years War. The mass migration of peoples was hardly unusual in the nineteenth century. In the decade following the famine of the 1840s, an estimated two million men, women, and children emigrated from Ireland. In 1850, the colonization of the three million slaves and free blacks in the United States probably seemed less unrealistic than immediate abolition.

For decades, the only full-length book on the subject was P. J. Staudenraus's, published in 1961. But the past few years have witnessed the appearance of a number of important works on colonization, including Eric Burin's history of the American Colonization Society, and Claude Clegg III's study of African Americans in Liberia. (Among other things, Clegg makes clear that, despite its rhetoric of enabling emigrating blacks to enjoy genuine freedom, the ACS seemed remarkably indifferent to the welfare of those it sent abroad. Emigrants suffered a high death rate from tropical disease. Long after it was clear that they had a better chance of survival if they settled at sites on high ground, the ACS regularly unloaded them at Monrovia, the malaria-infested coastal capital of Liberia.)[6]

Colonization was hardly a fringe movement. Thomas Jefferson and Henry Clay, the two statesmen most revered by Lincoln, favored colonization. So did John Marshall, James Madison, Daniel Webster, Andrew Jackson, Roger B. Taney, Stephen A. Douglas, and even Harriet Beecher Stowe (whose abolitionist novel *Uncle Tom's Cabin* ends with the hero, George Harris, affirming his "African nationality" and emigrating from the United

States). In an era of nation-building, colonization, among other things, formed part of a long debate about what kind of nation America was to be—about, that is, the composition of what Benedict Anderson calls the "imagined community." The dream of a white America was present from the very outset. The Naturalization Act of 1790, one of the first laws enacted by Congress after the inauguration of George Washington, prohibited all nonwhite persons (the majority of the world's population) from emigrating to the United States and becoming citizens.[7]

The first emancipation—the gradual abolition of slavery in the North—was not coupled with colonization. It seems to have been assumed that the former slaves would somehow be absorbed into Northern society. Not until 1816, just as slavery was embarking on its remarkable expansion into the Cotton Kingdom, did a society to rid the country of blacks altogether come into existence. But taking the nineteenth century as a whole, colonization needs to be viewed in the context of other plans to determine the racial makeup of American society, including removal of Native Americans and, later, Chinese exclusion. As late as 1862, the report of the House Committee on Emancipation and Colonization declared that "the highest interests of the white race" required the removal of blacks, so that whites could have possession of "every acre of our present domain."[8] In a sense, colonization was the mirror opposite of the movement to reopen the African slave trade in the 1850s. One sought to reduce the black population, the other to expand it; one viewed the nation's problem as a surplus of blacks, the other a surplus of poor whites who might rise into the middle class through slave ownership.

Recent literature has emphasized the complex, indeed contradictory, appeals colonizationists used in generating support for their cause. Advocates of colonization portrayed blacks, sometimes in the same breath, as depraved and dangerous outsiders, as Christian imperialists, as a class wronged by slavery, as potential trading partners, and as redeemers of Africa. The one constant was that they could not remain in America.[9]

In the South, colonization was generally directed primarily at free blacks, denounced as a degraded and dangerous population whose removal would actually strengthen the peculiar institution. At the meeting in the nation's capital that launched the American Colonization Society in 1816, Henry Clay, then speaker of the House, insisted that colonization applied to free blacks and that the movement must avoid the "delicate question" of emancipation. John Randolph, of Roanoke, added that colonization would in fact "materially tend to secure" the value of slave property. The official title of the ACS was the American Society for Colonizing the Free People of Color in the United States. Yet Clay also favored gradual emancipation and believed colonization would make slaveholders more willing to manumit their slaves. Indeed, gradual emancipation coupled with colonization formed essential parts of Clay's American System—his plan for regional and national economic development, which, he hoped, would reorient Kentucky into a modern, efficient, diversified economy modeled on the free-labor North. Slavery, he insisted, was why Kentucky lagged behind nearby states in manufacturing and general prosperity. Upper South planters and political leaders whose commitment to slavery sometimes appeared suspect dominated the American Colonization Society. This is why hostility to colonization became more and more intense in the Deep South as the nineteenth century wore on.[10]

In the North, colonization was presented as a means of abolishing slavery gradually, peacefully, and without sectional conflict. Colonizationists depicted blacks as doomed to permanent degradation in America because of white racism. But in Africa, they would be transformed into the bringers of modern civilization and Christianity. They would uplift a continent and achieve peoplehood for themselves. Some proponents of colonization, like Jefferson, argued that because of innate inferiority blacks could never be assimilated into republican citizenship. But most colonizationists were environmentalists. They insisted that blacks' status as slaves and unequal free persons arose from racism, not innate incapacity. Indeed, colonizationists and abolitionists agreed on one thing—that black men and women had the capacity for improvement. As one colonization publication put it: "There is nothing in the physical, or moral nature of the African, which condemns him to a state of ignorance and degradation. Extraneous causes press him to the earth. Light and liberty can, and do, under fair circumstances, raise him to the rank of a virtuous and intelligent being."[11] Where they differed was in whether those "fair circumstances" could ever be achieved in America.

Of course, some African Americans shared the perspective of the colonization movement. Almost every printed report of the ACS included testimonials from blacks who had either gone to Africa or were eager to do so. The ACS relied heavily on such testimony to develop sympathy for its program. Steven Hahn has recently emphasized the strength of grassroots emigrationist sentiment during and after Reconstruction. But, decades earlier, the black seafarer Paul Cuffee had settled small groups of blacks in Sierra Leone. John Russwurm, who in 1827 founded *Freedom's Journal,* the nation's first black newspaper, abandoned it after two years and moved to Liberia. In his final editorial, he explained why: "We consider it a waste of mere words to talk of ever enjoying citizenship in this country; it is utterly impossible in the nature of things; all, therefore who pant for this, must cast their eyes elsewhere." Interest in emigration revived in the 1850s among such early black nationalists as Martin Delany and Henry Highland Garnet.[12]

It is often forgotten that, between the Revolution and the Civil War, more blacks left the United States under auspices other than via the ACS. Between its founding in 1816 and 1860, the ACS transported about 11,000 persons to Africa, the majority slaves manumitted by their owners for the express purpose of removal to Liberia. But between 15,000 and 20,000 blacks, nearly all escaped slaves, evacuated with the British at the end of the War for Independence. They ended up in Nova Scotia, Sierra Leone, the West Indies, and even the German state of Hesse (home of the notorious Hessians).[13] The passage of the Fugitive Slave Act of 1850 created a crisis that led to the relocation of thousands of African Americans to Canada and rekindled interest in emigration to Africa. In other words, when presented with a choice between slavery in the United States and freedom elsewhere, many blacks chose freedom.

But the similarities between the rhetoric of colonizationists and of black emigrationists ought not to obscure the historical importance of the black mobilization against colonization that began immediately after the founding of the ACS and continued into the Civil War. Indeed, black hostility to colonization was one of the key catalysts for the rise of immediate abolitionism in the late 1820s and 1830s. The difference between colonization and abolitionism lay not only in their approach to getting rid of slavery, but in their view as to whether American racism should be considered intractable and whether blacks could hope to achieve equal citizenship in this country. Through the attack on colonization, the modern idea of equality as something that knows no racial boundaries was born.

It was in the response to colonization that free blacks articulated a radical abolitionist position that would soon become associated with William Lloyd Garrison and his followers. Indeed, Garrison's experience with the vibrant black communities of Baltimore and Boston between 1829 and 1831 inspired his conversion from colonization to abolition and racial equality. In its early issues, *The Liberator* devoted far more space to attacking colonization than advocating immediate emancipation. In his highly influential pamphlet, *Thoughts on African Colonization,* Garrison said that conversations with blacks had led him to change his mind about colonization. Like ACS publications, he compiled black statements, this time opposing colonization. The most potent objection to the idea, he wrote, was that it "is directly and irreconcilably opposed to the wishes of our colored population as a body."[14]

Militant abolitionism arose as the conjoining of two impulses—black anti-colonization and white evangelical Christianity and perfectionism. It was free blacks who first rejected colonization as a solution to the "problem" of race in America. The formation of the ACS was quickly followed by a convention in Philadelphia of three thousand blacks, who condemned the new society. The prominent black leader James Forten, who had supported Paul Cuffee's plan for emigration to Africa, was forced to reconsider his views because of the grassroots upsurge against colonization. The majority was "decidedly against me," he wrote. The meeting resolved not to separate from the slave population: "They are our brethren by the ties of consanguinity, of suffering, and of wrong." Free blacks challenged the racial and national assumptions at the heart of colonization. In asserting their own Americanness, they articulated a new vision of American society as a land of birthright citizenship and equality before the law, where rights did not depend on color, ancestry, or racial designation. Adopting the language of perfectionism, they denied that racism was immutable, that a nation must be racially homogenous, and that color formed an insurmountable barrier to equality.[15]

The mobilization against colonization led to the widespread abandonment of "African" in the names of black institutions. For two centuries, blacks in the North had tended to call themselves and their organizations "African" or "Free African." The formation of the ACS led them to avoid this word as dangerous. An 1835 black convention adopted a resolution calling on black people to "remove the title African from their institutions, the marbles of churches, etc." When the second black newspaper appeared in the late 1830s, it began as the *Weekly Advocate* but quickly took as its title *The Colored American.* The African Baptist Church of Boston, founded in 1806, changed its name in the 1830s to the First Independent Church of the

People of Color, because "the name African is ill applied to a church composed of American citizens." To take one further example: "We are Americans," declared the Address of the Rochester Colored Convention of 1853. "We address you not as aliens nor as exiles, but as American citizens asserting their rights on their native soil." The delegates demanded: "In our native land, we shall not be treated as strangers and worse than strangers."[16]

David Walker's *Appeal,* a key document of radical abolitionism, devoted its longest chapter to attacking the idea of colonization. America, Walker proclaimed, "is more our country, than it is the whites—we have enriched it with our blood and tears." He condemned those who had left for Africa for abandoning their brethren in America. Walker agreed with colonizationists that blacks lived in "abject" circumstances in America, but the cause was "the inhuman system of slavery," not innate incapacity or immutable prejudice. Jefferson had warned that whites' color-consciousness and blacks' resentment over the injustices they had suffered would make it impossible for the two races to live in harmony as free citizens. Walker disagreed. He addressed white Americans in scathing language, but insisted, "Treat us like men, and there is no danger but we will all live in peace and happiness together." America could become an interracial society of equals.

Walker confronted the most prominent advocates of colonization head-on. He devoted several pages to refuting Jefferson's musings on race in *Notes on the State of Virginia.* Jefferson had labeled blacks mentally inferior. "It is indeed surprising," Walker responded, "that a man of such great learning, combined with such excellent natural parts, should speak so of a set of men in chains." He blamed Jefferson for an increase in racism: "Mr. Jefferson's remarks respecting us, have sunk deep into the hearts of millions of the whites." Walker pointed out the absurdity of Jefferson's claim that Roman slaves, unlike American ones, produced great artists and writers, supposedly proving that blacks' degradation did not result from their condition. American slavery, he insisted, was far more oppressive than Roman, and freed slaves faced far greater barriers to advancement. Walker also cited Henry Clay's speech to the founding meeting of the ACS. He identified Clay as a slaveholder and not "a friend to the blacks. . . . [Slaves] work his plantation to enrich him and his family."[17]

Walker's comments on Clay offer an entry point into Abraham Lincoln's views on colonization. In some ways, Lincoln's views closely paralleled those of Clay, his "beau ideal of a statesman." Lincoln paraphrased some of Clay's statements on colonization, such as his insistence that public passions would forever prevent the two races from living together as equals and that it would therefore be better for blacks to have a nation of their own. Lincoln's first extended discussion of colonization came in 1852, in his eulogy after Clay's death. Unlike David Walker, Lincoln hailed Clay as an opponent of slavery, citing his support for gradual emancipation linked with colonization—returning blacks to their "long-lost fatherland." But he made clear that, for Clay, colonization was a way of ending slavery, not strengthening it, and that the "dangerous presence" in the United States was not free blacks, but slavery itself.[18]

Before the Civil War, Lincoln lived in a world in which support for colonization was a significant presence. Several of his close associates, including Judge David Davis and John T. Stuart, Lincoln's mentor and early law partner, belonged to the Illinois State Colonization Society. Lincoln himself addressed the Society's annual meetings in 1853 and 1855, and in 1857 he was elected one of its managers. But in some ways Lincoln's colonizationism proved quite different from other views of his time. He said nothing about the danger of racial mixing, except on occasion when, goaded by Democrats, he declared his opposition to interracial marriage and pointed out that the more slavery expanded the more likely it was for racial mixing to occur. Unlike Jefferson, Lincoln did not seem to fear a racial war if slavery were abolished, and unlike other colonizationists he expressed no interest in the Christianization of Africa. (Lincoln himself was a religious skeptic; his antislavery beliefs arose from democratic and free-labor convictions, not religious perfectionism.) Lincoln never spoke of free blacks as a vicious and degraded group dangerous to the stability of American society.[19]

Lincoln's views on colonization and its possible appeal to blacks may have been influenced by the Matson case of 1847, in which he represented the owner of plantations in Kentucky and Illinois who circumvented the laws of the latter state by bringing slaves in to work for a few months at a time. One slave mother and her four children escaped and secured abolitionist support. Lincoln defended Matson's claim to them, arguing that since Matson did not intend to keep them in Illinois permanently, he should recover his property. The court freed them, and eventually the family made their way to Liberia. (One may assume that Lincoln's role in defending Matson reflected a lawyer's desire to earn a fee rather than his own views of slavery. Yet it is noteworthy that, unlike his contemporaries Salmon P. Chase and

Lyman Trumbull, both of whom became major figures in the Republican Party, Lincoln never established a reputation for defending fugitive slaves and other blacks in court.)[20]

Springfield in the 1840s and 1850s was a small city (its population in 1860 had not reached 10,000) with a small free-black population. Lincoln could not have been unaware of the black presence. He and his wife employed at least three free-black women to work in their home at one time or another, and Lincoln befriended and gave free legal assistance to William Flourville, known as Billy the Barber. But unlike Garrison and many other white abolitionists, Lincoln had little contact with politically articulate free blacks before the Civil War. He said nothing when local blacks held a public meeting in 1858 to oppose the colonization movement. "We believe," they declared, "that the operations of the Colonization Society are calculated to excite prejudices against us, and they impel ignorant or ill disposed persons to take measures for our expulsion from the land of our nativity. . . . We claim the right of citizenship in this, the country of our birth. . . . We are not African." Later in that same year, Lincoln put together his "book" reiterating his support for colonization.[21]

During the first two years of the Civil War, Lincoln promoted a plan inspired by Clay—gradual emancipation in the border states with compensation financed by the federal government, coupled with voluntary colonization. He was hardly the only Republican to favor colonization. Two laws passed by the Republican Congress in 1862, providing for abolition in the District of Columbia and for the confiscation of the slaves of those who bore arms for the Confederacy—important steps on the path toward general emancipation—both included provisions for voluntary colonization. Congress appropriated $600,000 to aid in the removal of these African Americans.

During the Civil War, Lincoln's attention turned from Liberia to areas closer to home. In the 1850s, some Republican leaders, such as Francis P. Blair Jr., had promoted colonization in Central America as a way of establishing an American imperial presence there and forestalling Southern dreams of a Caribbean empire. In October 1861, Lincoln asked Secretary of the Interior Caleb Smith to look into possibilities for colonization in the Chiriqui region, now part of Panama. In his annual message to Congress, two months later, he proposed the voluntary colonization of "contrabands"—escaped slaves who had made their way to Union lines—as well as existing free blacks. A Washington newspaper suggested that the proposed black colony be called Lincolnia.[22]

Perhaps the most controversial or notorious moments of Lincoln's presidency came in August 1862, when he met at the White House with a hand-picked delegation of local black leaders and urged them to drum up support for colonization. "You and we are different races," he told them. Because of racism, "even when you cease to be slaves, you are yet far removed from being placed on an equality with the white race. . . . It is better for us both, therefore, to be separated." This was the only time Lincoln took the idea of colonization directly to blacks. He offered a powerful indictment of slavery—"Your race are suffering in my judgment, the greatest wrong inflicted on any people." But Lincoln refused to pass a similar moral judgment on racism, although he also declined to associate himself with it. Racism, he said, was intractable; whether it "is right or wrong I need not discuss."

Lincoln still found himself unable to include blacks within what one historian, in a different context, has called "the circle of the 'we'"—the definition of those who comprise American society. Indeed, he seemed to blame the black presence for the Civil War: "but for your race among us there could not be war," he observed, and he went on to offer their removal as the remedy. Although not mentioning Chiriqui by name, he touted Central America as an area of fine harbors and "rich coal mines" (although no evidence existed of either), where even a small band of colonists might succeed.[23]

A stenographer was present, and Lincoln's remarks quickly appeared in the nation's newspapers, as he undoubtedly intended. The prominent black abolitionist Frederick Douglass reacted with fury. "Mr Lincoln," he wrote, "assumes the language and arguments of an itinerant colonization lecturer, shows all his inconsistencies, his pride of race and blood, his contempt for Negroes and his canting hypocrisy. How an honest man could creep into such a character as that implied by this address we are not required to show." Of Lincoln's proposal to the black delegation, Douglass wrote, "It expresses merely the desire to get rid of them, and reminds one of the politeness with which a man might try to bow out of his house some troublesome creditor or the witness of some old guilt." Douglass pointed out that blacks had not caused the war; slavery had. The real task of a statesman, he concluded, was not to patronize blacks by deciding what was "best" for them, but to allow them to be free. But other blacks, while angered by Lincoln's words, embraced his proposal. Henry Highland Garnet, a long-time advocate of voluntary emigration, praised the Chiriqui plan as "the most humane, and merciful movement which this or any other administration has proposed for the benefit of the enslaved."[24]

The black delegation soon reported back to Lincoln that they could not support the idea of colonization. Heedless of their reaction, Lincoln pressed forward. As noted above, in his message to Congress in December 1862, Lincoln asked for a constitutional amendment authorizing Congress to appropriate funds for colonization—along with two others: one offering funds to states that provided for emancipation by 1900 (thirty-eight years in the future), and the other compensating owners of slaves who had gained freedom as result of the war. The first proposed amendment even considered the possibility that states might renege on emancipation, providing that if they did so, they would have to refund the money to the federal government. But at the same time, Lincoln directly addressed the racial fears of many whites, offering an extended argument as to why if freed slaves remained in the United States they would pose no threat to the white majority. The message was both a preparation of public opinion for the issuance of the Emancipation Proclamation less than a month hence and a last offer to the border and Confederate states of a different path to abolition—gradual, compensated emancipation coupled with colonization.

Lincoln had been promoting compensated emancipation since he drew up a proposed law for this purpose and presented it to Delaware late in 1861. That state took no action, but the bill abolishing slavery in Washington, D.C., did provide for compensation for loyal owners of about $300 per slave. Lincoln's scheme would have had the government issue interest-bearing bonds to be presented to slave owners, with the principal due when slavery ended in their state. In his December 1862 message, he offered an elaborate set of calculations to prove that, despite the economic value of slave property—more than three billion dollars, an enormous sum—the growth of the white population through natural increase and immigration would make the burden of taxation to pay off the bonds less and less onerous as time went on. Like other colonizationists, Lincoln was betting that the white population would grow faster than the black—an outcome that colonization would ensure. Without colonization, gradual emancipation held out the danger that the black population would grow as fast or faster than the white (as had happened in some Southern states before the Civil War), thus dramatically increasing the cost of the plan.[25]

On December 31, 1862, the day before he issued the Emancipation Proclamation, Lincoln signed a contract with a notorious speculator, Bernard Kock, to transport blacks to Ile â Vache, off Haiti. "This *Governor* Kock is an errant humbug . . . a charlatan adventurer," Attorney General Edward Bates, himself a supporter of colonization, had noted in his diary a month earlier. Bates made Lincoln aware of his opinion, but the president nonetheless arranged for Kock to be paid $50 each for transporting 5,000 blacks to the island. Some 500 hapless souls were taken there in 1863; the federal government rescued the 350 survivors in 1864. This is all that came of colonization during the Civil War.[26]

The Emancipation Proclamation represented a turning point in the Civil War—and in Lincoln's own views regarding slavery and race. In crucial respects, it differed markedly from Lincoln's previous statements and policies. It contained no mention of compensation for slave owners. It said nothing about colonization, although this had been included in the Preliminary Emancipation Proclamation of the previous September. It enjoined emancipated slaves to "labor faithfully" for "reasonable wages"—clearly envisioning their remaining in the United States. For the first time, it authorized the enrollment of black soldiers into the Union military (the Second Confiscation Act had envisioned using blacks as military laborers, not "armed service," as the Emancipation Proclamation provides). Thus, the Proclamation set in motion the process by which, in the last two years of the war, 200,000 black men served in the Union army and navy, playing a critical role in achieving Union victory.

After the issuance of the Emancipation Proclamation, Lincoln made no further public statements about colonization. The black abolitionist H. Ford Douglas had predicted that the raising of black soldiers would "educate Mr. Lincoln out of his idea of the deportation of the Negro," and I believe this in fact is what happened. Lincoln increasingly realized that, in fighting for the Union, black soldiers had staked a claim to citizenship in the postwar world. In addition, contact with articulate black spokesmen like Frederick Douglass—whom Lincoln met for the first time in 1863—changed his outlook. Lincoln's secretary, John Hay, noted in his diary in 1864: "I am glad that the President has sloughed off that idea of colonization. I have always thought it a hideous and barbarous humbug." This was not entirely accurate, as Hay, whose opinions generally reflected those of Lincoln, had favored the idea in 1862.[27]

By decoupling emancipation and colonization, the Emancipation Proclamation in effect launched the process of Reconstruction—that is, the adjustment of American society to the destruction of slavery and the reality of a biracial citizenry. For the first time, Lincoln began to think seriously of the role blacks would play in a post-slavery world, about what kind of labor system should replace slavery, and whether some blacks should enjoy the right to vote. In the Sea Islands, reformers were establishing schools for blacks and aiding them in acquiring land. In the Mississippi Valley, former slaves were being put to work on plantations. Lincoln expressed increasing interest in how these experiments fared. By 1864, Radical Republicans were pressing for a federal guarantee of blacks' equal rights before the law. Meanwhile, as Secretary of the Interior John P. Usher noted, blacks continued to show "little disposition . . . to leave the land of their nativity." Martin Delany, the most prominent emigrationist of the 1850s, would soon enroll in the Union army. In July 1864, Congress froze its previous appropriation for colonization. In the end, only $38,000 of the $600,000 allocated was spent.[28]

The dream of an all-white America did not die in 1865, nor did black emigration efforts or proposals by white racists to expel the black population. But the end of slavery meant the end of colonization. It was Frederick Douglass who during the Civil War offered the most fitting obituary. In a reply to an open letter by Postmaster General Montgomery Blair promoting colonization, Douglass dismantled one by one the arguments for the policy. There was no such thing as a people being naturally fitted for a particular climate—blacks had adapted to America and, more, had become Americans, not Africans. The idea of colonization allowed whites to avoid considering directly the aftermath of slavery. It was an "opiate" for a "troubled conscience," Douglass wrote, which deflected attention from the work of emancipation and denied free blacks the incentive of citizenship to inspire self-education and hard work. Only with the death of colonization could Americans begin to confront the challenge of making this a genuinely interracial democracy.[29]

As for Lincoln, the story of his long embrace of colonization and eventual abandonment of the idea illustrates how he was both a product of his time yet was able to transcend it—which is probably as good a definition of greatness as any. In April 1865, shortly before his death, he spoke publicly for the first time of suffrage for some blacks, most notably the men "who serve our cause as soldiers."[30] He had come a long way from the views he had brought together in 1858 in *Abraham Lincoln: His Book.*

Notes

This essay was originally delivered as a lecture in September 2006, and represents an early statement of my views on Lincoln and colonization. For a later examination of the subject, see my essay in Eric Foner, ed., *Our Lincoln: New Perspectives on Lincoln and His World* (New York, 2008).

1. J. McCan Davis, *Abraham Lincoln: His Book* (New York, 1903).

2. *The Collected Works of Abraham Lincoln,* ed. Roy P. Basler, 9 vols. (New Brunswick, NJ, 1953–55) [hereafter, Basler, ed., *Lincoln Works*], 2:255; 3:327–28.

3. Ibid., 5:534–35.

4. Lerone Bennett, *Forced into Glory: Abraham Lincoln's White Dream* (Chicago, 2000); Don E. Fehrenbacher, "Only His Stepchildren: Lincoln and the Negro," *Civil War History* 20 (December 1974), 307.

5. David Herbert Donald, *Lincoln* (New York, 1995), 160–61; Peter J. Parish, *The American Civil War* (New York, 1975), 240–42; Stephen B. Oates, *Abraham Lincoln: The Man behind the Myths* (New York, 1984), 101; Richard Striner, *Father Abraham: Lincoln's Relentless Struggle to End Slavery* (New York, 2006), 149–50; William Lee Miller, *Lincoln's Virtues: An Ethical Biography* (New York, 2002), 354; Doris Kearns Goodwin, *Team of Rivals: The Political Genius of Abraham Lincoln* (New York, 2005); Bennett, *Forced into Glory,* 127. See also Michael Vorenberg, "Abraham Lincoln and the Politics of Black Colonization," *Journal of the Abraham Lincoln Association* 14 (Summer 1993): 23–46.

6. P. J. Staudenraus, *The African Colonization Movement, 1816–1865* (New York, 1961); Eric Burin, *Slavery and the Peculiar Solution: A History of the American Colonization Society* (Gainesville, FL, 2005); Claude A. Clegg III, *The Price of Liberty: African Americans and the Making of Liberia* (Chapel Hill, NC, 2004). An important contribution to the renewed interest in colonization is David Brion Davis, "Reconsidering the Colonization Movement: Leonard Bacon and the Problem of Evil," *Intellectual History Newsletter* 14 (1992): 3–16.

7. Eric Foner, "Who Is an American?" in *Who Owns History* (New York, 2002), 151–53.

8. Quoted in George M. Fredrickson, *The Black Image in the White Mind: The Debate on Afro-American Character and Destiny, 1814–1917* (New York, 1971), 151.

9. Hugh Davis, "Northern Colonizationists and Free Blacks, 1823–1837: The Case of Leonard Bacon," *Journal of the Early Republic* 17 (Winter 1997): 651–75.

10. Isaac V. Brown, *Biography of the Rev. Robert Finley,* 2nd ed. (Philadelphia,

1857), 103–15; George M. Fredrickson, "A Man and Not a Brother: Abraham Lincoln and Racial Equality," *Journal of Southern History* 41 (February 1975), 43; Douglas R. Egerton, "Averting a Crisis: The Proslavery Critique of the American Colonization Society," *Civil War History* 43 (June 1997), 147; Daniel W. Howe, *The Political Culture of the American Whigs* (Chicago, 1984), 136.

11. Burin, *Slavery and the Peculiar Solution*, 22.

12. Steven Hahn, *A Nation Under Our Feet: Black Political Struggles in the Rural South, From Slavery to the Great Migration* (Cambridge, MA, 2003); Dickson D. Bruce Jr., "National Identity and African-American Colonization, 1773–1817," *The Historian* 58 (Autumn 1995): 15–28; Clegg, *Price of Liberty*, 22–25; Sandra S. Young, "John Brown Russwurm's Dilemma: Citizenship or Emigration," in *Prophets of Protest: Reconsidering the History of American Abolitionism*, ed. Timothy P. McCarthy and John Stauffer (New York, 2006), 90–114.

13. Burin, *Slavery and the Peculiar Solution*, 169; Simon Schama, *Rough Crossings: Britain, the Slaves, and the American Revolution* (London, 2005).

14. Staudenraus, *African Colonization Movement*, 193–200; William Lloyd Garrison, *Thoughts on African Colonization* (Boston, 1832), 5.

15. Young, "John Brown Russwurm's Dilemma," 101; Clegg, *Price of Liberty*, 35.

16. Sterling Stuckey, *Slave Culture: Nationalist Theory and the Foundations of Black America* (New York, 1987); James O. Horton and Lois E. Horton, *In Hope of Liberty: Culture, Community, and Protest among Northern Free Blacks, 1700–1860* (New York, 1997), 201; *The Life and Writings of Frederick Douglass*, ed. Philip S. Foner, 4 vols. (New York, 1950–55), 2:255.

17. Herbert Aptheker, *One Continual Cry: David Walker's Appeal to the Colored Citizens of the World* (New York, 1965), 72–91, 109–15.

18. Basler, ed., *Lincoln Works*, 3:29; 2:131–32.

19. Kenneth J. Winkle, *The Young Eagle: The Rise of Abraham Lincoln* (Dallas, 2001), 254–55, 265; Willard L. King, *Lincoln's Manager: David Davis* (Cambridge, 1960), 51.

20. Benjamin Quarles, *Lincoln and the Negro* (New York, 1962), 20–25.

21. Richard E. Hart, "Springfield's African-Americans as a Part of the Lincoln Community," *Journal of the Abraham Lincoln Association* 20 (Winter 1999): 35–54.

22. Vorenberg, "Abraham Lincoln and the Politics of Black Colonization," 28–31; G. S. Boritt, "The Voyage to the Colony of Lincolnia: The Sixteenth President, Black Colonization, and the Defense Mechanism of Avoidance," *The Historian* 37 (August 1975), 619; Basler, ed., *Lincoln Works*, 5:48.

23. Basler, ed., *Lincoln Works*, 5:370–75; David Hollinger, "How Wide the Circle of the 'We'? American Intellectuals and the Problem of the Ethnos since World War II," *American Historical Review* 98 (April 1993): 317–37.

24. Frederick Douglass, "The President and His Speeches," *Douglass' Monthly*, September 1862; James M. McPherson, "Abolitionist and Negro Opposition to Colonization during the Civil War," *Phylon* 26 (Winter 1965): 394–96.

25. Basler, ed., *Lincoln Works*, 5:530–35.

26. Ibid., 6:41; *The Diary of Edward Bates, 1859–1866*, ed. Howard K. Beale

(Washington, DC, 1933), 268; Vorenberg, "Abraham Lincoln and the Politics of Black Colonization," 44.

27. *The Black Abolitionist Papers,* ed. C. Peter Ripley, 5 vols. (Chapel Hill, NC, 1985–92), 5:167; John Hay, *Inside Lincoln's White House: The Complete Civil War Diary of John Hay,* ed. Michael Burlingame and John R. Ettlinger (Carbondale, IL, 1997), 217; John Hay, *Lincoln's Journalist: John Hay's Anonymous Writings for the Press, 1860–1864,* ed. Michael Burlingame (Carbondale, IL, 1998), 254–55.

28. Quarles, *Lincoln and the Negro,* 193–94; Burin, *Slavery and the Peculiar Solution,* 165.

29. Foner, ed., *Life and Writings of Frederick Douglass,* 3:285.

30. Michael W. Fitzgerald, "'We Have Found a Moses': Theodore Bilbo, Black Nationalism, and the Greater Liberia Bill of 1939," *Journal of Southern History* 63 (May 1997): 293–320.

The Theft of Lincoln in Scholarship, Politics, and Public Memory

✴   ✴   ✴   David W. Blight

We cannot escape history. We . . . will be remembered in spite of ourselves.

ABRAHAM LINCOLN, 1862

Since at least the attempt to steal Abraham Lincoln's body from his newly constructed tomb shortly after he was buried in Springfield, Illinois, in 1865, a myriad of appropriations, uses, inventions, and reinventions—thefts—of the sixteenth president's meaning and memory have ensued in American popular culture, in formal politics, in scholarship, and in public memory. The South's Lost Cause and the Confederate Legend, replete with ancestor worship, racist ideology, and a tenacious version of history that writes slavery out of the story of the Civil War, is a persistent, and probably eternal, myth in American culture. But in the hands of its persistent advocates and its detractors, the Lincoln Legend, in different forms, is perhaps equally as tenacious.

Almost all uses of the Lincoln image or legacy revolve in one way or another around themes of democracy, race, or the integrity of leadership. Everyone's Lincoln seems to be either the prophet or the opponent of someone's democracy; and everyone's Lincoln is either admired or disdained for his actions on emancipation. By revisiting the many uses of Lincoln in scholarship, and especially in the politics of public memory, we might grasp anew how much the Civil War and Lincoln's role in it sit squarely at the center of America's story—how much he and the conflict still tell us about what kind of racial democracy we live in.

Commercially, the Lincoln image has never been more popular, it would seem: he now appears on television advertisements for an insurance company that places the stovepipe-hatted one on a golf course, as a source of security and wisdom; and in a piece selling anti-foot-odor ingredients where his nose on the penny is turned up in disgust. Brunswick billiards tables were advertised on the televised Women's National Billiards Championships, with Civil War–era photos of the president, period music, and the pleas "Be a Lincoln" and "Buy a Brunswick." A pharmaceutical company has now used Lincoln's image on huge posters in airports and train stations, sitting knowingly, giving advice to use a certain sleeping pill. Any day now, we may see Lincoln's famous melancholia used to sell a new brand of antidepressant. H. L. Mencken warned sardonically of this never-ending trend in our culture in 1922, the year the Lincoln Memorial was unveiled. Lincoln, he said, "becomes the American solar myth, the chief butt of American credulity and sentimentality." Lincoln, according to Mencken, had been rendered a "mere moral apparition" by so much symbolic use, "a sort of amalgam of John Wesley and the Holy Ghost . . . fit for adoration in the chautauquas and Y. M. C. A.'s."[1] And that was only 1922!

Lincoln has long been infinitely malleable. He can be dour, pained, tragic, sorrowful, or the humorist and the raunchy storyteller; he can be Everyman or the Prince of our Democracy. He can be the distant intellectual; the political theorist who reimagined American race relations; or the racist demagogue who held back progress in race relations until only total war "forced" him into "glory," as Lerone Bennett has argued in a recent book. As the poet Carl Sandburg famously put it, Lincoln was a "man of both steel and velvet, who is as hard as rock and as soft as drifting fog, who holds in his heart and mind the paradox of terrible storm and peace unspeakable." Lincoln could do it all, and we still make him do so. He can serve as everyone's aid or tool in one struggle over historical memory after another. We all seem to keep him handy to use as we see fit. The reformer Ida Tarbell's remark still holds up well. Lincoln, she wrote, "is companionable as no public mind that I've ever known. . . . You feel at home with him, he never high hats you and he never bores you, which is more than I can say of any public man living or dead with whom I have tried to get acquainted. . . . I have kept him always on my work bench."[2]

Lincoln lovers and vilifiers alike need to use and re-use his words and his image. Is this because we are bereft of political poetry in our own time? Are we without thinkers and leaders to find the language to match the crises of our own bloodied and distracted era? Why couldn't Americans find any other poet of our own age to write and speak at the first anniversary of the September 11 attacks in New York? Did the Gettysburg Address really fit that commemorative moment, or was it simply too risky to leave such an occasion to the partisan whims of the speechwriters serving such inarticulate leaders as George Pataki and George W. Bush?

All presidents try to assume the mantle of Lincoln when they need him. One of the most eye-popping misuses of Lincoln came from former President Ronald Reagan at the 1992 Republican National Convention. As the Reagan Revolution seemed under threat from the Democratic challenger, Bill Clinton, the retired president trotted out four maxims that, he claimed, were cherished principles of Abraham Lincoln's:

> "You cannot strengthen the weak by weakening the strong."
> "You cannot help the wage earner by pulling down the wage payer."
> "You cannot help the poor man by destroying the rich."
> "You cannot help men permanently by doing for him what they could or should do for themselves."

Television cameras captured the thrilled faces and wild cheers of the Republican delegates as they watched their beloved Reagan draw Lincoln securely into their moral worldview. Lincoln, through Reagan's charm, would make them, as Rosalyn Carter once put it, "comfortable with their prejudices." The problem, however, was that Lincoln had never uttered any of these aphorisms. When members of the press pointed this out, Reagan's aides assured them that the president had, well . . . done his own "research." He had taken the quotations from *The Toastmaster's Treasure Chest*, by Herbert V. Prochnow. Prochnow had in turn taken them from a 1916 book, *Lincoln on Private Property*, by William John Henry Boetcker. Boetcker had made them up. His little book had been reprinted in many editions through the years and been passed down through Republican clubs. In this embarrassing misappropriation of Lincoln, Reagan was only beginning a new chapter in his party's spurious late twentieth-century effort to persuade voters that they were still the "party of Lincoln."[3]

The political Right, however, has had no monopoly on misquoting Lincoln. A favorite that seems to have nineteenth-century roots, and a good deal of staying power (appearing in the *Lincoln Encyclopedia* in 1950), is alleged to have been written in a letter by Lincoln to a Colonel Thomas Elkins, on November 21, 1864:

> I see in the near future a crisis approaching that unnerves me and causes me to tremble for the safety of my country. . . . Corporations have been enthroned and an era of corruption in high places will follow, and the money power of the country will endeavor to prolong its reign by working upon the prejudices of the people until all wealth is aggregated in a few hands and the Republic is destroyed.

Lincoln never wrote these words either. As Lincoln scholar Thomas Schwartz reports, the president's son, Robert, had earlier attempted to put this one to rest by suggesting that the quotation likely came from a séance in a small town in Iowa in the 1890s.[4]

Lincoln always seems to be there when we need him, relevant or not. As recently as September 2006, in "Bush and Lincoln," in the *Wall Street Journal,* former Speaker of the House Newt Gingrich argued that President Bush had not yet committed to a strategy of total "victory" and unconditional surrender in our current "World War III" against radical Islam and terror. In order to do so, claimed Gingrich, Bush must model his approach on Lincoln's war strategy to defeat the Confederacy, adopted in roughly the late summer of 1862. Other than the implication that Bush needed some of Lincoln's wisdom, and the courage to commit to true social sacrifice and mobilization for war, it is not clear how we connect the dots between Baghdad and Second Manassas, Antietam, and the Preliminary Emancipation Proclamation in this reach to stamp Lincoln's gravitas onto the disaster in Iraq. In the same week, in the *Washington Post,* E. J. Dionne suggested, in "The Rise of the Lincoln Democrats," that a "quiet counter-realignment" had been taking place in what he called the "Lincoln states" of the Northeast and the Midwest. Moderate, suburban Republicans, claimed Dionne, in states like Pennsylvania, New Jersey, Ohio, Minnesota, and Wisconsin, frightened off by the Tom Delay wing of the current Republican Party, would swing the House of Representatives to the Democrats in the fall 2006 elections. Dionne was on to something, but why these states needed to be called "Lincoln states" remains unclear. Bill Clinton carried many of these same voters twice, and Franklin Roosevelt attracted their parents or grandparents four times. But it was Lincoln's prestige, symbolism, or imprimatur that Dionne, like so many others, reached for to get our attention— the Lincoln as ingenious strategist and paragon of our democracy. I am reminded of the headline that appeared in the *Chicago Defender* in the 1936 election, urging blacks to shift their allegiance to FDR: "Abraham Lincoln is not Running in This Election!"[5]

One should exercise some restraint in casting aspersions on our current-day Lincoln thieves, since this process has ever been thus. Historian David Donald demonstrated this poignantly in his famous 1947 essay, "Getting Right with Lincoln." By the twentieth century, Donald showed, for American politicians of all parties, Lincoln could be "everybody's grandfather." Donald has sustained the image and the man he first wrote about with irony sixty years earlier; in Donald's work, Lincoln remains a towering political figure, characterized by his "essential ambiguity" and his "enormous capacity for growth."[6]

Despite all the efforts to pin Lincoln down ideologically, psychologically, religiously, legally, linguistically, sexually, and morally, it is the Lincoln of change, growth, and contradiction (and even of a self-described malleability) that makes possible his endurance as symbol and as scholarly subject. And despite the considerable labors of devotees of the political theorist Leo Strauss, who crave a principled and consistent Lincoln to advance their conservative agendas, his power over us derives from his splendid inconsistency. Certainly this is what has made Lincoln so useful to opposite ends of the political spectrum, to African Americans trying to preserve a usable past, and to right-wing ideologues, some of whom now find it politically impossible to operate without getting right, in their own way, with an emancipationist memory of the Civil War. There are many ways to "love" Lincoln. My own favorite comes from W. E. B. Du Bois. "I love him," Du Bois wrote in 1922 after expressing disgust at the nation's continuing adoration of Robert E. Lee, "not because he was perfect, but because he was not and yet triumphed. . . . The world is full of folk whose taste was educated in the gutter. The world is full of people born hating and despising their fellows. To those I love to say: See this man. He was one of you and yet became Abraham Lincoln." Like so many others, including Sandburg, Du Bois was drawn to Lincoln's embodiment of paradox. "There was something left," he said of Lincoln, "so that at the crisis he was big enough to be inconsistent—

cruel, merciful, peace-loving, a fighter, despising Negroes and letting them fight and vote, protecting slavery, and freeing slaves. He was a man—a big, inconsistent, brave man."[7]

Du Bois's Lincoln is the Lincoln of my own taste, choice, and use. Not a flavor of the month, but one for all time; it is Lincoln the flawed but changing democrat. But the revival of Lincoln scholarship and Lincoln memory in the past decade or so has given us many new variations on this theme, and we need to take notice of the political potential in the new thievery. As the bicentennial of Lincoln's birth arrives in 2009 and the United States Lincoln Bicentennial Commission plans its extensive commemorations, we will see only more grist for this mill. In the past few years, excellent books on Lincoln have emerged from liberal academic historians, libertarian pseudo-historians, a sexuality expert, legal scholars, literary theorists, political theorists, journalists, and psychologists. Many recent books have added notably and surprisingly to our knowledge of Lincoln as a thinker and writer, but many also sustain a trend that might be called "Lincoln triumphalism."[8]

One of the most celebrated works of the Lincoln establishment is Allen Guelzo's *Lincoln's Emancipation Proclamation: The End of Slavery in America*. Guelzo, however, seems so determined to protect Lincoln from critics that one wonders why the Emancipation Proclamation needs such a vehement defense in the early twenty-first century. It takes nothing away from the many recent good books on Lincoln to suggest that they (especially Guelzo's) may be efforts to defend Lincoln from those critics who have tried to take the mantle of Great Emancipator away from him and crush it in a wave of myth-busting from Left and Right. Lerone Bennett's *Forced Into Glory* (1999) spent over six hundred pages trying to demonstrate that Lincoln was a white supremacist first and always, and that traditional scholarship, political rhetoric, and the industry of memory and hero worship over time had created "the biggest attempt in recorded history to hide a man." Lincoln's defenders, claimed Bennett, had managed to turn "a racist who wanted to deport all blacks into a national symbol of integration and brotherhood," and had "fooled all the people all the time." But his selectively researched polemic gained great traction in black communities; its argument, strained as it is, has a new staying power at the grassroots, non-academic level of historical interest, a phenomenon no one should ignore. Bennett's book gained little respect in academic circles, however, and garnered few mainstream reviews. Yet, Guelzo also does not advance the debate over whether Lincoln alone freed the slaves or whether some slaves, by their own bravery, actually should be judged as "self-emancipated." Guelzo declares the self-emancipation thesis not worthy of the time of day, stating that it "asks too great a suspension of disbelief."[9] Numerous books and some slave narratives have demonstrated that slaves' volition in this story is more than worthy of our attention.[10]

It is as though Bennett stole the Great Emancipator from the halls of academe, and some Lincoln scholars have simply taken him back. Whether the two communities are even aware of each other's theft is another matter, since Bennett's and Guelzo's respective readers and advocates rarely speak to one another. The crucial questions about Lincoln on race and emancipation (as well as the colonization schemes launched by his administration) are far more complicated than polemical debate can settle. Lincoln the emancipator is one example of the intersection between scholarship and public memory that will forever witness volatile collisions. This is largely because it still very much matters how slavery ended in America, and how its aftermath in law, society, politics, and social psychology still infests our national memory with its most vexing dilemmas.

As long as we have a politics of race in America, we will have a politics of memory over Lincoln, the Civil War, and how and why black freedom came. And here we can see that Lincoln is still to some the president who held back racial change, while to many others he was the agent of great and lasting change. The argument is alive as a democratic one over just how much democracy Lincoln advanced or obstructed. In this sense, he and his actions are a pivot to American history that may forever be subject to contentious debate carried on in public memory far more than in scholarship.

Another community of historical writing on Lincoln and the Civil War emanates from the right wing, some of it white supremacist and neo-Confederate, and some of it staunchly libertarian, anti-statist, even utopian, where Lincoln-hating is the stand-in for the hated "big government." Two books stand out among a crowded subfield of neo-Confederate, pro-secession, largely ersatz scholarship. The first is Charles Adams's *When in the Course of Human Events: Arguing the Case for Southern Secession*; the second, Thomas J. DiLorenzo's *The Real Lincoln: A New Look at Abraham Lincoln, His Agenda, and an Unnecessary War*.[11]

Why pay attention to these books? The simple answer is that they sell well, better than some canonical works on Lincoln and the Civil War of recent years that might be considered part of a liberal orthodoxy forged around the books of James McPherson, Eric Foner, and others. But more importantly, along with such recent books as *The Politically Incorrect Guide to American History*, by Thomas E. Woods Jr., given huge publicity by Fox News, MSNBC, and other media outlets, and which had a stint on the *New York Times* bestseller list, these works provide a historical undergirding for a broadening conservative and libertarian attack on the actual legacies of the original Republican Party, the Progressive movement, the New Deal regulatory state, the Great Society, and the civil rights movement.[12] Moreover, carefully researched, well-written academic history (even by those authors who reach broad audiences) is merely one more target of a conservative network of enthusiasts who love Whiggish, happy, redemptive American history. Their real targets are the "liberal elites" who allegedly control the academy, brainwash generations of students, and too often remain in their cocoons, scorned and irrelevant to the ways history is used in the civic arena.

In a recent essay in *Reviews in American History*, Daniel Feller took on the Adams and DiLorenzo books, as well as a third, by Jeffrey Hummel, *Emancipating Slaves, Enslaving Free Men: A History of the American Civil War*. Feller points out that the Library of Congress catalogues my book, *Race and Reunion: The Civil War in American Memory*, right next to Tony Horwitz's *Confederates in the Attic* and Adams's defense of secession (with mine apparently in the middle). "Though Adams and Blight sit adjacent on the shelves," writes Feller, "the gulf between them, both in viewpoint and audience, is nearly bottomless. Contemplating that gulf provokes some disturbing thoughts."[13] In this essay, I have tried to at least peer across this disturbing gulf.

Adams, an economist by training, is self-described as the "world's leading scholar on the history of taxation." DiLorenzo teaches (also economics) at Loyola College in Maryland and has been active in the "League of the South." Both authors consider the slavery issue as a mere pretext for the larger reason Lincoln and the Republicans went to war—to advance the centralized, leviathan state. Both authors despise Lincoln, and they argue that the war's greatest legacy is federal "tyranny" over the states and especially over individual liberty. Secession was not only understandable, but right and holy. And Lincoln's war was vicious and "criminal." It was a war waged, in Adams's and DiLorenzo's view, for increased taxation, higher tariffs, and business profits. Adams compares Lincoln's ruthlessness in prosecuting a war to unconditional surrender to that of Stalin and Hitler in World War II. Adams considers Lincoln a virulent racist and calls the Second Inaugural "psychopathic," a mere cover for his larger motive—the total destruction of Southern civilization. During Reconstruction, according to Adams, the Union Leagues were the terrorist wing of the Republican Party and the Ku Klux Klan a harmless, necessary veterans' organization. Three of Adams's chapters had first been published in the white supremacist magazine, *Southern Partisan*.[14]

This is all standard Lost Cause dogma of a fairly extreme brand, and it could have been written in 1890 or 1913 by any number of first- or second-generation ex-Confederates. But, as Feller writes, it is not merely a "brainless rant." It has all the usual scholarly apparatus, footnotes, and a bibliographical essay. Adams's work is a screed full of some wild roundhouses, but it also reads much like a Bill O'Reilly monologue on Fox News, a Newt Gingrich news conference in 1994, or a Grover Norquist press release about the condition of the American polity circa 2004. It is history serving a political persuasion: facts spun into a compelling narrative for the scorned and rebuked white Christian conservatives of America who believe their faith in God, country, and righteousness is somehow under attack. Adams's Lincoln, like Norquist's lobbying, offers nourishment for the New Federalists and states' rightists who believe government and taxation to be America's great domestic enemies.[15]

DiLorenzo's book is even more extreme in its sheer hatred of Lincoln. *The Real Lincoln* may be taking some of its cues from a book of the same title published in 1901 by Charles L. C. Minor. That book, at the high tide of Lost Cause writing, trashed Lincoln as un-heroic, un-Christian, and a vulgar buffoon, a kind of counterexample to the noble Christian soldier Robert E. Lee. But primarily DiLorenzo twists Lincoln's presidency into a libertarian manifesto for an age of conservative complaint and ascendancy. DiLorenzo's Lincoln provoked the Civil War to bring into being the modern "welfare-warfare state." Rather than a Great Emancipator label, the sixteenth president should be remembered as the "great centralizer."[16]

What mainstream America celebrates in Lincoln's conception of the Civil War as the "rebirth" of freedom, DiLorenzo sees as the "death of federalism." His Lincoln is the dictatorial godfather of Big Government.[17] Leaders of secession were the Civil War's real heroes, according to DiLorenzo, because their cause had nothing to do with slavery—only with resisting federal tyranny. DiLorenzo's real subject is the economic legislation passed by the Lincoln administration and the Civil War Congress—protective tariffs, the Morrill Act (subsidized land-grant colleges), federal subsidies to railroads, nationalized money, the income tax, the Homestead Act, and, most egregious of all, emancipation by military force (the theft of individual property) and the huge extensions of federal power in the Fourteenth and Fifteenth Amendments.

There is no likelihood that the DiLorenzos of the Right will make significant numbers of Americans hate Lincoln, but much of his argument looks like only a slightly angrier, heightened version of the campaign manual of movement conservatives during the George W. Bush administration. They can never appear to hate Lincoln—and do not need to—but they do tend to hate government, and are very much interested in confirming judges and passing legislation that would roll back the activist-interventionist government, and the beginnings of the regulatory state, that the original Republicans created. In this instance, we can see again that struggles over historical memory—which version of the past or of a great president's legacy shall win out in public debates—are very much about how we define the nature of our democracy in relation to the past. Democratic debate does not always result in more democracy, despite the civic lessons we teach our young.

This makes all the more ironic the Republican National Committee's recent, well-funded, glitzy campaign to once again reclaim the mantle of the "party of Lincoln," to portray themselves as the true party of "civil rights." Early in 2005, just as President Bush was inaugurated for his second term, the Republican Party Policy Committee, led then by Christopher Cox (a California congressman later appointed head of the Securities and Exchange Commission), produced a four-color calendar that they distributed by the thousands to African American churches and other civic groups across the country. Called the "2005 Republican Freedom Calendar," its cover featured a majestic image of the Lincoln Memorial statue and twelve photographs of African Americans and other minority Republicans in American history. The calendar's subtitle leaves no doubt of its long-range historical claims: "Celebrating a century and a half of civil rights achievement by the Party of Lincoln."[18]

Cox's introduction offers a particular and curious version of history. It declares the Republican Party "the mightiest force for individual liberty in the history of the world" and "the most effective political organization in the history of the world in advancing the cause of freedom by staying true to its founding principles." And Cox makes clear to the black audience he hopes to reach who the enemy was and is. "We started our party," he says, "with the express intent of protecting the American people from the Democrats' pro-slavery policies that expressly made people inferior to the state." "Today," he continues, "the animating spirit of the Republican party is exactly the same as it was then: free people, free minds, free markets, free expression, and unlimited individual opportunity."[19] Libertarians in the guise of Free Soilers! It is a little hard to imagine the Bush White House of 2006–8, mired in a disastrous foreign war, ever aggressive in cutting the taxes of corporations and rich citizens, stumping for "intelligent design" in biology classrooms and against embryonic stem cell research in medical laboratories, as proponents of our collective "free minds" and "free expression." But the "party of Lincoln" has come to mean many things to many people.

Cox and his staff were determined to create a hated ideological enemy of both past and present. Cox continued, "Leading the organized opposition to these ideas [free markets and free minds] 150 years ago, just as today, was the Democratic Party. Then, just as now, their hallmarks were politically correct speech; a preference for government control over individual initiative (and of course slavery was the most extreme form of government control over individual initiative); and an insistence on seeing people as members of groups rather than as individuals." I know of no one who ever accused Stephen A. Douglas of using politically correct speech, but early twentieth-century Republicans are careful to invoke the symbol of Ronald Reagan (an odd kind of right-wing correctness of speech in our own era), as Cox did in this calendar, as the great spokesman of "the only country on earth to be based not on race or nationality, but on an ideal." For black audiences, not to mention millions of whites and others with historical memories, these are odd claims to make for Reagan, the most racially divisive president in modern American history. But the "Freedom Calendar" leaves one impression above all others: black voters, and whites who need to feel better about being Republicans, should draw a clear, uninterrupted line from Harriet Tubman and Frederick Douglass to Condoleezza Rice and Colin Powell, and American history ought to be seen as a consistent struggle of the Republican Party to sustain a society where the "individual is master and the government is servant." This sophistry has many parallels and antecedents. After President Franklin Roosevelt had captured a majority of the black vote in 1936 (the first time a Democrat had ever done so), he remarked with derision: "Does anyone maintain that the Republican party from 1868 to 1938 (with the possible exception of a few years under Theodore Roosevelt) was the party of Abraham Lincoln?" With even more derision, we might say today: "Does anyone really believe that the Republican Party from 1964 to 2008 was the party of Abraham Lincoln?"[20]

It is easy to simply laugh away such slippery, ahistorical versions of the past century and a half of American political history. But incredulity is hardly enough against the realization that millions of Americans either believe this story or are blissful in their ignorance. Such a twisted, sleight-of-hand history of the Republican Party (sinless, indeed, righteous on race) has not yet swayed (at least through the 2008 elections) even a few percent more African Americans to vote for Bush-era Republicans. Indeed, we have seen quite the opposite, with a decisive number of white moderate Republicans moving over to vote for Barack Obama in the 2008 election. What is also clear is that it makes a reeking irony of recent attacks by Dick Cheney, Condoleezza Rice, President Bush, and others on so-called "revisionist history" among those who opposed their policies. The racial rhetoric and action of the Bush-era Republican Party not only backfired, it may have, along with a declining economy, sealed its own doom at the dawn of the Obama era. And is it indeed this embarrassing history, or simply an embedded racism, that drives Republican spokesmen—conservative white males all—such as Karl Rove, Newt Gingrich, and Rush Limbaugh to sully President Obama's nominee to the Supreme Court, Sonia Sotomayor, as herself the "racist" because of her occasional remarks about the unique potential of a Hispanic woman's worldview? Those who howl against reverse racism had better clean their own house first.

Moreover, if the Republicans' record is so pure, why did the party chairman, Ken Mehlman (until his resignation in 2006), travel the country in search of black support? Indeed, it may be evidence that the facile "calendar" strategy backfired, since Mehlman went to the NAACP annual convention in July 2005 in Milwaukee largely to apologize for the Republican record on race and civil rights, especially its notorious "Southern strategy," begun under Richard Nixon but manipulated by no one more adroitly than

Ronald Reagan, and to a lesser extent, by President George H. W. Bush. Mehlman pleaded guilty to the Republicans' "trying to benefit politically from racial polarization." "I am here today," he told the suspicious NAACP delegates, "to tell you we were wrong." Meanwhile, on the same day, July 14, 2005, President Bush was speaking to "business leaders" at the Indiana Black Expo, emphasizing gains for African Americans in education, faith-based initiatives, and private enterprise. "Racial polarization" would seem to have suddenly become a thing of the distant past, rendered no longer operative by a passive voice from a Republican leadership eager to make the past fit its present. In his speech to the NAACP, Mehlman used the phrase "party of Abraham Lincoln" no less than six times.[21] A Lincoln currency no longer buys anything among African Americans who know something about the recent history of civil rights and which side most Republicans were on.

Further evidence that the Republicans desperately need something more serious to truly attract black allegiance, especially in the wake of Hurricane Katrina, stems from President Bush's July 2006 speech to the annual convention of the NAACP, an organization he had snubbed for four years. Bush's speechwriters placed a remarkable document in his hands. This time, it was based on some history written in the last forty years. He called the civil rights movement a "second founding" of the United States, and the movement's leaders the new "founders." He acknowledged racism to be the "stain we have not yet wiped clean." And the only reference to the "party of Lincoln" was in an open admission of his party's failures in race relations. "I understand that many African Americans distrust my political party," said Bush. "I consider it a tragedy that the party of Abraham Lincoln let go of its historic ties to the African American community. For too long my party wrote off the African American vote, and many African Americans wrote off the Republican party."[22] So much for the calendar strategy and the selling of nonsense as history. Only a short time after launching the calendar effort and its related outreach to black voters, the official Republican Party all but admitted the implausibility of their own arguments. Sometimes history is whatever you can make people believe in the political marketplace, and sometimes not. Here President Bush seemed to need to get right not only with Lincoln but also with the facts. Can the post-Bush Republicans, led now by a beleaguered African American national chairman, Michael Steele, find a new history in which to live? We shall see.

In thus reaching out in 2006, it is as though Bush's aides decided that, for this symbolic moment at least, it was time to disown part of the political heritage of his biological father (George H. W. Bush) as well as his political father (Ronald Reagan). No matter how malleable, no matter how ambiguous, perhaps deep in the legacies of the original father of the Republican Party, there is one ghost that will not down: Lincoln possessed a genuine sense of tragedy, and from it he learned and grew. Whether former President George Bush has a sense of the tragic, or of history generally, is open to debate. Whether his party will ever overcome its late twentieth-century and early twenty-first-century politics of resentment on race remains to be seen.

We could attribute all of this simply to the twisted ways politicians use history. But this broad manipulation of history by Republicans has been, of course, nothing new. The various thefts of Lincoln from the Right, and even to some extent in mainstream scholarship, are part of a larger distortion of the story of emancipation in the First Reconstruction and the story of the civil rights revolution in the Second Reconstruction. It is a bold attempt by the conservative movement to gain control of the master narrative of American history in order to reverse many of the gains of both revolutions.

It is possible that a new master narrative emerged on the night of November 4, 2008, when Barack Obama and his family strode out onto the stage in Grant Park in Chicago. All the world watched as an African American was elected president of the United States, in the country where his wife's ancestors had been slaves and where he found a home for his multiracial, multinational experience. Something in excess of 50 percent of Americans that night wept and cheered with joy and wonder as the new president-elect quoted both Lincoln and Martin Luther King Jr. as visionaries, but especially as healers. He reminded Republicans directly of their origins, and of their "values of self-reliance, individual liberty, and national unity." He wanted the world to know, via Lincoln's famous Gettysburg refrain, that government "of the people, by the people, for the people has not perished from the earth." And from Lincoln's First Inaugural, of March 1861 (the beginning of the conflict), Obama drew the inspiring appeal to Republicans and all who had opposed him: "We are not enemies, but friends . . . though passion may have strained, it must not break our bonds of affection."[23] As so many people wept, on television, in the streets, and in their living rooms, it was as though the legacies of so much awful racial history were being washed away with the tears. One wonders how many Republican Party leaders thought then, or since, about just how much history was coming back to haunt them.

The New Right has abandoned the racism of the Old Right and has found a new narrative in "color-blind conservatism." Color-blind conservatism gave us the most ardent states-rightist on the Supreme Court in Clarence Thomas, and it has now put the black ardent libertarian Janice Rogers Brown on the U.S. Court of Appeals. And though the stories of the Iraq War and torture policies have not yet played out, it has all but made a fool of Colin Powell, and perhaps Condoleezza Rice as well. Color-blind conservatism has fashioned a master narrative in which American history is a morality tale of progress—from the Emancipation Proclamation to the Fourteenth Amendment; from the 1964 Civil Rights Act to Secretary of State Rice; from the rollback of Social Security, tax cuts for rich people, and the abolition of the estate tax in the name of "liberty," to a slow demise of environmental regulation—all as legacies, somehow, of the "party of Lincoln." In the America of the early twenty-first century, we can all feel as if we freed the slaves, we all participated in the Underground Railroad, we all cheered for the civil rights movement (even if a few of us got "polarized"), while small majorities voted to erode many of its achievements in favor of the free market and the vilification of "liberals"—the arch-enemies of all this progress, rather than its architects.

As Republicans tried to steal the meaning of American history and ride Lincoln's coattails while hating the government he imagined, they have sought what all insurgent political movements need—a *warrant of the past.* That warrant is one of the chief prizes in all political contests. Whether Republicans—moderates hoping for a new inclusive vision, or the rock-ribbed, narrow-thinking right wing that seemed to fall temporarily in love with Sarah Palin, and their friend and now-silent partner, President Bush—can ever again win this struggle over storytelling remains a pivotal question for American voters. Millions of them care and read about Lincoln, and as the sixteenth president's bicentennial may have demonstrated, the concept of the "party of Lincoln" may now receive more scrutiny than the creators of the "Freedom Calendar" ever intended. It is as though that calendar came back in the mail, labeled "undeliverable," like a political letter bomb.

A tragic overreach on so many fronts by the Republican Party and the Bush White House has denied them, for the time being, any secure control over America's story. The Iraq War, with many more years of consequences to unfold, may have swallowed Rove's dream of a "permanent Republican majority." The heterosexual and homosexual habits of gay-bashing Republican senators and congressmen may also have waylaid this historic "party of civil rights." One of the tests of the extent of our democracy now is just how equal gay Americans will be under law. A tide of hypocrisy may have all but banished homophobia from the Republican playbook just when it seemed to have won some victories for the "rights" of heterosexual couples. Moreover, the detainees at Guantanamo Bay and official defenses of "torture" may have sidelined Republican cant about their civil rights history for some time to come. But in politics the past is forever malleable. Indeed, President Obama now faces his own personal and Democratic Party challenge on the issue of gay civil rights.

As he considered Karl Rove's immediate legacy in recent American political history, the Bush administration critic Frank Rich chose George Allen's "macaca moment" (the Virginia U.S. senator's reference to a dark-skinned Asian American in an audience during his unsuccessful reelection campaign in 2006) as "a single symbolic episode to encapsulate the collapse of Rovian Republicanism." It works as well as any other, although in its directness it lacks the cynicism and sophistry of the Bushites' presentation of themselves as the "party of Lincoln" to the sufferers in New Orleans's Superdome and its Ninth Ward, or even of the first President Bush's appointment of Clarence Thomas to the Supreme Court. But Rich captured in a phrase the nature and meaning of the Republican Party's attempted theft of the past, and of reason itself: a "monochromatic whiteness at the dark heart of Rovian Republicanism" tried to steal the country.[24]

Deep in the heart of the modern GOP lies a history it hardly wishes to know, and that past, recent and long-term, has everything to do with why not a single black Republican serves in 2009 in the United States Congress. Republicans will likely continue to scramble to assume the mantle of the "party of Lincoln." But the Republicans' founder had a warning for them. In his "Annual Message to Congress," December 1, 1862, Lincoln famously said: "Fellow-citizens, we cannot escape history. We of this Congress and this administration, will be remembered in spite of ourselves."[25]

Notes

This essay originally appeared, in a slightly different form, in *Our Lincoln,* edited by Eric Foner (©2008 by David W. Blight. Used by permission of W. W. Norton & Company, Inc.).

1. H. L. Mencken, *Prejudices: Third Series* (New York, 1922), 174.

2. Carl Sandburg quoted in Merrill D. Peterson, *Lincoln in American Memory* (New York, 1994), 371; Ida Tarbell quoted in ibid., 155.

3. Herbert V. Prochnow, *The Toastmaster's Treasure Chest,* 2nd ed. (New York, 1988). For Reagan's use of the four aphorisms, see Mario M. Cuomo, *Why Lincoln Matters: Today More Than Ever* (New York, 2004), 13–16; and Herbert Mitgang, "Republicans in Houston: For the Record, Reagan Put Words in Lincoln's Mouth," *New York Times,* August 19, 1992. Boetcker's work is sometimes referred to as a "leaflet."

4. Thomas F. Schwartz, "Lincoln Never Said That," *For the People: A Newsletter of the Abraham Lincoln Association* 1, (Spring 1999): 4–6. For a particularly egregious misquoting, or fabrication, of Lincoln on the Iraq War, by Republican partisans, see Eric Foner, *The Nation,* March 12, 2007.

5. Newt Gingrich, "Bush and Lincoln," *Wall Street Journal,* September 7, 2006; E. J. Dionne, "The Rise of the Lincoln Democrats," *Washington Post,* September 5, 2006.

6. David Herbert Donald, "Getting Right with Lincoln," in *Lincoln Reconsidered: Essays on the Civil War Era* (New York, 1947), 16, 18; David Herbert Donald, *Lincoln* (New York, 1995), 14.

7. W. E. B. Du Bois, "Abraham Lincoln," *The Crisis,* May 1922; and W. E. B. Du Bois, "Lincoln Again," *The Crisis,* September 1922, both in W. E. B. Du Bois, *Writings: The Suppression of the African Slave-Trade; The Souls of Black Folk; Dusk of Dawn; Essays and Articles from "The Crisis,"* ed. Nathan Irvin Huggins (New York: Library of America, 1986), 1196, 1198.

8. See Allen C. Guelzo, *Lincoln's Emancipation Proclamation: The End of Slavery in America* (New York, 2004). Other recent important Lincoln books, very selectively, include Harold Holzer, *Lincoln at Cooper Union: The Speech that Made Abraham Lincoln President* (New York, 2004); Douglas L. Wilson, *Honor's Voice: The Transformation of Abraham Lincoln* (New York, 1998); Douglas L. Wilson, *Lincoln's Sword: The President and the Power of Words,* (New York, 2006); William Lee Miller, *Lincoln's Virtues: An Ethical Biography* (New York, 2002); Daniel Farber, *Lincoln's Constitution* (Chicago, 2003); and George P. Fletcher, *Our Secret Constitution: How Lincoln Redefined American Democracy* (New York, 2001).

9. Lerone Bennett Jr., *Forced Into Glory: Abraham Lincoln's White Dream* (Chicago, 2000), preface; Guelzo, *Lincoln's Emancipation Proclamation,* 9.

10. See David W. Blight, *A Slave No More: Two Men Who Escaped to Freedom, Including Their Narratives of Emancipation,* (New York, 2007). Many recent books develop, to varying degrees, the "self-emancipation" thesis, but for a beginning, see Ira Berlin et al., *Slaves No More: Three Essays on Emancipation and the Civil War* (New York, 1992).

11. Charles Adams, *When in the Course of Human Events: Arguing the Case for Southern Secession* (Lanham, MD, 2000); Thomas J. DiLorenzo, *The Real Lincoln: A New Look at Abraham Lincoln, His Agenda, and an Unnecessary War* (New York, 2002).

12. See James M. McPherson, *Battle Cry of Freedom: The Civil War Era* (New York, 1988); Eric Foner, *Reconstruction: America's Unfinished Revolution, 1963–1877* (New York, 1987); Thomas E. Woods Jr., *The Politically Incorrect Guide to American History* (Washington, DC, 2005). For a review that exposes Woods's falsehoods and right-wing political agenda, as well as simply sloppy pseudo-scholarship, see David Greenberg, "History for Dummies: The Troubling Popularity of *The Politically Incorrect Guide to American History*, March 11, 2005, on *Slate.com*, http://slate.msn.com/id/2114713. Greenberg points out that some conservative academics have denounced Woods's book, while right-wing television hosts Sean Hannity and Pat Buchanan offered it praise and considerable air time. The book demonstrates, Greenberg asserts, that the Far Right of the Republican Party increasingly exhibits a "scorn for intellectual authority altogether."

13. Daniel Feller, "Libertarians in the Attic, or a Tale of Two Narratives," *Reviews in American History* 32 (June 2004), 184.

14. Adams, *When in the Course of Human Events*, 109–25, 151–55, 205.

15. Feller, "Libertarians in the Attic," 189. On Norquist, the leader of the advocacy group, and "Americans for Tax Reform," see John Cassidy, "The Ringleader: How Grover Norquist Keeps the Conservative Movement Together," *The New Yorker*, August 1, 2005, 42–53.

16. On Charles L. C. Minor's book, *The Real Lincoln*, see Peterson, *Lincoln in American Memory*, 193; and DiLorenzo, *The Real Lincoln*, 233.

17. DiLorenzo, *The Real Lincoln*, 264, 6.

18. "2005 Republican Freedom Calendar: Celebrating A Century and a Half of Civil Rights Achievement by the Party of Lincoln," Republican National Committee, Washington, DC, www.policy.house.gov. Much of the text of the calendar was the work of Michael Zak (see "Back to Basics for the Republican Party," a history of the GOP, available at www.republicanbasics.com).

19. Christopher Cox, "About the Calendar," "2005 Republican Freedom Calendar."

20. Ibid. Roosevelt is quoted in Donald, "Getting Right with Lincoln," 14.

21. Anne E. Kornblut, "Bush and Party Chief Court Black Voters at 2 Forums," *New York Times*, July 15, 2005; James Dao, "Republican Party Is Backing Black Candidates in Bid to Attract Votes," *New York Times*, July 1, 2005; "Morning Edition," National Public Radio, July 15, 2005.

22. "President Bush Addresses NAACP Annual Convention, Washington, DC, July 20, 2006, www.whitehouse.gov/news/releases.

23. Text of Obama election night speech, in *Chicago Sun-Times*, November 5, 2008.

24. Frank Rich, "He Got Out While the Getting Was Good," *New York Times*, August 19, 2007.

25. Abraham Lincoln, "Annual Message to Congress," December 1, 1862, in *Abraham Lincoln, Slavery, and the Civil War: Selected Writings and Speeches,* ed. Michael P. Johnson (Boston, 2001), 217.

III WILSON

American Sphinx

Woodrow Wilson and Race

✦   ✦   ✦   John Milton Cooper Jr.

The title of this essay is not original with me. I have copied it from Joseph Ellis's biographical study of Thomas Jefferson, *American Sphinx*—for
two reasons. First, and most important, those arresting words capture what
strikes me as the essence of Woodrow Wilson's attitude toward race; and
second, the phrase invites a linkage between Wilson and Jefferson. Let me
reverse the order and take up the second reason first.[1]

In many ways, Wilson and Jefferson seem a well-matched pair. Both men
were born not many miles apart in the same part of Virginia. Both were intellectuals who wrote inspiring and immortal words. Wilson felt Jefferson's
influence throughout his life, including when he studied at the university
that "Mr. Jefferson" founded. It would be wrong to push those similarities
too far. Unlike Jefferson, Wilson loved and trusted political power. At an
early age he broke with the prevailing orthodoxy of state rights and limited
government that was then being preached in Jefferson's name in their native
South. "Ever since I have had independent judgments of my own," Wilson
once declared, "I have been a Federalist(!)." By that, he meant a devotee
of strong, centralized government, and he often confessed that his favorite among the founders of the Republic was, not Jefferson, but Alexander
Hamilton.[2]

Still, profound as those differences were, they do not outweigh several
significant similarities. Like Jefferson—and unlike both Hamilton and Wilson's own great rival Theodore Roosevelt—Wilson believed that human
happiness and the fulfillment of the individual person's gifts and potential
formed the chief ends of government and sole route to the achievement of

the good society. More simply put, Wilson was a liberal, not a conservative. Equally important, in their historical achievements and reputations, he and Jefferson shared the same pair of Achilles' heels: race and civil liberties. On race, Jefferson was the greater sinner, and on civil liberties, Wilson was the bigger transgressor. Why both men fell short in these areas is especially puzzling in light of their liberalism. These were not men who took a dim view of human nature and sanctioned inequality and repression as immutable aspects of man's (and woman's) fate. Why, then, did they violate their own deepest convictions? To try to answer the question about Wilson and race is to try to solve the riddle of this American sphinx.

The first task in this effort is straightforward. It is necessary to establish a basis of facts about Wilson's racial views and how he came by them. For most interpreters, this effort begins and ends with Wilson's birth and upbringing. He was a white Southerner who was born on the eve of the Civil War and raised during that war and Reconstruction. Plenty of testimony appears to make those circumstances the key to understanding his subsequent thought and action with respect to race. The most widely quoted statement of Wilson's about these origins is something he said in 1909: "It is all very well to talk of detachment of view, and of the effort to be national in spirit and purpose, but a boy never gets over his boyhood, and never can change those subtle influences which have become part of him, that were bred into him when he was a child. So I am obliged to say again and again, that the only place where nothing has to be explained to me is the South."[3]

That statement might appear to unlock the door to understanding and dispel any notion of mystery about Wilson's racial attitudes. Coming of age during the most intensely racist time in the history of the South, what could be expected of him except that he would believe in the inequality of African Americans and discriminate against them? Such a view, however, is not sufficient. The influences of his white Southern background on Wilson were not straightforward, and it is not easy to pin them down and show how they shaped his thought and action. Wilson made that statement after having lived in the North for almost a quarter of a century. After the age of eighteen, he lived in the South for only four years, when he studied law at the University of Virginia and then practiced law in Atlanta. Neither of those experiences filled him with unalloyed joy. In fact, living and working in the unofficial capital of the New South disgusted him. "I can never be happy unless I am enabled to lead an intellectual life," he told a friend, "and who can lead an intellectual life in ignorant Georgia?" Soon after writing those words, Wilson fled north to graduate school at Johns Hopkins and the academic career that took him to Pennsylvania, Connecticut, and New Jersey. Not even what was for him the most tempting academic post in the South—the presidency of the University of Virginia—could persuade him to come back to his native region.[4]

Clearly, then, Wilson felt ambivalent about his origins. In fact, there are grounds for questioning how much of a Southerner he was. For one thing, as his classmates at Princeton remembered, he did not have a Southern accent. That may have reflected the influence of his close-knit family, with his parents having come from Ohio not long before his birth. More likely, the lack of an accent sprang from Wilson's having trained himself as a speaker from an early age, which appears to have included ridding himself of pronunciations that he thought unattractive, including a flat "a." He later tried, unsuccessfully, to get his Georgia-born wife to rid herself of her Southern accent. More important, young Wilson's becoming a Hamiltonian admirer of strong centralized government was an act of political apostasy. He did not keep his less-than-orthodox Southern views to himself. When he came to Charlottesville to study law, he published an essay in a student magazine that celebrated the defeat of the Confederacy: "I yield to no one in precedence in love of the South. But *because* I love the South, I rejoice in the failure of the Confederacy." Successful secession would have perpetuated slavery, which had been "enervating our Southern society and exhausting our Southern energies. . . . Even the damnable cruelty and folly of Reconstruction was to be preferred to helpless independence." This was a different kind of Southerner, to say the least.[5]

Perhaps most unusual in Wilson's youthful attitudes was that he rarely appears to have thought about race at all. The documentary record of his youth has next to nothing to say on the subject. This is truly bizarre. Wilson grew up surrounded by African Americans. In keeping with the custom among Presbyterian ministers, his family did not own slaves, but the household included slaves whom the church leased from parishioners; later, the family had African American servants. The places where he lived for most of the first two decades of his life—Augusta, Georgia, and Columbia, South Carolina—had large black populations, and South Carolina had a black majority. That state also had one of the longest-lasting Republican Reconstruction governments and the largest number of black officeholders. Yet the record of Wilson's early life reflects none of those circumstances. For him, it seems, the African American truly was, in Ralph Ellison's immortal words, "the invisible man."

That invisibility is not simply an artifact of the sparseness of the documentary record of Wilson's youth. Happily for those who study him, Wilson's first and official biographer, Ray Stannard Baker, was a journalist who did what came naturally in his profession: he interviewed people who had known Wilson, and he actively solicited recollections of Wilson's youth. This was a full generation before academic historians woke up to these practices and coined the term "oral history." Yet the recovered memories that Baker gathered contain only a few scattered, inconsequential references to African Americans. This is truly puzzling because, unusual among white Northern journalists of his time, Baker knew and cared about race relations. As one of the famed "muckrakers," he had mounted a major investigation that was published as a magazine series and a book, both of which were titled *Following the Color Line*.

Just one exception lifts this silence about race among the recollections of Wilson's youth. Another journalist-biographer, William Allen White, interviewed David Bryant, a black man who worked for the Wilson family when they lived in Wilmington, North Carolina. Bryant knew his employers well. Using Wilson's boyhood nickname, he told White, "Outside Mr. Tommy was his father's boy. But inside he was his mother all over." Interestingly, too, in a photograph taken of the family in Wilmington shortly after Wilson's mother's death, two black female servants identified as "Nannie" and "Minnie" are shown standing just behind "Tommy," who now called himself "Woodrow."[6]

During the first fifty-odd years of his life, Wilson left only widely separated and occasionally contradictory indications of what he thought about race. During his twenties, as he later told a friend, some black people had seemed awestruck when they watched him practice oratory in the pulpit of his father's church in Wilmington. "I'm Southern," Wilson commented, "but I have very little ease with coloured [*sic*] people or they with me. Why is it? For I care enormously about them." Wilson may have believed that, but his words and deeds did not bear out the claim. In his one serious historical work, *Division and Reunion*, published in 1893, he portrayed the antebellum South in a kindly light, viewing slavery as generally benign—except when it broke up families—but economically inefficient and wasteful. In that book, Wilson again had no patience for secession, but he also damned Reconstruction as an attempt to graft such alien practices as black suffrage and office-holding onto the South. In 1897, he wrote in an article in the *Atlantic Monthly,* "Even the race problem in the South will no doubt work itself out in the slowness of time. . . . Time is the only legislator in such matters."[7]

Wilson did make one gesture toward racial enlightenment during these years. In 1902, he invited Booker T. Washington to his inauguration as president of Princeton. The Tuskegee principal marched in the academic procession along with the representatives of other colleges and universities, and he was one of the speakers at a gala dinner after the inaugural ceremony. Wilson's daughter Jessie later recalled that Washington's presence "scandalized" one of her mother's relatives from Georgia, who "said if she had known he was to be there she wouldn't have gone." Wilson, however, maintained that Washington's speech "was the very best at the dinner afterwards bar none."[8]

Having a distinguished black guest briefly at Princeton for a ceremonial occasion was one thing; having African Americans there for a longer time in any other capacity was something else altogether. Although Wilson appointed the first Jew and first Catholic to the faculty, it never seems to have occurred to him to appoint a black person. During his second year as Princeton's president, he received an inquiry about an African American applying for admission as a student, and he answered, "I would say that, while there is nothing in the law of the University to prevent a negro's entering, the whole temper and tradition of the place are such that no negro has ever applied for admission, and its [*sic*] seems extremely unlikely that the question will ever assume a practical form." Toward the end of his presidency, he would again discourage an African American from applying for admission. "Regret to say that it is altogether inadvisable for a colored man to enter Princeton," he wrote in a memorandum. "Appreciate his desire to do so, but strongly recommend his securing education at a Southern [Negro] institution." Princeton would continue to draw a tight color line long after Wilson left its presidency. It would be the last of the schools in what came to be called the Ivy League to have black students. In 1947, a veteran of the World War II Navy V-12 program, John Leroy Howard, would become the first African American to receive a bachelor's degree from Princeton. That same year, the first regularly admitted peacetime black student, Joseph

Ralph Moss, would enroll; he would graduate four years later in the class of 1951. The first black faculty member would be Charles Davis, a professor of English appointed in 1957.[9]

Wilson could also show that he shared the reigning white racial views of the time. When he traveled abroad in the summer of 1908, the daughter of some of his English friends recorded in her diary that their visitor regretted that President Theodore Roosevelt had recently appointed an African American to a high-ranking federal post in South Carolina. It was, Wilson said, "too much for them [whites] to stand. And intermarriage would degrade the white nations for in Africa the blacks were the only race who did not rise. . . . Social intercourse would bring about intermarriage." Publicly, Wilson presented a more moderate face. The following year, speaking at an African American church in Princeton, he argued that "the so-called 'negro problem' is a problem, not of color, but capacity; not a racial, but an economic problem." He praised the work being done by Booker T. Washington's Tuskegee Institute and "many smaller institutions conducted along similar lines."[10]

Those utterances and actions comprise virtually everything that survives to document Wilson's thinking about race before he entered politics in 1910 at the age of fifty-three. This change of careers did not immediately bring him into contact with racial matters. In his first campaign—his successful bid for governor of New Jersey—Wilson does not appear to have said anything to or about African Americans. The state had a fair-sized black population, but the adult males among them who could vote made up a reliable bloc of supporters for the Republicans, not Wilson's Democrats.

His first encounters with the politics of race came two years later, when he ran for president. Curiously, when he sought his party's nomination, his Southern background worked both for and against him in his native region. Wilson's supporters there were reconstructed Southerners, high-toned centrists who wanted to promote educational and economic progress and sectional harmony. His opponents were unreconstructed Southerners, who clustered at the opposite ends of the political spectrum. Conservatives, or "Bourbons," correctly suspected that Wilson did not worship at their Jeffersonian altar of state rights and limited government. Agrarian radicals incorrectly suspected that he was soft on big business, and correctly suspected that he could be friendly to city folk. The common thread linking those opponents was resentment at Wilson for having left the South, having become an "expatriate" and, therefore, no longer a "real" Southerner. Those opponents included the most virulent racists of the time, particularly the demagogues Tom Watson and James K. Vardaman.

After Wilson won the Democratic nomination, racial politics played a small but telling role in his subsequent campaign. In September 1912, a group of prominent blacks, led by W. E. B. Du Bois and Bishop Alexander Walters of the African Zion Church, came out publicly in support of the Democratic nominee. They were fed up with repeated Republican efforts to distance the party from African Americans in order to court white Southern votes, and they felt equally offended by Theodore Roosevelt's lily-white Southern strategy in organizing his new Progressive Party. Wilson accepted this black support. He declined, however, to speak to Walters's and Du Bois's group. Instead, he sent a letter assuring them of "my earnest wish to see justice done in every matter," and promising that "they may count on me for absolute fair dealing and for everything by which I could assist in advancing the interests of their race in the United States." Privately, he told a white Democrat, "I do not believe I ought to make any statement on the negro question. I think it ought to suffice Bishop Walters that he himself knows my mind in this matter and can count on my impartiality." Such guarded words and arm's-length treatment portended bad times ahead for African Americans.[11]

Those bad times began almost as soon as the new president entered the White House. Between the election and his inauguration, Wilson talked about sectional reconciliation and worried about the predominantly Southern flavor of his party. Although half of his Cabinet hailed from the South, he fretted about journalistic comments on the Dixified political atmosphere. "We shall have to be careful not to make the impression that the South is seeking to keep the front of the stage and take possession of the administration," he told one congressional leader. Wilson also encouraged Oswald Garrison Villard, a white civil rights leader and grandson of the abolitionist William Lloyd Garrison, to pursue the idea of a government commission to investigate race relations. However, those words and gestures notwithstanding, Wilson raised no objections a month into his administration when three of his Cabinet secretaries floated ideas about introducing segregation into the workplaces in their departments. "The President said he made no promises to negroes, except to do them justice," Secretary of the Navy Josephus Daniels recorded in his diary after a Cabinet meeting in April 1913, "and he did not wish them to have less [*sic*] positions than they have now, but he wishes the matter adjusted in a way to make the least friction." Despite that expression of presidential sentiment, nearly all departments began to reduce the number of black-held positions, including lower-level jobs.[12]

The plans to segregate federal departments stirred up protests from the newly organized National Association for the Advancement of Colored People, of which Villard was a founder and Du Bois was editor of its magazine, *The Crisis*. Villard took those protests directly to Wilson. "I cannot exaggerate the effect this [segregation] has had upon the colored people at large," he told the president, adding that Negroes had taken from his campaign slogan, the New Freedom, "the belief that your democracy was not limited by race or color." Wilson responded waspishly, "It is as far as possible from being a movement *against* negroes," but he also threw cold water on the idea of a race commission, protesting the press of other business. In November 1913, Wilson consented to meet with a mixed-race delegation of critics of the segregation plan. Their spokesman, the sharp-tongued black editor from Boston, William Monroe Trotter, delivered a stinging indictment of administration policies and challenged the president: "Wipe out the blot, apostle of 'New Freedom,' put no limitation on any being for race." Wilson answered evasively, "I am not familiar with it all. . . . Now, mistakes have probably been made, but those mistakes can be corrected." The segregation plans were put on hold, but the reduction in positions continued.[13]

Limp words and a partial retreat did not satisfy black leaders, who continued to criticize Wilson and his administration. A year later, the president met with another delegation of critics, again headed by Trotter. The Boston editor challenged the president again: "Only two years ago you were heralded as perhaps the second Lincoln, and now the Afro-American leaders who supported you are hounded as false leaders and traitors to their race. What a change segregation has wrought!" Wilson once more tried to evade the issue: "Nobody can be cocksure about what should be done. . . . We must not allow our feelings to get the upper hands of our judgments." Trotter would have none of it: "We are not here as dependents. We are here as full-fledged American citizens, vouchsafed equality of citizenship by the Federal Constitution." Trotter also reminded the president of the black support he had received in 1912, and that set Wilson off: "Your tone, sir, offends me. You are an American citizen, as fully an American citizen as

I am, but your [*sic*] are the only American citizen that has ever come into this office who has talked to me with a tone with a background of passion that we evident." Trotter shot back, "I am from a part of the people, Mr. President." Wilson answered, "You have spoiled the whole cause for which you came."[14]

This was a momentous encounter, although it was not made public for many years. It probably marked the nadir of relations between Wilson and African Americans, although there was not much of an upswing afterward. It was certainly the most unpleasant face-to-face exchange Wilson ever had in the White House, and one of the worst in his whole life. He instantly recognized that he had mishandled the meeting. Secretary of the Navy Daniels later recalled that the president said to him, "Daniels, never raise an incident into an issue. When the negro delegate threatened me, I was damn fool enough to lose my temper and to point them to the door. What I ought to have done would have been to have listened, restrained my resentment, and, when they had finished, to have said to them that, of course, their petition would receive consideration. They would have withdrawn quietly and no more would have been heard about the matter. But I lost my temper and played the fool."[15]

That statement was both sad and revealing. It was sad that Wilson, even in regret, did not respond to what Trotter said about the facts of racial injustice. Wilson regretted only the way he handled himself. He had violated the cardinal principle of his personal philosophy that he transferred to groups and nations—self-control. Wilson had given in to what he accused Trotter of bringing into the presidential office—"passion." It was revealing that he suffered this breakdown in self-control during the grim months following the death of his first wife, Ellen, which also coincided with the outbreak of World War I. Grief and larger anxiety clearly affected him. Nothing like this would happen again while Wilson was president, except in smaller ways following the stroke that he suffered five years later. His use of the word "passion" also revealed something about his underlying attitude toward race. Wilson had separated himself early from the political attitudes of his native region, and he had sought a larger vision that was more national, more rational, and, above all, more self-controlled. Race offered an uncomfortable reminder of all that he sought to put behind him.

Wilson implicitly tried to make amends for that encounter. A month later, he received a delegation at the White House from the University

Commission on the Southern Race Question, an organization of white racial moderates. "There isn't any question, it seems to me, into which more candor needs to be put, or more thorough human good feeling, than this," the president told his visitors. "I know myself, as a southern man, how sincerely the heart of the South desires the good of the Negro and the advancement of his race on all sound and sensible lines. . . . And our object is to know the needs of the Negro and sympathetically help him in every way that is possible for his good and our good." Those words were not a cry to action, but it is interesting to speculate whether Wilson might have made some attempts to mend fences with African Americans if other events had not intervened.[16]

The biggest of these events was the war in Europe. Early in 1915 the Germans opened submarine warfare, and in May they sank the *Lusitania*—the war generation's equivalent of September 11, 2001. From then on, foreign affairs increasingly crowded other matters from Wilson's mind. Before that happened, however, a specific incident had publicly soured Wilson's relations with African Americans. The NAACP was protesting against and trying to block the showing of D. W. Griffith's film *Birth of a Nation.* Thomas F. Dixon Jr., author of *The Clansman,* the scurrilous racist novel on which the movie was based, had once been a student of Wilson's at Johns Hopkins. As a ploy to get publicity and counter the NAACP protests, Dixon slyly hoodwinked the president into showing the film at the White House. He later admitted his hidden agenda. "Of course, I didn't dare allow the President to know the real purpose back of my film," Dixon explained to Wilson's secretary, Joe Tumulty, *"which was to revolutionize Northern sentiments by a presentation of history that would transform every man in my audience into a good Democrat!* . . . What I told the President was that I would show him the birth of a new art—the launching of the mightiest engine for moulding public opinion in the history of the world."[17]

On February 18, 1915, Dixon and a projection crew gave the president, his family, and guests a showing in the East Room. How Wilson reacted to the film is a matter of dispute. Over twenty years later, a magazine writer claimed that he said, "It is like writing history with lightning. And my only regret is that it is so terribly true." It is doubtful that Wilson ever uttered those words. Revealingly, Dixon did not quote them in his memoirs. In 1977, Arthur Link interviewed Marjorie Brown King, the last person living who had been present at the film showing. She recalled that the president had not seemed to pay much attention to the movie and left when it was over without saying a word. Still, Dixon and Griffith touted the event and insinuated that *Birth of a Nation* enjoyed a presidential seal of approval.[18]

The White House showing only redoubled NAACP protests, which began to embarrass some Democrats. Two months later, Tumulty showed Wilson a clipping about protests organized by Trotter and advised the president to write "some sort of a note showing that he did not approve of the 'Birth of a Nation.'" Wilson responded, "I would like to do this if there were some way in which I could do it without seeming to be trying to meet the agitation which in the case referred to in this clipping was stirred up by that unspeakable fellow Tucker [*sic*]." Wilson found a way to do this by drafting a statement that he had Tumulty give out under his name: "It is true that 'The Birth of a Nation' was produced before the President and his family at the White House, but the President was entirely unaware of the character of the play before it was presented and has at no time expressed his approbation of it. Its exhibition at the White House was a courtesy extended to an old acquaintance."[19]

Wilson's regret over this incident was of a piece with his blowup at Trotter. A few months later, he commented to Dixon about his proposed next movie, *The Fall of a Nation,* a flag-waving call to arms and an attack on pacifists: "I think the thing a great mistake. I should deeply regret seeing any sort of excitement stirred in so grave a matter." About *Birth of a Nation,* he would tell Tumulty three years later, "I have always felt that this was a very unfortunate production, and I wish most sincerely that its production might be avoided in communities where there are so many colored people." Once more, Wilson was deploring stirring up emotions, bad manners, and loss of control, rather than condemning the racist message of Dixon's novel and Griffith's film. The juxtaposition with Dixon's project to inflame belligerent sentiment was noteworthy, too. Wilson had urged Americans to be "neutral in thought as well as in action" and "too proud to fight." In both race and foreign affairs, he desperately wanted to avoid "passion."[20]

More than the segregation plan, the showing of *Birth of a Nation* made Wilson anathema among African Americans. This movie would inspire a boosterish white man in Atlanta, William J. Simmons, to found anew the Ku Klux Klan—a twisted tribute to the cultural influence of the new medium of film. This influence would lead, in turn, to a kind of guilt by association, and for years afterward some African Americans would believe that

Wilson had been a Klansman. A recent example of this abysmal reputation was the effort in Maryland to remove Wilson's name from the Interstate 95 bridge that spans the Potomac between Alexandria, Virginia, and Prince George's County, Maryland.[21]

Effectively, Wilson's engagement with the politics of race ended in 1915 with the outcry following the showing of *Birth of a Nation*. For the rest of his presidency, he lapsed back into his sphinxlike silence about anything to do with African Americans. When Wilson ran for reelection in 1916, no prominent blacks supported him. Villard reluctantly backed him, because of the president's reform legislation and his having kept the country out of war; those accomplishments outweighed a sense of betrayal on race, even for a founder of the NAACP. W. E. B. Du Bois was not so forgiving. On behalf of the NAACP, he wrote to Wilson to challenge him to live up to his assurances to Negroes in 1912: "We received from you a promise of justice and sincere endeavor to forward their interests. We need scarcely to say that you have grievously disappointed us." Wilson did not reply to Du Bois, but he instructed Tumulty "to answer this letter for me and say that I stand by my original assurances and can say with a clear conscience that I have tried to live up to them, though in some case my endeavors have been defeated."[22]

Race did enter into Wilson's thinking on two occasions at the end of his first term as president. At the beginning of January 1917, his confidant Col. Edward M. House tried to get the president to contemplate entering the world war. House recorded in his diary that Wilson responded: "This country does not intend to become involved in this war. We are the only one of the great White nations that is free from war today, and it would be a crime against civilization for us to go in." A month later, when the Germans unleashed their submarines, Wilson discussed the danger of war with the Cabinet, and some of the men present remembered him saying the same thing. Secretary of State Robert Lansing recorded in a memorandum that Wilson "had been more and more impressed with the idea that 'white civilization' and its domination in the world rested largely on our ability to keep this country intact, as we would have to build up the nations ravaged by the war. He said that as this idea had grown upon him he had come to the feeling that he was willing to go to any lengths rather than to have this nation actually involved in the conflict." Secretary of Labor William B. Wilson later recalled the president saying, "With the terrible slaughter taking place in Europe, if we also entered the war, what effect would the depletion of man power [*sic*] have upon the relations of the white and yellow races? Would the yellow races take advantage of it and attempt to subjugate the white races?"[23]

At first blush, these would appear to be straightforward expressions of white-supremacist and imperialist thinking. Others in America, most notably Madison Grant, the purveyor of pseudo-scientific Nordic views, also opposed entering World War I because they feared its impact on their favored white groups. In Wilson's case, this is a matter of taking the sour with the sweet. One of his noblest efforts as president was his struggle to spare his country from the death and destruction of the war. Perhaps it was strange that less-noble facets of his thought would enter into that effort. But here, too, there are elements of mystery. Wilson had once briefly been an imperialist, but he had changed his views and now looked forward to the gradual end of colonialism and the spread of self-government. Also, this seems to be the only time that he ever raised the specter of the "yellow peril." As president of Princeton, he had welcomed students from East Asia. One of them, who studied with Wilson personally for his doctorate in political science, was the future president of South Korea, Syngman Rhee. At the peace conference after the war, Wilson would block the Japanese attempt to insert a racial-equality clause into the Covenant of the League of Nations, but that move sprang from the twists and turns of international politics rather than his racial views. This concern for "white civilization," on the brink of entering World War I, was an odd, one-time expression of one man's inner turmoil as he grappled with the greatest crisis of his presidency.

Race relations and the politics of race did not stand still during Wilson's second term. The entry of the United States into World War I accelerated the already swelling Great Migration of African Americans out of the South and into Northern cities. And over the course of the war, several hundred thousand African Americans served in the armed forces, some of them in combat roles. That combat role, together with the training of a small number of black officers, came about thanks mainly to pressure exerted by the NAACP. On the domestic front, the term "white backlash" would not be coined for another half-century, but as a matter of fact it began during these years. The first so-called race riot outside the South occurred in East St. Louis, Illinois, in 1917. Two years later, during the summer of 1919, Northern cities exploded in a string of "race riots"—which were really acts of white mob aggression against newly arrived blacks. Those months earned the name "Red Summer"—not because of the anti-radical hysteria of the "Red Scare," which occurred later, but because of the blood, mainly black blood, that flowed in the streets of those cities. The worst and longest-lasting racial violence occurred in Chicago and Washington, D.C.

Clearly, this was a time of racial change and ferment, but no one who heard or read the president's words during these years would have known much about these changes. Wilson acquiesced in a greater role for African Americans in the armed forces, but despite pleas from supporters, he said nothing about the East St. Louis violence. Persistent pressure from Robert Moton, who was Washington's successor at Tuskegee, finally prodded the president into speaking out against the tidal wave of lynching that swept over the South in 1918 and 1919. "I say plainly that every American who takes part in the action of a mob or gives it any sort of countenance is no true son of this great democracy, but its betrayer," Wilson declared, and he asked governors and law enforcement officers to act "to make an end to this disgraceful evil." In 1919, the only reference that he made to the "Red Summer" came in a side comment during his speaking tour to promote American membership in the League of Nations: "I hope you won't think it inappropriate if I stop here to express my shame as an American citizen at the race riots that have occurred at some places in this country, where men have forgot humanity and justice and orderly society and have run amuck. That constitutes a man, not only the enemy of society, but his own enemy, and the enemy of justice." Once again, he played the sphinx on race.[24]

The problem remains, How does one read this riddle? Despite Wilson's own occasional references to his Southern background, that did not bend the twig and shape the tree. During his second term, he selectively purged agrarian radicals among the Southern Democrats in Congress, including Vardaman, and his wartime invocations of "one hundred per cent Americanism" were aimed more often at Southerners than at recent immigrants. On other matters, Wilson showed enlightenment and growth. Although he had frosty relations with his party's mainly Irish American city bosses, that did not reflect ethnic or religious prejudice. As his political right-hand man, he relied on an Irish American Catholic, Joe Tumulty, whose presence at the president's side infuriated anti-Catholic bigots, including Tom Watson, who opposed nearly all of Wilson's policies and actions, including intervention in World War I. On gender issues, Wilson hung back at first, despite having begun his career as an academic at a woman's college, Bryn Mawr, and despite having two college-educated daughters who ardently supported woman suffrage and did not hide their views from their father. Wilson came out in favor of the suffrage for women on the state level in 1915, and he inserted a plank favoring state action in the 1916 Democratic platform. Continued agitation by the suffrage organizations and their conspicuous participation in the war effort eventually won him over to a Constitutional amendment, and he played an important part in securing the passage of the Nineteenth Amendment.[25]

Why, then, with his liberal views and enlightened stands on other issues, did Wilson remain cold and deaf to pleas for racial justice? The answer, I believe, lies partly in the man himself and partly in the larger context of American politics. For his part, that deep-seated desire to eschew "passion" and practice self-control and rationality made him recoil from touching the question that excited the hottest and most violent passions in the public arena. Likewise, his problematic relationship with his native region made him reluctant to challenge Southern racism. Racial justice seems to have been something that Wilson just did not know how to handle. For him, race was what Daniel Patrick Moynihan later called Social Security—"the third rail of American politics."

Nor was Wilson alone in not wanting to touch that potentially fatal issue. Wariness about race formed a seemingly fixed star in the political firmament of the first half of the twentieth century. Wilson's greatest rival, Theodore Roosevelt, showed no profile in courage when racial questions arose, as witnessed by the Brownsville affair, the diplomatic controversy over Japanese immigration, and the lily-white Progressives. Wilson's greatest successor, Franklin Roosevelt, shied away from confronting racism even after substantial numbers of African Americans started joining the Democratic Party. None of these comparisons can excuse Wilson for his shortcomings, but they do locate his problem in a broader contest. Neither the best of the twentieth-century presidents politically—which is to say, Franklin Roosevelt—nor the brightest intellectually—which is to say, Theodore Roosevelt and Woodrow Wilson—were willing to attempt to cut the Gordian knot of racial injustice. Each of them hid behind his own style of the sphinxlike pose.

Real breakthroughs in the politics of race would require other events and other presidents, cut from different cloth. The other events would be the rise of nonwhite peoples in Africa and Asia and the anti-racist lessons instilled by the war against Nazism. Interestingly, despite his bitter disappointments with Wilson, Du Bois supported him in his greatest cause—the creation of the League of Nations. Du Bois presciently discerned that, despite its shortcomings, the League marked the beginning of the end of colonialism and white world domination. The other presidents would be less refined, less intellectual men than Wilson. Harry Truman, a grandson of Confederates from Missouri, would be the first of them to take political risks to combat racism, both because he had learned the lessons of World War II and because he believed there might be political gain as well as loss in supporting civil rights. Another grandson of Confederates, Lyndon Johnson, would take further risks and would break the back of legalized white supremacy, both because he grasped the simple justice of racial equality and because he believed that he and his party could not evade a clear choice, even at grievous political cost. Those presidents played the part of Oedipus, who solved the riddle of the Sphinx—and later suffered for that feat. On race, it is those latter-day Oedipuses who deserve honor, not the sphinxes.

Notes

1. Joseph J. Ellis, *American Sphinx: The Character of Thomas Jefferson* (New York, 1998).

2. Woodrow Wilson to Albert Bushnell Hart, June 3, 1889, in *The Papers of Woodrow Wilson*, ed. Arthur S. Link, 69 vols. (Princeton, NJ, 1966<->94) [hereafter, *PWW*], 6:243.

3. Wilson speech at Chapel Hill, N.C., January 9, 1909, ibid., 18:631.

4. Wilson to Richard Heath Dabney, May 9 [*sic*, May 10], 1883, ibid., 2:349.

5. Wilson, "Mr. Gladstone: A Character Sketch," *Virginia University Magazine* (April 1880), ibid., 2:642.

6. William Allen White, *Woodrow Wilson: The Man, His Times, and His Task* (Boston, 1924), 59. The photograph with the identification of the servants is in Eleanor Wilson McAdoo, *The Woodrow Wilsons* (New York, 1937), 41.

7. Wilson quoted in Edith Gittings Reid, *Woodrow Wilson: The Caricature, the Myth, and the Man* (New York, 1934), 22.

8. Jessie Wilson Sayre to Ray Stannard Baker, [April 27, 1925], Ray Stannard Baker Papers, box 121, Library of Congress, Washington, DC.

9. Wilson to John Rogers Williams, September 2, 1904, in *PWW*, 15:462; Wilson memorandum, ca. December 3, 1909, ibid., 18:149. On Joseph Ralph Moss, see "A Princeton Pioneer," *Princeton Alumni Weekly* 106 (June 7, 2006): 28–30.

10. Entry, July 31, [1908], Mary Yates Diary, in *PWW*, 18:386; *Princeton Press*, April 3, 1909, ibid., 19:149.

11. Wilson to Alexander Walters, [October 21, 1912], ibid., 25:449; Wilson to Robert S. Hudspeth, [October 21, 1912], ibid., 25:450. On the black overture to Wilson, see David Levering Lewis, *W. E. B. Du Bois: Biography of a Race* (New York, 1993), 424–25; and Arthur S. Link, *Wilson: The Road to the White House* (Princeton, NJ, 1947), 501–6.

12. Wilson to Oscar W. Underwood, January 21, 1913, in *PWW,* 27:66; entry, April 11, 1913, Diary of Josephus Daniels, ibid., 27:291. On the efforts to introduce segregation and reduce black appointments, see Arthur S. Link, *Wilson: The New Freedom* (Princeton, NJ, 1956), 246–52; Kathleen L. Wohlgemuth, "Woodrow Wilson's Appointments Policy and the Negro," *Journal of Southern History* 24 (November 1958): 457–71; and Morton P. Sosna, "The South in the Saddle: Racial Politics in the Wilson Years," *Wisconsin Magazine of History* 54 (Autumn 1970): 30–49.

13. Villard to Wilson, July 21, 1913, in *PWW,* 28:60–61; Wilson to Villard, August 19, 1913, ibid., 28:64; Trotter statement, November 6, 1913, ibid., 28:491–95; Wilson response, November 6, 1913, ibid., 28:496–99.

14. Transcript of White House meeting, November 12, 1914, ibid., 31:301–8.

15. Daniels to Franklin D. Roosevelt, June 10, 1933, quoted in ibid., 31:309n2.

16. Wilson remarks, [December 15, 1914], ibid., 31:464–65.

17. Thomas Dixon to Joseph P. Tumulty, May 1, 1915, ibid., 32:142n5.

18. See ibid., 32:267n1. The "history with lightning" remark first appeared, without attribution, in Milton McKaye, "The Birth of a Nation," *Scribner's Magazine* 102 (November 1937), 69.

19. Tumulty to Wilson, April 24, 1915, in *PWW,* 33:68; Wilson to Tumulty, [April 24, 1915], ibid.; Wilson to Tumulty, April 28, 1915, ibid., 33:86.

20. Wilson to Dixon, September 7, 1915, ibid., 34:426–27; Wilson to Tumulty, [ca. Apr. 22, 1918], ibid., 47:388n3.

21. Evidence of the belief that Wilson was a Klansman came in the telephone calls to the CSPAN television program on him in the network's Presidents series, which aired in September 1999.

22. Du Bois to Wilson, October 10, 1916, in *PWW,* 38:459; Wilson to Tumulty, [ca. October 17, 1916], ibid.

23. Robert Lansing, "Memorandum on the Severance Of Relations with Germany," February 4, 1917, ibid., 41:120; William B. Wilson to Ray Stannard Baker, September 17, 1932, Ray Stannard Baker Papers, Series I, box 58, Library of Congress, Washington, DC. Secretary of Agriculture David F. Houston also remembered Wilson worrying about what effect going to war would have on the white race (see Houston, *Eight Years with Wilson's Cabinet, 1913 to 1920* [Garden City, NY, 1926], 229–30).

24. Wilson statement, July 28, 1918, in *PWW,* 44:98; speech at Helena, Montana, September 11, 1919, ibid., 43:196.

25. On Wilson's wartime purge of Southern Democrats, see Anthony Gaughan, "Woodrow Wilson and the Rise of Militant Interventionism in the South," *Journal of Southern History* 65 (November 1999): 771–808; and on his conversion on woman

suffrage, see Christine A. Lunardini and Thomas J. Knock, "Woodrow Wilson and Woman Suffrage: A New Look," *Political Science Quarterly* 95 (Winter 1980–81): 655–71.

W. E. B. Du Bois, Woodrow Wilson, and the Dilemma of Democracy and Race in the Progressive Era

✹   ✹   ✹   Manning Marable

In much of the literature of American race relations during the Progressive era, many of the retreats from racial justice in the years from 1913 to 1921 are attributed to the actions or attitudes of President Woodrow Wilson. As early (historiographically) as 1940, for example, Ralph Bunche observed, "The introduction of segregation into the civil service was one of the blackest and abominable spots on the Wilson Administration."[1] The president's second term witnessed the notorious "Red Summer of 1919," in which thousands of rioting whites destroyed and ransacked dozens of black communities throughout the country. In one case, in Omaha, Nebraska, on September 28, 1919, five thousand whites surrounded and overwhelmed a county courthouse to seize an African American accused of assaulting a white girl. The mob mutilated the black man, shooting him literally more than a thousand times, and then burned the bullet-riddled body.[2] In "The Jim Crow Policies of Woodrow Wilson," Kenneth O'Reilly presents a litany of examples illustrating Wilson's racism: that the first Southerner elected since the Civil War had once described Reconstruction as "nothing more than 'a host of dusky children untimely put out of school'"; that "many of Wilson's Cabinet members were militant segregationists who enjoyed the 'darky stories' that Wilson sometimes told in dialect at their meetings"; and that "Wilson helped create the climate for the first major wartime riot by accusing the Republicans of 'colonizing' black voters in East St. Louis, and other cities."[3]

Although these condemnations and criticism are historically accurate, there nonetheless remains the question of whether Wilson was largely or only partially responsible for the political climate of racial reaction. Perhaps a more effective way to judge Wilson's record is through the political lens of his interactions with the premier African American intellectual of the period, W. E. B. Du Bois, and the organization he co-founded in 1910, the National Association for the Advancement of Colored People (NAACP). What seems clear is that the election of 1912, which elevated Wilson to the presidency, did not suddenly usher in a new age of American apartheid. Racial segregation already had become pervasive in federal government offices under Republican administrations in the years before Wilson's presidency, and in the South it had become codified and incorporated into civic practices at state and local levels as well, in the 1890s and early twentieth century. Yet the bitter disappointment that black activists such as Du Bois and the journalist/editor William Monroe Trotter suffered because of Wilson's attitude and performance on racial matters illustrates the deep divide that separated liberals and progressives regarding the place of African Americans in public life.

Following Reconstruction, the vast majority of African American males permitted to exercise the franchise naturally supported the Republican Party in national elections. It was not simply the sense of obligation that they felt toward Lincoln's Emancipation Proclamation, or the Republican Party's sponsorship and support for the constitutional amendments protecting blacks' rights during Reconstruction. Rather, it was more generally a matter of practical politics. From the 1890s to the outbreak of the First World War, the most influential African American politician was Booker T. Washington. The founder and principal of Tuskegee Institute constructed a black political machine of editors, clergy, and businessmen who worked in coalition with national Republicans to bring resources to black communities. It was under the presidential administrations of Theodore Roosevelt and William Howard Taft that black Republicans benefited demonstrably from their alliance with the national Republican leadership. Charles Anderson, a supporter of Washington and a prominent New York politician, was named Collector of Internal Revenue in New York, serving from 1905 to 1915. Washington's chief lieutenant in Tennessee, the businessman J. C. Napier, served as Register of the Treasury (1911–13). There were others examples, all of them aligned with the "Tuskegee Machine." R. L. Smith, the founder of the Texas Farmers Improvement Society and a state representative in the Texas legislature (1894–96), was subsequently named a U.S. marshal for the Eastern Texas District; attorney Robert H. Terrell, a Harvard graduate, was appointed a magistrate for the District of Columbia; and the novelist and lawyer James Weldon Johnson, co-author of the Negro national anthem, "Lift Ev'ry Voice and Sing," held consular posts in Venezuela and Nicaragua.[4]

Despite his prominence, Washington never managed to silence his critics within the black community. His most vehement critic was the Harvard-trained journalist William Monroe Trotter, editor of the *Boston Guardian.* And with the 1903 publication of the classic collection of essays, *The Souls of Black Folk,* Du Bois emerged as Washington's major rival. From the vantage point of history, the Washington-Du Bois conflict was about ideology, but it was also, at least in part, about patronage. It reflected the divergent interests of a growing African American entrepreneurial and professional middle class. The faction that favored Washington—especially the entrepreneurs based in the National Negro Business League, along with the political elites tied to the national Republican Party—opposed direct confrontations against legal segregation. They recognized that Jim Crow codes enforced segregation, but that, in so doing, the codes restricted the incursion of white capital into black consumer markets, thus creating spaces for black-owned business growth and development. Washington perceived black success in the context of an ever expanding, capitalist economy, especially in the South. Consequently, he opposed black participation in, and support for, trade unions and strikes. Conversely, the Du Bois-Trotter faction, geographically based more in the Northeast and Middle West than the Tuskegee Machine's key leaders, vigorously rejected Jim Crow law enforcement and urged blacks to defend their voting rights. They favored liberal and professional educational curricula for the training of the African American middle class, eschewing Tuskegee's emphasis on industrial and vocational education. In 1905, the Du Bois-Trotter faction consolidated its anti–Tuskegee Machine program by establishing the Niagara Movement. The group's initial manifesto called for "freedom of speech and criticism" and "the recognition of the principle of human brotherhood as a practical present creed."[5]

Despite its spirited defense of civil rights, the Niagara Movement failed to consolidate itself as a broad popular force for the African American middle class. By mid-1906, fewer than two hundred blacks had officially joined the group—and most of them were educators, lawyers, and clergy. For his part, Washington and his allies used a variety of tactics to undermine the Niagara Movement's activities. One newspaper aligned with Washington dubbed Du Bois the "Professor of hysterics." Ministers who publicly opposed Tuskegee's public-policy positions frequently were ousted from their posts. Educators who had joined the Niagara Movement found it nearly impossible to obtain funds from white philanthropy for their schools, owing to Washington's influence. When Judson W. Lyons, also a register of the U.S. Treasury, expressed support publicly for some of William Monroe Trotter's arguments, Washington's lieutenant, Emmett J. Scott, wrote an anonymous press release claiming that Lyons's office was being used for partisan political purposes. The white press picked up the false charges and President Roosevelt fired Lyons. Du Bois himself became the target of a series of smears and innuendoes. In 1906, when his name was suggested as the potential assistant superintendent of the public school system of Washington, D.C., Du Bois would later write, one local black leader who was loyal to Washington went to Roosevelt, to emphasize "the danger of [my] appointment."[6]

The Niagara Movement's demise began in the autumn of 1907 over a conflict between Trotter and a Du Bois ally, Clement Morgan. Trotter had called for Morgan's removal as a state leader of the Niagara Movement, and he secured the support of its executive committee. Du Bois then threatened to resign his post as the Niagara Movement's general secretary if Morgan was removed. By 1908, many of the movement's adherents had become overwhelmed by the political bickering between personalities and factions, and simply stopped participating in the organization. In 1908, Trotter, the Reverend Alexander Walters, and a number of former Niagara Movement members established the National Negro American Political League; its purpose was to galvanize the black vote in Northern states around the 1908 presidential election. The league endorsed the Democratic candidate, William Jennings Bryan, in his third run for the presidency. Booker T. Washington and the Tuskegee Machine supported William Howard Taft.[7] Du Bois disliked both Bryan and Taft, so at first he was unprepared to offer blacks any advice. In his small quarterly magazine *Horizon,* in February 1908, he urged African American voters to defeat both Bryan and Taft; thus, he appeared to embrace the radical candidacy of the Socialist Eugene V. Debs. "In all cases remember that the only party today which treats Negroes as men, North or South, are the Socialists," counseled Du Bois.[8] In March

1908, he revised his position, suggesting that if the national election was to be decided between Taft and Bryan, then it was the Democratic candidate who was preferable.[9] In the *Horizon* issue of November–December 1908, following Taft's victory, Du Bois reflected: "We did not happen to have the power in the last election of deciding who should be President but we will have the power in certain future elections."[10]

Taft's presidency (1909–13) represented a major disappointment to most African Americans, many of whom had voted for him under the advice of Booker T. Washington. While Taft did continue to provide federal patronage positions to blacks allied with the Tuskegee Machine and the national Republican Party, the number of posts was curtailed. In the South, Taft Republicans aligned themselves with the lily-white faction of the Republican Party, which promoted racial segregation and the elimination of black voters in order to appease the white racist electorate. In the federal government and at the Capitol offices, patterns of racial segregation that had begun under Roosevelt expanded greatly. Black federal employees and the general African American public gradually found themselves excluded from lunchrooms and restaurants on the basis of race. Black employees began to be denied access to lavatories, and were increasingly forced to do their work assignments in racially restricted zones. In 1910, racial segregation was imposed upon employees in the Census Bureau and in the White House dining room.[11]

As the political status of African Americans deteriorated across the country, some concerned white liberals rallied to the cause of racial fairness. The socialist William English Walling, in a widely read essay published in September 1908, called for the construction of a new anti-racist movement: "Either the spirit of the abolitionists, of Lincoln and Lovejoy, must be revived and we must come to treat the Negro on a plane of absolute political or social equality or Vardaman and Tillman will soon have transferred the Race War to the North."[12] Walling and two other white liberals, Mary White Ovington and Dr. Henry Moskowitz, initiated a conference, in May 1909, dedicated to examining the future status of African Americans in the United States. The prominent newspaper publisher Oswald Garrison Villard, grandson of the abolitionist William Lloyd Garrison and formerly an advocate of Booker T. Washington, expressed his support for the white liberal venture. Other white liberals and socialists pushed for the creation of a new organization on behalf of Negro rights. These included the literary critic William Dean Howells, historian John Spencer Bassett, and the progressive social worker Jane Addams. Du Bois attended the conference and generally approved the character of the debate and discussions. A national steering committee was formed; within a few months, it reached a consensus that a new national rights organization had to be established. In May 1910, at a second conference, the group launched the National Association for the Advancement of Colored People. From the beginning, the NAACP was largely dominated by whites. The liberal reformer Moorfield Storey was chosen as national president; Walling was elected chair of the association's executive committee, with Villard serving as national treasurer. Du Bois was the only African American chosen as a national officer, but he soon would become, in effect, the organization's voice. Leaving his faculty position at Atlanta University, Du Bois arrived in New York City in August 1910, where he quickly established the NAACP's monthly journal, *The Crisis.* Although a majority of the Niagara Movement members eventually joined the NAACP, some felt that white leaders such as Villard and Storey were too ideologically close to Washington. Meanwhile, Trotter, Waldron, and some Niagara supporters renamed their group the National Independent Political League and continued to pursue a strategy of cooperation with the Democratic Party.[13]

As the presidential campaign of 1912 unfolded, Du Bois and many NAACP supporters were deeply troubled by the major party candidates. "I was and had been for years utterly disgusted with the treatment which the Republican Party had meted out to its Negro supporters," Du Bois recalled in 1939, concerning the 1912 campaign. "But it was difficult to get them to vote anything but the Republican ticket." For a brief time, he considered endorsing Theodore Roosevelt, the "Bull Moose" presidential candidate of the newly formed Progressive Party. Du Bois submitted a "plank" document calling for fairness to the Negro to the Progressives' convention in Chicago. "It was turned down flatly," Du Bois observed. "Roosevelt not only distrusted me personally but thought that he had a chance to capture the South, and flirted with the 'lily whites' to his ultimate disaster."[14]

In a sense, that left the only other major presidential candidate, New Jersey's Democratic governor, Woodrow Wilson. Du Bois respected Wilson as an intellectual and was familiar with his ideas. At Atlanta University, where Du Bois had taught from 1898 to 1910, he had assigned Wilson's book, *The State,* in his political science courses. Wilson and Du Bois also had both contributed essays to a symposium on the Civil War and Reconstruction, published in the *Atlantic Monthly*.[15] Yet there remained the troubling record of Wilson's tenure as president of Princeton University (1902–10). By 1900, seven of the eight Ivy League schools had admitted African Americans as students; the sole exception was Princeton. Under Wilson, that university adhered to its "steadfast segregationist" policies.[16] Throughout his Princeton presidency, all blacks who applied to the college were coerced into withdrawing from consideration. Historian Henry Blumenthal has suggested that the central issue to Wilson was not fair consideration and opportunity extended to black applicants, but the maintenance of "the social peace of the university which, he feared, would have been disturbed" by the admission of African Americans. Ideologically, Wilson's position on African American advancement was strikingly similar to the public posture of Booker T. Washington. Wilson believed in "the gradual elevation of the colored masses through education, vocational training, and improved economic opportunities." During Wilson's campaign for governor in 1910, the Newark Negro Council had sought unsuccessfully to obtain assurances regarding the Democratic candidate's position on blacks' rights. Consistently, Wilson tried to sidestep racial issues. In his inaugural address as New Jersey's governor, he promised to exercise authority "without fear or favor."[17] Between 1911 and 1913, Wilson proposed no new legislation to the state legislature pertaining to the special problems of black citizens. Still, despite these troubling signs, William Monroe Trotter and a number of African American liberals championed Wilson as a friend to blacks' interests.[18]

On July 16, 1912, Wilson met with a small delegation of African Americans, including Trotter and the Reverend J. Milton Waldron. If elected, he assured them, he would most certainly be "President of the whole nation—to know no white or black; no North, South, East or West." Wilson conveyed the impression that black Democrats would receive their fair share of patronage positions in the federal bureaucracy, just as black Republicans had under Theodore Roosevelt.[19] On August 13, 1912, Wilson met for three hours with Oswald Garrison Villard, who, beyond his NAACP connections, was also publisher of the *New York Evening Post*. Their conversation was surprisingly cordial. Villard came away convinced that Wilson, once elected to the presidency, would "speak out against lynching." The candidate followed up this session by informing Bishop Walters that his black supporters should be told "they may count on me for absolute fair dealing. . . . My earnest wish [is] to see justice done them in every matter, and not merely grudging justice. My sympathy with them is of long standing."[20]

In 1911 Du Bois had joined the Socialist Party, like a number of his white progressive associates in the NAACP had done. His party membership committed him publicly to support its presidential candidate, Eugene V. Debs, in the 1912 national campaign. However, based on Wilson's vague but hopeful statements regarding Negro rights, Du Bois made the difficult decision. He resigned from the Socialist Party and added his name to the Democrat's list of endorsers. In the August 1912 issue of *The Crisis,* he stated that the fundamental choice for the presidency was between the Republican Party and the Democrats; given that reality, the Democrats were clearly preferable. Perhaps Wilson's governance of the nation will "reflect his learning rather than his background" as a Southerner. Du Bois added that if he could "assure the presidency" to Debs he would do so, because among all major candidates he alone, "by word and deed, starts squarely on a platform of human rights regardless of race or class."[21]

With the Republican electorate split between Roosevelt and Taft, Wilson easily captured a plurality of votes and the White House. There was some historical significance to Wilson's triumph: he was only the second Democrat, and the first Southerner, elected as the nation's chief executive since the Civil War. In the November 1912 issue of *The Crisis,* Du Bois speculated hopefully that perhaps the Democratic Party under Wilson would dare to be "Democratic when it comes to black men. . . . We are willing to risk a trial."[22] In the following month, Du Bois wrote that Wilson's victory could be partially attributed to the fact that approximately one hundred thousand African Americans had voted for him.[23] To mark the inauguration on March 4, 1913, Du Bois released an "Open Letter to Woodrow Wilson." The statement combined flattery and black militancy. "Your elevation to the chief magistracy of the nation at this time shows not simply a splendid national faith in the perpetuity of free government in the land, but even more, a personal faith in you." Du Bois also pointedly reminded the president that African American votes "helped to put you in your high position." He explained the black support for Wilson as a result of their growing desire to gain political independence and "put into power a man who today has the power to become the greatest benefactor of his country since Abraham Lincoln."[24]

Du Bois's central argument was that the so-called "Negro problem" could be solved by bold presidential leadership. "You cannot make 10,000,000 people at one and the same time servile and dignified, docile and self-reliant, servants and independent leaders," Du Bois wrote. Racial segregation had crippled and destroyed the capacity of African Americans to play meaningful roles in the national economy and society. He continued:

A determination on the part of intelligent and decent Americans to see that no man is denied a reasonable chance for life, liberty, and happiness simply because of the color of his skin is [the] simple, sane and practical solution of the race problem in this land. The education of colored children, the opening of the gates of industrial opportunity to colored workers, absolute equality of all citizens before law, the civil rights of all decently behaving citizens in places of public accommodation and entertainment, absolute impartiality in the granting of the right of suffrage—these things are the bedrock of a just solution of the rights of man in the American Republic. . . . But it is not the offices at your disposal, President Woodrow Wilson, that is the burden of our great cry to you. We want to be treated as men. We want to vote. We want our children educated. We want lynching stopped. We want no longer to be herded as cattle on street cars and railroads. We want the right to earn a living.[25]

Wilson's victory among white Southerners was generally perceived as a triumph for the regime of Jim Crow. Although African Americans were acknowledged as part of the electoral constituency of the national Democratic Party in the Northern states, they were extended no influence in terms of public policy whatsoever. Wilson named prominent proponents of segregation to his Cabinet, including William McAdoo as Secretary of the Treasury and Albert S. Burleson as Postmaster General. McAdoo and Burleson almost immediately ordered racial segregation in their departments' offices across the board—in lavatories, waiting rooms, and restaurants. Within weeks, Jim Crow restrictions were extended to the Bureau of Engraving and Printing. Collectors of internal revenue and postmasters were allowed to fire black employees outright, or otherwise reduce their ranks and salaries.[26] Despite these actions, many liberals still held out hope that Wilson could be a moderating force. Villard again approached the president and urged him to establish a "National Race Commission." Ideally, such a presidential advisory body would include blacks and whites and would be charged to develop a constructive program for facilitating race relations. Wilson initially liked the idea, but in August 1913 he informed the newspaper publisher that "it would be politically inadvisable to raise the issue."[27]

In late July 1913, the Register of the Treasury, an African American, resigned in protest from his department rather than enforce the new segregation policies. Wilson at first nominated a black man as the replacement for the position, belatedly recognizing that some measure of patronage had to be extended to Negro Democrats. Almost immediately, the appointment was challenged by Southern legislators who, in effect, demanded a "lily-white policy" for the federal bureaucracy. Wilson then withdrew the nomination, capitulating to the white supremacists. According to historian Henry Blumenthal, Wilson "did not want to lose Southern support by starting a bitter controversy" over the issue of race. Policies over tariffs and currency reform were far more important than the presence of Negroes within the federal government. "In his judgment," Blumenthal observed, "the Negroes' interests would in the long run be best served by the adoption of reforms in the national interest."[28]

Wilson's capitulation on racial fairness deeply concerned the NAACP. In an open letter signed by Moorfield Storey, Villard, and Du Bois, dated August 15, 1913, the association declared: "Never before has the Federal government discriminated against its civilian employees on the ground of color. Every such act heretofore has been that of an individual State." The statement implored the president to repudiate the policy of color prejudice in federal employment, reminding him that he had campaigned for the presidency on his New Freedom slogan. "Shall ten millions of our citizens say that their civil liberties and rights are safe in your hands?" the statement asked. "They desire a 'New Freedom' too, Mr. President, yet they include in that term nothing else than the rights guaranteed them by the Constitution under which they believe they should be protected from persecution based upon a physical quality with which Divine Providence has endowed them."[29]

Du Bois followed this appeal with "Another Open Letter to Woodrow Wilson," published in *The Crisis* in September 1913. In a related editorial, "The Fruit of the Tree," he argued that the "fruit" of the doctrine of black accommodation to white supremacy was "disfranchisement, segregation, lynching. . . . Is it not time to swear by the Eternal God we will NOT be slaves, and that no aider, abettor and teacher of slavery in any shape or guise can longer lead us?"[30] The real object of Du Bois's scorn in the editorial was Booker T. Washington, not Wilson; however, the NAACP's feud with the Wilson administration over racial policies and Du Bois's 1912 endorsement of the Democrat had forced him to display a more assertive, militant posture to his own constituency. His growing radicalism soon contributed to new tensions and controversies within the NAACP's national leadership.

It became depressingly clear to Du Bois that racism was so entrenched within both the Democratic and Republican Parties that African Americans should consider a strategy of "group segregation"—the establishment of all-black institutions to provide goods and services to black consumers, and the creation of racially exclusive social and political organizations to promote African American interests. "The Strength of Segregation," published in December 1913, thus called upon blacks to unite "together like one great fist for their own ends, with secret understanding, with pitiless efficiency and resources for defense which will make their freedom incapable of attack from without." By creating a powerful independent black movement, Du Bois insisted, African Americans could fight more effectively against lynching and disenfranchisement. "What can America do against a mass of unshaken troops in their battle?" he asked, and in answer, declared: "Nothing."[31] The February 1914 issue of *The Crisis* featured another Du Bois editorial, "The South in the Saddle," a polemical attack on Wilson. The president had not kept his promises to black Americans, Du Bois wrote, because of the inordinate political clout of the white South, which was based on black disenfranchisement.[32]

Villard and other moderate whites in the NAACP's leadership found Du Bois's racial militancy more than they could handle. Villard resigned from the chairman's post in January 1914, but maintained his position on the national board. In April 1914, he insisted that Du Bois, who was employed as the Director of Research as well as *The Crisis* editor, should have his authority sharply reduced. Du Bois effectively appealed to his closest ally, Mary White Ovington, and warned, "I should regard the adoption of the proposed provision a vote of lack of confidence and I shall immediately resign my position."[33] The threat pressured the majority of the NAACP board members to reject Villard's demands. But even Du Bois's allies remained angry. Joel Spingarn charged that Du Bois would prefer to have his own way, "rather than accept another way, even when no sacrifice of principle is involved."[34]

While Wilson's actions outraged Du Bois, William Monroe Trotter felt betrayed and humiliated. Trotter had promoted the national political aspirations of Princeton's former president since 1910; he had used his own political organization to endorse Wilson in 1912, and had convinced perhaps tens of thousands of African Americans to vote for him. On November 6, 1913, Trotter and a small number of African American leaders were granted a private meeting with Wilson at the White House. Trotter tried hard to maintain a level of civility, but he had little recourse except to be blunt. "There can be no equality, freedom or respect from others, in [racial] segregation," he began. Segregated toilet facilities, for example, could only be justified if those who are "segregated are considered unclean, diseased or indecent as to their parents." If such was the motivation, "the federal Government thereby puts an insult upon its own citizens, equal by law, unparalleled in the history of any nation." Trotter explicitly condemned Treasury Secretary McAdoo's requirement of segregated dining facilities for his employees, and then gave the following account of recent events across many departments:

> All this is true of segregation at desks or in rooms already notorious under the auditors of the Post Office, the Navy, in the Post Office Department, the Bureau of Engraving, and elsewhere. Secretary McAdoo admits a rule against "enforced and unwelcome juxtaposition of white and Negro employees." This is segregation, and of African-American employees at the behest of the prejudice of all other racial classes of employees. It is clear and definite subjection of one element of citizens to the race prejudice of other citizens. It denies equality of citizenship to the former, in fact, unsettles their citizenship altogether. For the rule is open to abuse and African-American employees are thus exposed to possible discrimination of any kind.[35]

Trotter reminded Wilson of the multitudes of African Americans who had "so overcome traditional fear of party and section as they did last year in voting for you. Thousands and thousands of them were your friends, and so will remain if there be no segregation and injustice, no stain upon your record and that of your administration." Wilson listened patiently to Trotter and then stalled for time with platitudes. "Now, mistakes have probably been made," the president admitted, "and you ought to assure those of your own people who are misinformed about these things that they must wait for the judgment of the long run to see what exactly happened." Wilson refused to state whether the actions of McAdoo and other officials were taken on their own authority or with his support. Frustrated, Trotter then made a tactical error, saying curtly, "Mr. President, we simply wanted an assurance that it will be worked out." Probably relieved, Wilson replied: "I assure you it will be worked out." At that point, the meeting ended.[36]

In 1913–14 Villard frequently communicated privately with both Wilson and McAdoo, pleading that blacks should not be segregated in the federal bureaucracy or be demoted or dismissed on the basis of race. Wilson wanted to avoid controversy and sought to mollify the criticisms of black Democrats. But in the end, he personally was convinced that racial segregation was in "the best interest of the colored people."[37] The specter of restrictive racial quotas emerged in May 1914 when the Civil Service Commission issued a new requirement for the completion of Civil Service examinations: all applicants would in the future attach a photograph of themselves with their examination forms. In 1910, African Americans comprised 6 percent of all United States Civil Service employees. By 1918, after four years of the mandatory-photograph policy, the percentage of blacks in the Civil Service had fallen to 5 percent.[38]

Trotter and other African American Democrats secured a second meeting with the president, on November 12, 1914. A transcript reveals a forty-five minute confrontation, primarily between Trotter and Wilson. One year had elapsed since their last exchange, Trotter began, and during that time racial "segregation of government employees of African extraction [was] still practiced in the treasury and post office buildings, and to a certain extent [had] spread into other government buildings." Trotter's larger point, however, was that black Americans as a group recognized that, "If they can be segregated and thus humiliated by the national government at the national capitol, the beginning is made for the spread of that persecution and prosecution which makes property and life itself insecure in the South." The black leader's demeanor and the sharpness of his arguments indicated that he had lost all patience for compromise. He demanded an executive order, signed by the president, outlawing "all segregation of government employees because of race and color." "We await your reply," said Trotter, "that we may give to the waiting citizens of the United States of African extraction."[39]

Nothing in Wilson's personal or professional life had prepared him for this unprecedented confrontation with Trotter and the other articulate, professional African American leaders. He could scarcely fathom that these blacks had presumed to criticize the nation's chief executive, and in his own office. Wilson explained that the imposition of racial segregation in federal buildings was designed "to prevent any kind of friction between the white employees and the Negro employees." The objective of Secretary McAdoo and others "was not to do what you gentlemen seem to assume—to put the Negro employees at an uncomfortable disadvantage." Wilson then explained to his guests that it would take "generations" for Americans to transcend racial biases, and so accommodations had to be made. Again he affirmed his willingness "to do anything that is just." But, he continued, "I am not willing to do what may turn out to be unwise." Wilson emphasized his desire to support African American advancement, but he supported that expression of support from the continuation of Jim Crow policies: "I want to help the colored people in every way I can, but there are some ways, some things that I could do myself that would hurt them more than it would help them."[40]

As Trotter and his companions disputed vigorously with him, President Wilson finally lost his patience and decorum and snapped, "You have spoiled the whole cause for which you came." Even so, Trotter persisted in his arguments against Jim Crow policies. Blacks who had "led this movement" backing Wilson, like himself, "are today, among our people, branded as traitors to our race on segregation," he continued, and again denounced the segregationist policies as a form of "degradation." "I don't think it's degradation," Wilson shot back. "That is your interpretation of it." He was especially incensed by Trotter's warning that African American Democrats might abandon both the president and his party if the administration did not overturn its Jim Crow policies. "Politics must be left out in any consideration of racial segregation because, don't you see, to put it plainly, that is a form of blackmail," Wilson averred. "When you call upon an officer and say that you can't get certain votes if you don't do certain things, that is the kind of course which ought never to be attempted."[41]

Trotter's altercation with Wilson in the White House became widely known throughout black America. The incident apparently hardened Wilson regarding his approach to African Americans' rights. Reflecting back on the controversy in 1939, Du Bois recalled: "It took a hard fight with letters, interviews and publicity to secure even a mild breaking down of these barriers and to this day some of them remain. The attempt on the part of Negroes to plead with the President and secure his sympathy in this matter was on the whole unsuccessful."[42] In February 1915, Du Bois editorialized in *The Crisis* that "Wilson's racism is now unambiguous" and represents "one of the most grievous disappointments that a disappointed people must bear."[43] Between 1909 and 1915 an average of seventy African Americans were lynched across the South each year; Wilson's response was cold silence. Now even Booker T. Washington was forced to acknowledge that the system of Jim Crow segregation was inherently unjust and that, in the long run, it could not be sustained in a democratic society. In his last major essay before he died suddenly in December 1915, Washington argued that racially restrictive residential codes would inevitably be outlawed. African Americans and whites could only advance collectively on the basis of racial fairness: "In the gain or loss of one race, all the rest have equal claim."[44] In August 1916, under the auspices of NAACP leader Arthur Spingarn, the Washington and Du Bois factions met in Amenia, New York, and achieved a rapprochement of sorts. In the absence of Washington's powerful personality, black moderates grudgingly acknowledged the common political ground they shared with black liberals like Du Bois. Within another four years, one of Washington's brilliant supporters, James Weldon Johnston, was named executive secretary of the NAACP. By 1919, Du Bois's *The Crisis* had achieved a circulation in excess of one hundred thousand; and, politically, he was the most influential African American leader in the country.[45]

Du Bois used his growing influence to criticize the Wilson administration at almost every opportunity. In the March 1916 issue of *The Crisis,* he condemned the administration's failure to act on a report by the University Commission on Southern Race Problems, which had called for federal legislation to end lynching.[46] In his October 1916 editorial, "The Presidential Campaign," Du Bois admitted that he had little enthusiasm for Republican presidential candidate Charles Evans Hughes, yet the New York Republican was preferable to the "insufferable Wilson." Once again the editor praised the Socialists' program, regretting that the party had little chance of winning the election. Faced with dire alternatives in electoral politics, African Americans "must either vote as a unit or continue to be politically emasculated as at present," he observed, suggesting that they might have to initiate a "Negro Party."[47] On the eve of the election, Du Bois wrote that supporters of Hughes claimed their candidate was "all right" on blacks' issues, despite his silence on such matters. Thus, while Du Bois might have had reservations about Hughes, he had no doubts regarding the incumbent: No African American "can vote for Wilson."[48] Du Bois was undoubtedly disappointed when, by a narrow margin, California's electoral votes secured the president's reelection.

With America's entry into the World War in April 1917, the domestic terrain of racial politics became far more complicated for Du Bois and the NAACP. A majority of white liberals affiliated with the NAACP generally supported the U.S. war effort. For example, John Dewey and Joel Spingarn praised Wilson and supported the war. Villard actually joined the army and received an officer's commission with the rank of major; and NAACP member Charles Edward Russell, recently the Socialist candidate for mayor of New York, not only resigned from the party but urged that all anti-war Socialists "be driven out of the country." Under the Espionage Act of June 1917, Congress targeted the Socialist Party and other radicals. Anti-war labor leaders were harassed, tarred and feathered, and jailed. Many Socialist newspapers ceased publication, and many of the party's adherents, including Debs, were eventually imprisoned. In some instances, "patriotic socialists" actively participated in government suppression of the anti-war Left. The assault against the American Socialist Party in 1917–19 permanently crippled the organization and reduced social democracy to a marginal political status forever after.[49]

The social patriotism of white liberals who were also NAACP supporters influenced Du Bois's shifting attitudes about World War I. These left-leaning intellectuals numbered among his closest friends within the socialist movement, and he valued their judgment. Du Bois remained outraged by what he considered the Wilson administration's racist practices in the training and deployment of black troops. He was also overwhelmed by the terrible tragedies of the infamous white racist attack against a black neighborhood in East St. Louis, Illinois, and the hanging following courts martial of thirteen Negro soldiers in the wake of racial unrest in Houston in 1917. Nevertheless, the vast majority of the NAACP and its leadership continued to support the war. The organization endorsed the creation of a segregated camp for the training of black officers and campaigned for decent conditions for all black draftees. Arthur Spingarn, who had also accepted an officer's commission, actively lobbied the War Department for Du Bois's appointment as a captain, and Du Bois responded that he "would accept" such a position, so long as he could "retain general oversight of *The Crisis* magazine." The NAACP board of directors had difficulty with Du Bois's latter demand but recognized that, in light of the war effort, he "must accept" the captaincy. Although the offer was later withdrawn in 1918, he was by then caught up in the frenzy of patriotism. Arthur Spingarn "wanted me and my people not merely as a matter of policy, but in recognition of a fact, to join wholeheartedly in the war," Du Bois subsequently explained in *Dusk of Dawn*. "It was due to his advice and influence that I became during the World War nearer to feeling myself a real and full American than ever before or since." Although he was still, "in principle, opposed to war," he had become convinced that America's involvement would become a "fight for democracy including colored folk and not merely for war investments." He also believed that any "passive resistance" by the NAACP "would have fallen flat and perhaps slaughtered the American Negro body and soul."[50]

In July 1918, Du Bois wrote in *The Crisis* a famous, controversial editorial, "Close Ranks," in which he urged African Americans to rally behind their country. In a sentence he later deeply regretted, he declared: "Let us, while this war lasts, forget our special grievances and close our ranks shoulder to shoulder with our own white fellow citizens and the allied nations that are fighting for democracy."[51] Many a veteran of the Niagara Movement could hardly believe he had written these words. Byron Gunner, then president of Trotter's National Equal Rights League, wrote Du Bois that he was "unable to conceive that said advice comes from you. It seems to me that the impossible has happened and I'm amazed beyond expression." Gunner insisted that the war was "the most opportune time for us to push and keep our 'special grievances' to the fore."[52]

As the war concluded on November 11, 1918, the public careers of Woodrow Wilson and W. E. B. Du Bois crossed paths a final time. "I saw Woodrow Wilson but once [more] in my life," Du Bois recalled in 1939:

> I was standing at the edge of the Place de la Concorde in Paris when he rode through in December, 1918. He had come to attend the Congress of Versailles and he was at the moment without doubt the foremost figure in the world. He had just been wildly acclaimed in London and

Rome, and Paris was no whit behind. He enjoyed the adulation. He smiled and bowed right and left and seemed to have no apprehensions of the difficulty, perhaps the impossibility, of the task that lay before him.[53]

Wilson's campaign to achieve global peace and to bring the United States into the soon-to-be-formed League of Nations would fail of course. Yet it was Wilson's call for "self-determination" and the inalienable right of all oppressed nations to be granted freedom and independence that motivated Du Bois to travel to Paris; it was also both the cause and the occasion for initiating an international movement among intellectuals and politicians throughout the African diaspora. With the political assistance of the Senegalese politician Blaise Diagne, Premier Georges Clemenceau of France gave the approval for hosting an unprecedented "Pan-African Congress." Despite U.S. opposition and U.S. military surveillance of Du Bois during his stay in Paris, the first Pan-African Congress met on February 19, 1919, with fifty-seven delegates from fifteen countries in all. The representatives included sixteen Americans, twenty-one delegates from the Caribbean, and twelve representatives from African territories. The Congress's moderate manifesto demanded that all people of African descent must be "governed" democratically; that capital in African colonies must be "regulated as to prevent the exploitation of the natives and the exhaustion of the natural wealth of the country"; and that every African child must "learn to read and write his own language" as well as have access to "higher technical and cultural training." In one address to the Congress, Du Bois invoked the Covenant of the League of Nations, in a discourse on racial equality and the depredations of imperialism. And, in his "Manifesto to the League of Nations," on behalf of the Congress, he requested that the International Labor Organization (a significant portion of the Treaty of Versailles) address "the condition and needs of native Negro labor." In the same document, despite his disappointment with Wilson for other reasons, Du Bois suggested that the mandate system of the League could hasten the end of colonialism, and he urged that a Negro man, "properly fitted in character and training," be appointed to the Mandates Commission at the earliest opportunity. Thus, the great promise of Wilson's League, by Du Bois's lights, lay in its "vast moral power" to advance the cause of "the absolute equality of races." The 1919 Pan-African Congress led to similar international gatherings—in 1921,

1923, and 1927—and, most important, in October 1945, in Manchester, England. These meetings set into motion the independence movements of black people throughout Africa and the Caribbean, and indirectly aided the development of the black freedom struggle to overthrow segregation in the United States. Ironically, then, in this way, Woodrow Wilson's passion for global democracy and internationalism ultimately played an important role in accelerating the struggle for Pan-Africanism and black freedom, ideals central to the spirit and substance of W. E. B. Du Bois.[54]

Notes

1. August Meier and Elliott Rudwick, "The Rise of Segregation in the Federal Bureaucracy, 1900–1930," *Phylon* 28 (Summer 1967): 178–84. See also Nancy J. Weiss, "The Negro and the New Freedom: Fighting Wilsonian Segregation," *Political Science Quarterly* 84 (March 1969): 61–79. A more comprehensive study of Wilson's racial policies throughout the federal administration is Eric Steven Yallin, "In the Nation's Service: Racism and Federal Employees in Woodrow Wilson's Washington," Ph.D. diss., Princeton University, 2007.

2. Manning Marable and Leith Mullings, *Freedom* (London, 2002), 101.

3. Kenneth O'Reilly, "The Jim Crow Policies of Woodrow Wilson," *Journal of Blacks in Higher Education* 17 (Autumn 1997): 117–19.

4. Manning Marable, *Black American Politics* (London, 1985), 158–59.

5. Manning Marable, *W. E. B. Du Bois: Black Radical Democrat* (Boston, 1986), 55.

6. Ibid., 53–58.

7. Ibid., 66–69.

8. W. E. B. Du Bois, "To Black Voters," *Horizon* 3 (February 1908): 17–24.

9. W. E. B. Du Bois, writing in *Horizon* 3 (March 1908), 8.

10. W. E. B. Du Bois, wwriting in *Horizon* 4, (November–December 1908), 1–14.

11. Meier and Rudwick, "The Rise of Segregation in the Federal Bureaucracy," 178–81.

12. Marable, *W. E. B. Du Bois,* 71.

13. Ibid., 69, 71–75.

14. W. E. B. Du Bois, "My Impressions of Woodrow Wilson," *Journal of Negro History* 58 (October 1973): 453–59 (quotations, 453).

15. Ibid., 453.

16. Henry Blumenthal, "Woodrow Wilson and the Race Question," *Journal of Negro History* 48 (January 1963): 1–21, (quotation, 2).

17. Ibid., 2.

18. Christine A. Lunardini, "Standing Firm: William Monroe Trotter's Meetings with Woodrow Wilson, 1913–1914," *Journal of Negro History* 64 (Summer 1979):

244–64 (quotation, 244); see also Arthur S. Link, "The Negro as a Factor in the Campaign of 1912," *Journal of Negro History* 32 (January 1947): 81–99.

19. Blumenthal, "Woodrow Wilson and the Race Question," 4.

20. Ibid., 4–5.

21. W. E. B. Du Bois, "Politics," *The Crisis* 4 (August 1912): 180–82.

22. W. E. B. Du Bois, "The Last Word in Politics," *The Crisis* 5 (November 1912): 29.

23. W. E. B. Du Bois, "Editorial," *The Crisis* 5 (December 1912): 75–78.

24. W. E. B. Du Bois, "Open Letter to Woodrow Wilson," *The Crisis* 5 (March 1913): 236.

25. Ibid.

26. Blumenthal, "Woodrow Wilson and the Race Question," 8; Meier and Rudwick, "The Rise of Segregation in the Federal Bureaucracy," 181.

27. Blumenthal, "Woodrow Wilson and the Race Question," 9.

28. Ibid., 6.

29. Du Bois, "My Impressions of Woodrow Wilson," 456.

30. "Another Open Letter to Woodrow Wilson," *The Crisis* 6 (September 1913): 232–33, 236; and "The Fruit of the Tree," *The Crisis* 6 (September 1913):232.

31. Marable, *W. E. B. Du Bois*, 77.

32. W. E. B. Du Bois, "The South and the Saddle," *The Crisis* 7 (February 1914): 186–90.

33. Marable, *W. E. B. Du Bois*, 80.

34. Ibid.

35. Lunardini, "Standing Firm," 244–64 (quotations, 244, 246–47).

36. Ibid., 249–50.

37. Blumenthal, "Woodrow Wilson and the Race Question," 8–9.

38. Ibid., 7.

39. Lunardini, "Standing Firm," 256.

40. Ibid., 256–58.

41. Ibid., 258–62.

42. Du Bois, "My Impressions of Woodrow Wilson," 457.

43. W. E. B. Du Bois, "The President," *The Crisis* 9 (February 1915): 181–84.

44. Marable, *W. E. B. Du Bois*, 81–82.

45. Ibid., 82–83.

46. W. E. B. Du Bois, "Editorials," *The Crisis* 11 (March 1916): 240–44.

47. W. E. B. Du Bois, "The Presidential Campaign," *The Crisis* 12 (October 1916): 267–71.

48. W. E. B. Du Bois, "Editorial," *The Crisis* 13 (November 1916): 18.

49. Albert Fried, ed., *Socialism in America: From the Shakers to the Third International* (Garden City, NY, 1970), 506–9; John Diggins, *The American Left in the Twentieth Century* (New York, 1973), 82–86.

50. W. E. B. Du Bois, *Dusk of Dawn* (New York, 1940), 247–57. See also Mark Ellis, "Federal Surveillance of Black Americans during the First World War," *Immigrants and Minorities* 12 (March 1993): 1–20.

51. W. E. B. Du Bois, "Close Ranks," *The Crisis* 16 (July 1918), 111.

52. Byron Gunner to W. E. B. Du Bois, 25 July 1918; and Du Bois to Gunner, 10 August 1918, in *The Correspondence of W. E. B. Du Bois,* ed. Herbert Aptheker, 3 vols. (Amherst, MA, 1973–78), 1:228. See also William Jordan, "'The Damnable Dilemma': African-American Accommodation and Protest during World War I," *Journal of American History* 81 (March 1995): 1562–83.

53. Du Bois, "My Impressions of Woodrow Wilson," 433.

54. Manning Marable, "The Pan-Africanism of W. E. B. Du Bois," in *Black Leadership* (New York, 1998), 75–96; Clarence G. Contee, "Dubois, the NAACP, and the Pan-African Congress of 1919," *Journal of Negro History* 57 (January 1972): 13–28; David Levering Lewis, *W. E. B. Du Bois: The Fight for Equality and the American Century, 1919–1963* (New York, 2000), 44–47, 113–14.

"Peoples of Many Races"

The World beyond Europe in the Wilsonian Imagination

Erez Manela

> On the one hand stand the peoples of the world,—not only the peoples actually en-
> gaged, but many others who suffer under mastery, but cannot act; peoples of many
> races and in every part of the world.
>
> WOODROW WILSON, Address at Mount Vernon, July 4, 1918

In contrast to Thomas Jefferson and Abraham Lincoln, whose views and
policies on racial issues are interesting largely in the context of domestic
U.S. history, Woodrow Wilson is remembered also—perhaps more so—
for his influence on U.S. relations with the world at large. Therefore, the
question of the influence of his racial views, on his perceptions of the world
outside the United States and on his policies toward that world, is central
to any understanding of their significance. This is especially so since his
views on race are often perceived, as they are in the domestic context, as
coming into direct conflict with the ideals for which he claimed to stand
in international affairs, especially his well-known advocacy of the equality
of all nations and of their right to self-determination. Can Wilson's racial
views be reconciled with the forceful advocacy of liberal internationalism
for which he was widely hailed at the time and for which he is most often
remembered today?

Wilson appeared on the international stage near the end of the Great
War of 1914–18, which not only extinguished millions of lives and caused
unprecedented devastation, but also brought in its wake expectations for a
postwar world entirely different from what came before it. These expectations found their icon in Wilson, who appeared as a prophet of the new
world order and came, however briefly, to symbolize to millions worldwide

their own hopes and aspirations. Wilson's apparent promise of a new world order, articulated in a series of eloquent and widely circulated speeches, captured not only the imaginations of Americans and Europeans, but also those of many in Asia and Africa. The American war propaganda machine, of unprecedented scope and efficiency, also facilitated the dissemination of his words, and the messages they carried amplified and often exaggerated their meaning. The salesmen of the American creed saw Wilson's idealistic language and image as defender of right against might as a major asset in convincing the world of the righteousness of America's war effort and its plans for the peace. In the wake of a war, Wilson's words captured the attention of millions of nonwhite peoples and seemed to many of them to carry the promise of self-determination.

In Egypt, under British rule, men and women took to the streets to call for cheers for country, liberty, and President Wilson. In Korea, under the heavy hand of Japan, rumors spread that Wilson would swoop down from the sky, flying into Seoul on an airplane to declare Korean self-determination. In China, long the target of imperialist depredations, Wilson's wartime addresses were widely circulated in Chinese translation, and many schoolchildren could quote passages of the Fourteen Points address verbatim. In India, hopes that Wilson would support Indian home rule were widespread, and one editorial writer exclaimed that it would "be a sin if India does not lay her ailments before Dr. Wilson."[1] Across Asia, the Middle East, and Africa, then, subject peoples saw in the American president a potential champion of their struggles for self-determination.[2] An American president had never before spoken, as Wilson did during the war, on such a grand stage, to such a broad audience, and with such a widespread effect. Arguably, none has done so since.[3]

The Elements of the Wilsonian Imagination

Wilson's peace plan had numerous components that changed and evolved considerably in the course of the war and its aftermath, but several central, consistent elements in the plan tended to stand out for those groups who were colonized or marginalized in prewar international society. Those elements included, first, Wilson's oft-repeated call for the "equality of nations," asserting that small, weak nations were entitled to the same treatment and rights in international society as the great powers. A related second prin-

ciple, summarized by its proponents at the time as "right over might," was
that international disputes should be resolved through peaceful means, relying on international law and mechanisms such as arbitration, rather than
through a resort to armed conflict. And third, perhaps most celebrated and
best known of the Wilsonian mantras, was the rejection of any international arrangements that would not receive the consent of the populations
concerned. This was the principle of the "consent of the governed," a term
for which, for reasons explained below, Wilson began after February 1918 to
substitute what would become his most famous and memorable phrase: the
right of peoples to "self-determination."

These elements were already there in the first major public address in
which Wilson detailed a plan for the postwar settlement, delivered in Washington, D.C., on May 27, 1916, almost a year before the U.S. entry into the
war. In it he called for political arrangements, whether national or international, anchored in popular legitimacy, or, in the phrase Wilson favored,
"the consent of the governed," and he asserted the notional equality of the
political units constituted through such arrangements of consent. "We believe," Wilson declared then, "that every people has a right to choose the
sovereignty under which they shall live," and that "the small states of the
world shall enjoy the same respect for their sovereignty and for their ter-
ritorial integrity."[4] This was the essence of the principle of "the equality of
nations," which would later be eagerly reiterated by representatives of weak
nations such as China. Eight months later, in his famous "Peace Without
Victory" address, on January 22, 1917, Wilson urged that law and morality replace raw power in governing international relations. The "balance of
power" must make way for a "community of power," and this new international society must be constituted on the basis of "an equality of rights" that
would "neither recognize nor imply a difference between big nations and
small, between those who are powerful and those that are weak."[5]

The basic premise, clearly, was the need to universalize the American
creed. The ideals on which American society was founded, Wilson had no
doubt, would appeal to all peoples. They were quintessentially American—
the United States, he said, "could stand for no others"—but at the same
time they could and should be applied globally. These ideals held "the af-
fections and convictions of mankind" and were shared by "forward looking
men and women everywhere, of every modern nation, of every enlightened
community." Their implementation would respond to the popular will of

the world's people, and was therefore a practical necessity for the achievement of lasting peace. Any arrangement that contravened them was bound to fail, since it would fail to muster popular consent, sparking resistance among "whole populations" who "will fight subtly and constantly against it, and all the world will sympathize."[6] The principles of equality and of consent, then, were inextricably bound together.

Rule by popular consent rather than fiat, Wilson insisted, must serve as a basis for the international legitimacy of governments, and for the legitimacy of the international system as a whole. "No peace can last, or ought to last," he intoned on that same occasion in January 1917, in a phrase that representatives of the colonized peoples later repeated often, "which does not recognize and accept the principle that governments derive all their just powers from the consent of the governed, and that no right anywhere exists to hand peoples about from sovereignty to sovereignty as if they were property." International peace required that no one nation seek to dominate another, but that every people should be left to determine their own form of government, their own path of development, "unhindered, unthreatened, unafraid, the little along with the great and powerful."[7] This principle, Wilson believed, had been at the heart of the foreign policy of the United States since the promulgation of the Monroe Doctrine in 1823. His own project was, in essence, to extend the reach of that doctrine over the entire globe.

The "Peace Without Victory" address, the most complete and detailed plan for the postwar world articulated by any major statesman until that time, quickly became widely known and discussed around the world and affirmed Wilson's stature as a leading figure in the international arena.[8] The logic inherent in Wilson's argument that a durable peace required that governments rule by popular consent raised a direct challenge to the arrangements of imperial rule or influence that spanned much of the world at the time. Indeed, one historian has concluded that the address constituted "the first time that any statesman of stature" had launched what amounted to a "penetrating critique of European imperialism."[9]

Still, though Wilson articulated his vision in terms of universal maxims—no right *anywhere* exists—he was clearly referencing the situation in Europe, with little thought of dependent territories elsewhere. In the "Peace Without Victory" address itself, he gave the restoration of an independent Poland as an example of the principle of consent. Yet, imperialist powers could still take some comfort in Wilson's words if they parsed them carefully enough. His liberal use of qualifiers such as "enlightened" and "modern," for example, to describe those groups who could appreciate such principles and should enjoy their benefits left the door wide open for exclusion of groups deemed to lack those characteristics. If certain groups were not sufficiently "modern," certain communities not fully "enlightened," they would not take part, at least for the time being, in the brave new world that the president envisioned.

The Fourteen Points and the Rise of "Self-Determination"

By the spring of 1917, Wilson's voice was becoming increasingly prominent in the international arena. On March 5, in the inaugural address of his second term in office, the president again declared that international order and cooperation could not last long unless it stood on the principles of equality of nations and government by consent. The United States, then, would insist both on "the actual equality of nations in all matters of right and privilege" and on the principle that "governments derive all their just powers from the consent of the governed." A month later, when he came before Congress to ask for a declaration of war against Germany, the president said that the United States would fight "for democracy, for the right of those who submit to authority to have a voice in their own governments, for the rights and liberties of small nations."[10]

It was not until February 1918, however, that he had uttered in public the phrase "self-determination," with which he would soon become so closely associated and which would come to serve as the rallying cry for nationalists the world over. The phrase in fact came from socialist thought and was introduced into the rhetoric of Allied war aims in late 1917 by the Russian Bolsheviks.[11] Wilson adopted it only after it was used by British Prime Minister David Lloyd George in a speech he gave in early January 1918.[12] Contrary to popular perceptions both at the time and later, the term "self-determination" itself was nowhere to be found in the text of Wilson's famous Fourteen Points address, given on January 8, 1918. However, several of the points, like the call for the "readjustment of the frontiers of Italy" along "clearly recognizable lines of nationality" and for reconstituting a Polish state along similar lines, seemed to imply Wilson's support for that principle, at least in some instances.

The address, moreover, included for the first time an explicit reference to colonial questions, calling for any settlement of colonial issues to take into account the interests of colonial populations. Colonial claims, Wilson said in Point Five of the fourteen, would have to be resolved in a "free, open minded, and absolutely impartial" manner. Their resolution, he added, would be "based upon a strict observance of the principle that in determining all such questions of sovereignty the interests of the populations concerned must have equal weight with the equitable claims of the government whose title is to be determined."[13] But the phrasing of this principle was ambivalent, since it suggested that it was the "interests" of colonial peoples rather than their wishes or preferences that should be taken into account, and thus left open the question of just who would decide what those interests were: the people themselves, or a "benevolent" colonial power? As if to emphasize the point, Wilson also balanced those "interests" against the "equitable claims" of the colonial governments, which would receive equal consideration.

Still, the inclusion of a reference to the interests of colonial peoples, however tentative and equivocal, signaled the president's dissatisfaction with the reigning imperial order in international society. Wilson did not draft the Fourteen Points address alone, and many of the points followed the recommendations of a memorandum authored by members of a panel of experts assembled by Wilson's close adviser, Colonel House. But the memorandum made no mention of colonial issues, and it was Wilson himself who added this reference to the text of the address.[14] "At first it was thought we might have to evade this [colonial question] entirely," House told his diary, "but the President began to try his hand on it and presently the paragraph which was adopted was acceptable to us both, and we hoped would be to Great Britain." Wilson did not consult the Allies on this question, so germane to their interests, and House was clearly concerned about their reaction.[15] The decision to refer to the colonial question and to the interests of colonial peoples was Wilson's alone.

Why did he make that choice? Was it primarily a tactical decision, reflecting specific wartime considerations, or an important element of Wilson's overall vision for the postwar world order? One influential interpretation has argued that the Fourteen Points address was essentially a response—a "countermanifesto"—to the challenge that Lenin and Trotsky had presented with the announcement of their own radical peace plan.[16] In this context, Point Five might be seen as a rejoinder, albeit a hedged, tentative one, to the Russian Bolsheviks' sweeping call for self-determination for colonial peoples. But the call made in Point Five was also entirely consistent with Wilson's previous wartime pronouncements, as well as with his long-standing position on the nature and purpose of colonialism. The specific timing of the Fourteen Points address reflected the recent Bolshevik challenge, but its content drew on principles that had long been part of his basic worldview. The essential elements of the Wilsonian scheme for world order, both in the colonial realm and elsewhere, had been part of his rhetoric long before the Bolshevik challenge emerged, expressed in his assertions of the right to "self-government" and the requirement that governments receive the "consent of the governed."[17]

Wilson's position on the colonial question in the Fourteen Points was still hedged and equivocal, but his rhetoric soon grew bolder, and five weeks later he used the phrase "self-determination" in public for the first time. On February 11, 1918, the president came before Congress again to outline the principles of the American peace plan. In the coming settlement, he said, "national aspirations must be respected" and people may be "dominated and governed only by their own consent." "Self-determination," he emphasized, was not "a mere phrase," but rather "an imperative principle of action, which statesmen will henceforth ignore at their peril." In invoking the principle of "self-determination," Wilson realized that he was incorporating a novel term into his wartime ideological lexicon. Nevertheless, he adopted this phrase as his own and assimilated it into his program for the postwar international order. Calls for a peace based on self-determination would henceforth largely replace in Wilson's wartime rhetoric references to the "consent of the governed." This switch aimed to neutralize Bolshevik critiques of the Allied war aims by co-opting their language, but it did not change the essence of Wilson's vision in his own mind. To him, the term "self-determination" was simply synonymous with "self-government." And he added qualifications: only "well-defined national aspirations" would receive consideration, and only to the extent that they would not create or perpetuate "elements of discord."[18]

Thus, although Wilson borrowed the term "self-determination" itself from the Bolsheviks, he gave it a different meaning and used it for a different purpose. For the Bolsheviks, who always talked specifically about "national" self-determination, it was a call for the revolutionary overthrow of colonial and imperial rule through an appeal to the national identity and aspirations of subject peoples. Wilson, on the other hand, rarely if ever uttered the specific term "national self-determination"; rather, he used the more general, vaguer phrase "self-determination," and usually equated the term with popular sovereignty, conjuring an international order based on democratic forms of government. He did at times, as in the cases of Poland or Italy, advocate redrawing borders according to ethnic lines, but as a matter of prudence or convenience rather than of principle. Indeed, acutely aware as he was of the multiethnic character of American society itself, it was always popular consent, rather than ethnic identity, that stood at the center of Wilson's understanding of self-determination.[19]

In addition, while Lenin saw self-determination as a revolutionary principle and sought to use it as a wrecking ball against the reactionary multiethnic empires of Europe, Wilson hoped that self-determination would serve in precisely the opposite role: as a bulwark against radical, revolutionary challenges to existing orders, such as those he saw in the Russian and Mexican Revolutions. If revolution, as Wilson and other Progressives believed, was a reaction to oppression by autocratic, unaccountable regimes, then the application of self-determination, defined as government by consent, would largely remove the revolutionary impulse and promote change through rational, gradual reforms. In the case of colonialism, as already noted, he envisioned that self-determination would emerge through gradual processes of reform, with the acceptance and cooperation of the colonial powers, rather than through the abrupt overthrow of colonial rule.[20]

These distinctions between Wilson and Lenin, however compelling they are in retrospect, were hardly so clear-cut at the time. To many around the world, and especially in the nonwhite world, Wilson and Lenin appeared more similar than different. Both advocated a new, open diplomacy; both were sharply critical of imperialism; both called for a radical transformation of international relations; and both relentlessly advocated a peace based on the principle of self-determination.

Moreover, by the summer of 1918, as the tide of the war began to turn decisively in favor of the Allies, Wilson's rhetoric grew bolder still. On the Fourth of July, in a brief Independence Day address at George Washington's estate at Mount Vernon, he invoked the legacy of the Founding Fathers in support of his own mission. They had "entertained no private purpose" and "desired no particular privilege" in their historic endeavors, he said, but were "consciously planning that men of every class should be free," and striving to make America a haven for "the rights and privileges of free men." The United States' participation in the European war was an extension of that self-same mission: it would secure not only the liberty of the United States "but the liberties of every other people as well."[21] This address, though based on a rather generous interpretation of the purposes of the American Revolution, nevertheless presented Wilson's boldest formulation yet of his postwar plans, and it resonated widely around the world, far beyond the president's intended audiences in the United States and Europe.

Wilson and the World beyond Europe

Although Wilson in his wartime utterances did not explicitly exclude non-European or colonial populations from the right to be governed by consent, he did not elaborate at any length on his views on colonial questions, nor explain how and to what extent that principle applied in colonial situations. Some of Wilson's advisers, at least, clearly believed that the principle of self-determination, whatever its merits, was inapplicable to most colonial populations. Secretary of State Robert Lansing, for instance, was an early critic of Wilson's advocacy of self-determination as "dangerous to peace and stability." Lansing noted with alarm "the frequent repetition of the phrase in the press and by members of certain groups and unofficial delegations, who were in Paris seeking to obtain hearings before the Conference," which made him all the more convinced of "the danger of putting such ideas" as self-determination "into the minds of certain races," where it was bound to stir up "impossible demands" and "create trouble in many lands."[22] Even those who advocated self-determination "as a great truth," he added, did not "claim it for races, peoples, or communities whose state of barbarism or ignorance deprive them of the capacity to choose intelligently their political affiliations."[23]

When Wilson initially wanted to include a reference to the principle of self-determination in the League of Nations Covenant, many of his own advisers balked at the idea because of what it might mean for the future of international relations, especially for the place of nonwhite peoples within them. General Tasker Bliss, an American peace commissioner who was usually an ardent supporter of the president's peace plan, wondered incredulously upon seeing Wilson's draft of the Covenant whether its provisions "contemplate the possibility of the League of Nations being called upon to consider such questions as the independence of Ireland, of India, etc., etc.?"[24] David Hunter Miller, the international lawyer who was the chief American legal expert responsible for negotiating the final text of the League Covenant, warned the president that his ideas for continuous adjustment of boundaries in accordance with the principle of self-determination would make "dissatisfaction permanent," compelling "every power to engage in propaganda" and legalizing "irredentist agitation." When Miller met his British counterpart in order to merge the various American and British proposals for the League Covenant into a single document, the two quickly agreed that this section of Wilson's draft simply had to go.[25]

Some historians have noted the failure of the great powers, including the United States, to apply in the peace settlement the principle of self-determination meaningfully outside Europe, and they have therefore concluded that Wilson "believed that national self-determination applied almost exclusively to Europeans." Colonial peoples who expected any support from the American president, they argue, were simply naive.[26] But this conclusion may be too simple, since it conflates results with intent and since it ignores other elements that shaped Wilson's policies during those years. Indeed, the decisions made in Paris that are often taken as evidence of Wilson's racism are in fact more easily and fully explained by other factors at play. Wilson's rejection of the Japanese demand to insert a "racial equality" amendment into the League of Nations Covenant, often cited as conclusive evidence of his racism, is one such case in point. In fact, scholars who have studied this decision agree that it was a combination of two factors—pressure from British dominions like Australia and New Zealand, and domestic opposition in the United States to the Asian immigration that the Japanese proposal was intended to protect—that explain why Wilson felt compelled, after long delays, to exclude the amendment from the League Covenant.[27]

That Wilson in Paris largely ignored the pleas for self-determination of nonwhite peoples, in particular those who made claims that stood to injure the interests of his European allies, is also taken as evidence of racism. But Wilson ignored similar pleas from white Europeans, such as the Irish and the Catalans, when they appeared to him irrelevant to the specific issues that the peace conference had to settle. Such claims, he believed, would be dealt with in the future by the League of Nations. Indeed, this sense of the limited scope of what the conference itself could accomplish is the main reason that Wilson insisted on the establishment of the League as its first order of business. The conference could do only so much, and the rest, he assumed, would be sorted out in due course by the League of Nations. Explaining his position on the demands of Irish leaders for independence, he said that the League, once organized, would "afford a forum not now available for bringing the opinion of the world and of the United States in particular to bear on just such problems."[28] Subject populations, both in Europe and elsewhere, would eventually have self-determination, but they would get there through gradual reforms and international institutional and legal processes, not violence and revolution. This was the logic behind Wilson's struggle in Paris to establish colonial "mandate" territories, in which the powers, supervised by the League of Nations, were to serve as "trustees" of populations deemed not yet ready to govern themselves.[29]

None of this, of course, proves that Wilson was not a racist, but it does suggest that his racism provides neither the only nor even the leading explanation for his policies toward the demands of nonwhite peoples in 1919. Beyond the establishment of the mandate principle, Wilson did not give much thought during his time in Europe to colonial questions. Britain and France, the main colonial powers among the Allies, were naturally unwilling to entertain discussion of their own colonial possessions and policies at the peace table. The conference dealt with only those colonial issues that arose directly from the war, largely those related to former German and Ottoman possessions outside Europe, and in any case, Wilson focused most of his energy and attention in Paris on the complex issues of the European settlement.[30] A broader perspective on the development of his thinking on colonial issues is therefore needed if one is to probe the conceptual world behind Wilson's advocacy of self-determination and gain a better understanding to what extent, and in what fashion, he might have seen his principles as applicable to non-Europeans. Wilson's attitude toward the United States' own imperial possessions, initially as a prominent academic and then as a political leader, is especially relevant in this regard.

Wilsonian Theory: Between Imperialism and Consent

Woodrow Wilson, as others in this volume have noted, was a son of the American South, born in 1856 in antebellum Virginia and raised in Georgia, where he lived through the Civil War as a boy, and later in South Carolina.

He was clearly imbued with the racial assumptions typical of that time and place, and throughout his life he viewed blacks as his inferiors and generally disapproved of social mixing between the races. Wilson's racial prejudices were occasionally on display in his public orations, as when he entertained white audiences with jokes and anecdotes that featured uneducated, simple-minded "darkies."[31] Wilson's perception of African American inferiority appeared to be a matter of intellectual and social habit, and he never seems to have seriously questioned it nor rebelled against it.

As a scholar and intellectual, however, Wilson said and wrote little that was explicitly about race relations, and even less about U.S. foreign relations or imperialism prior to the Spanish-American War of 1898. It was only when the question of overseas expansion moved to the forefront of the American political debate with the acquisition of the Philippines, Cuba, Puerto Rico, and Guam as a result of that war, that Wilson, by then already a prominent academic at Princeton University, set his mind to it. Initially, he was not an ardent expansionist, but once the annexation of the Spanish possessions by the United States was settled, Wilson spoke in its favor, asserting that America's new role as a colonial power would be good both for the United States and for the native populations of its new colonial possessions. In the United States, an imperial role would help overcome domestic divisions and "restore the unity of national purpose to the American people and government," and the duties of empire would offer an outlet for the energies of American youth, affording the "impetuous, hot-blooded young men of the country" an opportunity to make their mark on the world. To the native populations, American rule would bring progress, both material and political. Indeed, such rule would be justified only if it pursued this purpose.[32]

In his earliest statements on U.S. rule in the Philippines, Wilson emphasized that its ultimate goal must be to prepare the islanders for self-government, but that attaining that goal would require time and training, and hence a significant period of direct rule. It would not be enough for the United States merely to institute the forms of constitutional government in the Philippines and then leave. Free institutions could not be "spread by manuscripts," and the United States would have to install and nurture them for a considerable period.[33] The Filipinos were not yet ready to exercise responsibly the rights that come with a full-fledged democracy, and therefore should not have those rights: "Freedom is not giving the same government to all people, but wisely discriminating and dispensing laws according to the advancement of a people." Cautioning against attempts to implement the American system of government in the Philippines prematurely, he warned that the United States would "have to learn colonial administration, perhaps painfully." At the same time, he spoke against the colonial authorities' initial efforts to suppress Filipino criticisms of America's imperial policies. The United States should "do everything openly and encourage those in our new possessions to express freely their opinions," in order to prove to Filipinos that it had "only their welfare at heart."[34] Americans should teach the rudiments of democracy by example and work to earn the goodwill of the native population.

Wilson also criticized American anti-imperialists, who opposed the annexation of the islands, as irresponsible. Their argument that the United States was constitutionally ill-suited for colonial rule and should leave the Philippines to another power reminded him, he told one audience, of a vain woman who had recently found religion. When asked about her newly plain appearance, she replied: "When I found that my jewelry was dragging me down to hell, I gave it to my sister."[35] It was America's duty to govern the Philippines for the advancement of the native population, and it could not shirk it. Those anti-imperialists who compared Emilio Aguinaldo, the leader of the Filipino resistance to the American occupation, to George Washington misunderstood, he thought, the true nature of liberty. In this context, Wilson was fond of quoting one of his favorite thinkers, Edmund Burke, in his quip on the French Revolution. How, Burke had asked, had France's "new liberty" been "combined with government; with the discipline and obedience of armies; with the collection of an effective and well-distributed revenue; with morality and religion; with the solidity of property; with peace and order; with social and civil manners"? Aguinaldo, Wilson continued, offered the Philippines liberty without order, and that was not true liberty at all.[36] Filipinos could have liberty eventually—they were not inherently incapable of it—but only by a process of gradual, measured progress, supervised by the United States.

A conservative Burkian sensibility permeated Wilson's thinking on the Progressive mission overseas. Wilson summarized the task of the United States in the Philippines and Puerto Rico as the establishment of self-government, "if they be fit to receive it,—so soon as they can be made fit." A long-time admirer of the British political system, Wilson held British colonial administration in high regard. The United States, he thought, should follow in that tradition in order to instruct "less civilized" peoples in "order and self-control in the midst of change" and in the "habit of law and obedience." The ultimate goal was to lift the colonized to the level of the colonizers and make them, as he said in one case, "at least equal members of the family of nations,"[37] but it would be a gradual process which might take as long as three or four generations and would require conceptual flexibility and sensitivity to cultural difference. Despite his later image as an unreconstructed "idealist," Wilson saw democracy as historically contingent and organically evolving rather than as a mechanism that could be made universal by an act of human will. The Anglo-American form of self-government, Wilson often reminded audiences, emerged out of historically specific political traditions, and so self-government in the Philippines could well look quite different from that in the United States.[38]

But could colonial rule be reconciled with the principle of government by consent, which Wilson saw as the bedrock of legitimate government? This was precisely what a former student wrote to Wilson in September 1900 to ask, how the principle of consent might apply to the new American possession in the Philippines. Ever the courteous professor, Wilson replied that he had not studied the question and so he could not give a firm opinion. Nevertheless, he suggested that the principle could not possibly mean the same thing, nor apply in the same manner, to Americans and Filipinos:

> "The Consent of the Governed" is a part of constitutional theory
> which has, so far, been developed only or chiefly with regard to the
> adjustment or amendment of established systems of government. Its
> treatment with regard to the affairs of politically undeveloped races,
> which have not yet learned the rudiments of order and self-control,
> has, I believe, received next to no attention. The "consent" of the Filipi-
> nos and the "consent" of the American colonists to government, for
> example, are two radically different things,—not in theory, perhaps,
> but in practice,—and practice is the "whole duty of man" in politics,—
> i.e. what is practicable, workable. But this difference has, unfortunately
> for some thinkers (or would-be thinkers) never been fully or adequately

explained. You will have to work on your own muscle,—and I shall be very much interested to know where your thinking lands you. I shall have to tackle the problem myself more formally than I have yet tackled it.[39]

This statement is important since it illustrates the central difficulty that Wilson, like other progressives, had in resolving the conflict between the universal scope of his ideals and the narrowness, in terms not only of race but also of class and gender, of their practical application. Wilson admitted that, "in theory," Filipinos had as much right to government by consent as Americans; "in practice," however, which Wilson described as the essence of politics, there was a difference: Filipinos were unable to exercise in practice that right of self-government which they possessed in theory, and therefore more-developed nations had a duty of tutelage until such time that they could. This tension between the theoretical equality of people and of nations and their perceived practical inequality, both as individuals and as groups defined by race, gender, or class, is, of course, a central conundrum of all liberal thought. As his reply shows, Wilson was well aware of this problem as it applied to the relations of the United States with nonwhite peoples, and he had a well-established opinion about how to solve it in practice through "benevolent" imperialist tutelage. In theory, however, he could not resolve it to his satisfaction: What indeed was the difference between the consent of the Filipinos and that of the American colonists? Though he promised his correspondent that he would "tackle the problem" more formally, he never did. Soon after the letter was written, he became president of Princeton, and then governor and U.S. president, and his time was taken up ever more with matters of practice, not theory.

The view that many, if not all, of the nonwhite "races" were, either inherently or developmentally, unfit for self-government was a common one in American public discourse, as it was in Europe, in the early decades of the twentieth century. Some opponents of imperialism invoked that view to argue that nonwhite populations, inherently "savage," could not be "developed" and should therefore be left alone.[40] For Wilson, however, the lack of fitness for self-government of many nonwhite populations was a result of their stage of development rather than the result of permanent racial deficiencies, and could therefore be remedied by time and training, though he usually stressed that the process would take many years. During the turn-of-the-century debates over the acquisition of an overseas colonial empire, then, Wilson believed that U.S. colonial rule could be useful for both colonizers and colonized, and that its goal was to allow colonial populations eventually to exercise self-government. In the meantime, however, the position of the colonized would be akin to students to be taught, or children to be raised, by their American masters. Independence would come eventually, but only through a lengthy period of tutelage and cultural and institutional development.

Wilsonian Practice: The Philippines, Haiti, and Beyond

In the decade from 1902 to 1912, Wilson said little, and apparently thought little, about colonial issues as he rose quickly in the world, first becoming president of Princeton University, then in 1911 governor of New Jersey, and finally the Democratic candidate for president in 1912. Despite his earlier writings in favor of colonial rule, during the presidential campaign Wilson adopted the anti-imperialist planks of the Democratic platform, and upon taking office his administration moved quickly to implement them. He appointed Francis Burton Harrison, a liberal-minded Democrat, governor of the islands, with instructions to give Filipinos majorities in both houses of the Philippine legislature and to respect the decisions of that legislature.[41] This, Wilson explained in his first annual message to Congress, would allow Filipinos to prove their "sense of responsibility in the exercise of political power," and, if successful, would allow them to proceed toward full independence. The United States would gradually extend and perfect the system of self-government on the islands, testing and modifying it as experience required, giving more control to the indigenous population, and eventually establishing their independence. Americans were beginning to gain the confidence of Filipinos, Wilson believed, and the colonial officials would rely on the counsel and experience of the Filipinos in order to learn how best to serve them, and how soon they could withdraw.[42]

For Wilson, success in this task was more than just an issue of domestic interest. It was a practical test of American ideals and principles, conducted before a global audience. The eyes of the world, Wilson said, were on the American experiment in the Philippines, and the United States had the opportunity, indeed the obligation, to instruct the whole world on how to manage the benevolent transformation of a backward people.[43] Outlining his view on America's role as a "trustee" of overseas territories, Wilson emphasized that the United States was not there to do as it pleased or to further narrow interests. A new era had dawned in relations between the advanced powers and developing regions: "Such territories, once regarded as mere possessions, are no longer to be selfishly exploited; they are part of the domain of public conscience and of serviceable and enlightened statesmanship." The aim of U.S. policy in the Philippines must be the Filipinos' ultimate independence, and the transition to independence must move forward "as steadily as the way can be cleared and the foundations thoughtfully and permanently laid."[44] Already here the outlines of what in 1919 would become the mandate principle were clear, and also its contradictions. The "civilizing" colonial power had to stay in control in order to allow it, eventually, to relinquish control and leave. Colonial populations had a right to self-government, but the implementation of that right could be deferred, perhaps indefinitely.

Besides his policy on the Philippines, the most obvious test case of the influence of Wilson's racial thinking on his foreign policy would appear to be the U.S. invasion and occupation of Haiti, the only black republic in the Western Hemisphere. In the summer of 1915, Wilson authorized a military invasion of Haiti in the name of restoring order on the Caribbean island, precipitating an American occupation that lasted until 1933. Indeed, scholars who have studied the occupation have found that U.S. racial attitudes, and especially Southern Jim Crow ideas and practices, were central in shaping the U.S. presence on the island and the interactions of U.S. soldiers and administrators with the Haitians.[45] However, a close examination of the terms through which Wilson himself articulated his policy on Haiti proves surprising, inasmuch as they lacked any explicit racial references. In both official and private correspondence, Wilson repeatedly admitted that the question of Haiti caused him "anxieties" and left him "perplexed," and once he even called it "a pretty mess" in a letter to his future wife, Edith Galt. But while he referred to Haiti as a "small republic," he did not make any reference to its racial makeup.[46] This, of course, is not conclusive evidence that racial attitudes had no influence on his policy, but if there were such influence he was reluctant to articulate it, even in private, perhaps even to himself. As in the case of the Philippines, in the case of Haiti, too, Wilson the progressive intellectual and politician articulated his thinking in terms of development, order, and progress, and not in terms of race.

In addition, the world war itself, especially after the U.S. entry into it, transformed Wilson's conception of America's world role, and as a result exerted significant influence on his thinking and attitudes toward nonwhites, both within and outside the United States. Already in 1916, as the administration launched its preparedness program and the president began to contemplate the possibility of entering the conflict, colonial policy became even more directly linked in his mind to the larger context and goals of the United States' growing world role. In its actions and policies in the Philippines, Wilson declared in February 1916, the United States had to prove its disinterested and benevolent attitude toward peoples of all races and in all regions of the globe. What America had to give the world, he announced, was of universal value, explicitly transcending differences of geography, ancestry, or race. The American flag "stands for the rights of mankind, no matter where they be, no matter what their antecedents, no matter what the race involved; it stands for the absolute right to political liberty and free self-government, and wherever it stands for the contrary American traditions have begun to be forgotten."[47] Self-government, then, at least in theory, was a universal right, not a privilege limited to specific geographical regions or racial groups.

Among other things, the war heightened tensions within American society and led Wilson to think more deeply than he had before about the multiethnic composition of American society and the concomitant need for the American creed to transcend boundaries of race, ethnicity, or background. Thus, despite his long-standing admiration of "Anglo-Saxon" ideas and traditions as the font of American liberty and political culture, Wilson now saw clearly that these ideals had to be severed from their supposed "racial" origins. In an interview with a British journalist soon after his arrival in England in December 1918, Wilson made this point clear:

You must not speak of us who come over here as cousins, still less as brothers. We are neither. Neither must you think of us as Anglo-Saxons, for that term can no longer be rightly applied to the people of the United States. Nor must too much importance in this connection be attached to the fact that English is our common language. . . . No, there are only two things which can establish and maintain closer relations between your country and mine: they are community of ideals and of interests.[48]

The pressures introduced by the war also led Wilson to voice a more forceful opposition than he had previously to racist practices, such as lynching, that were in clear breach of the principles for which, he tried to convince the world, the United States stood. If the United States was going to be a light unto the world—the antithesis of the militarism and barbarity that Wilson attributed to the Central Powers—then American society had to be a model, and the stakes involved in domestic race relations were higher than ever before. No longer were they crucial only for the future of American society, but for the future of the world. Thus, in July 1918 the president for the first time publicly denounced lynching, both of African Americans and, as happened on numerous occasions during the war, of those deemed "German sympathizers." The perpetrators of such acts, he charged, were emulating the "disgraceful example" of Germany and harming the war effort by sullying the image of the United States abroad:

> We proudly claim to be the champions of democracy [but] every American who takes part in the actions of a mob [is] its betrayer, and does more to discredit her by that single disloyalty to her standards of law and of right than the words of her statesmen or the sacrifices of her heroic boys in the trenches can do to make suffering people believe her to be their savior. How shall we commend democracy to the acceptance of other peoples, if we disgrace our own by proving that it is, after all, no protection to the weak?[49]

The statement had a practical purpose—to allay the discontent among African American soldiers fighting in Europe—but the fact that Wilson framed his condemnation of lynchings in the context of the U.S. world role was nevertheless revealing. And Wilson's wartime conception of America's global responsibilities helped change his attitude not only on questions of race, but also on those of gender. Initially reluctant to support a constitutional amendment guaranteeing women the vote, he changed his position by 1918, telling the Senate in September that the amendment was necessary in order for the United States to retain the faith and trust of the common people of the world. "The plain, struggling, workaday folk . . . are looking to the great, powerful, famous Democracy of the West to lead them to the new day for which they have so long waited; and they think, in their logical simplicity, that democracy means that women shall play their part in affairs alongside men."[50] Wilson, then, had come to view the major social and political issues within the United States as intimately connected to the global role he envisioned for it in the postwar world. The next day, the amendment came up for a vote in the Senate and fell only two votes short of achieving the requisite two-thirds majority. It was finally passed the following summer and ratified in August 1920.

Conclusion

The world beyond Europe, then, had a deeply ambivalent place in the Wilsonian imagination. In theory, its peoples were to become part of the new international order of self-determining states that Wilson advocated. In practice, however, they would join that order only through a slow, deliberate process of colonial reform, overseen by the League of Nations and dependent, to a significant extent, on the good will of colonial powers. In the end, it was not Wilson's intent but the perceptions, goals, and contexts of his often unintended audiences that defined the receptions and implications of his rhetoric among nonwhite peoples in Asia, the Middle East, and elsewhere. The interpretations and import given to Wilson's words there often went far beyond his own beliefs. The message stood independently of the man, and could be used without regard—sometimes in conscious disregard—of his intent.

As others in this volume have suggested, perhaps no one knew better the limits of Wilson's liberalism than William Monroe Trotter, the black leader whom Wilson had thrown out of his White House office several years earlier for urging him to fulfill his promises to African Americans. But despite that experience, in 1919 Trotter was quick to adopt the language of self-determination to make the case for black liberation, within the United States and elsewhere. The peace conference, he believed, "with its talk of democracy and self-determination," could "provide a stage from which to tell the world about the plight of blacks in the United States." Overcoming State Department objections, Trotter arrived in Paris in April 1919 to launch a campaign for black self-determination, inundating the assembled press and conference delegates—including Wilson—with letters and memoranda aimed at "letting the world know that the Negro race wants full liberty and equality of rights." Black Americans, Trotter argued, were "an ethnical minority denied equal rights," and they demanded the same rights as everyone else.[51] Like anticolonial nationalists across the ocean, Trotter enlisted Wilsonian language on self-determination for purposes different and more radical than Wilson himself had imagined.

Notes

1. *Hindi Brahmin Samachar,* November 25, 1918; and *Kesari* (Poona), n.d., both in India Office Records, L/R/5/200, p. 596, British Library, London.

2. For full details of the responses to the "Wilsonian moment" in Egypt, Korea, China, and India, see Erez Manela, *The Wilsonian Moment: Self-Determination and the International Origins of Anticolonial Nationalism* (New York, 2007).

3. Franklin Delano Roosevelt's advocacy of the United Nations in the last years of the Second World War may have come close (see Elizabeth Borgwardt, *A New Deal for the World: America's Vision for Human Rights* [Cambridge, MA, 2005]).

4. An Address in Washington to the League to Enforce Peace, May 27, 1916, in *The Papers of Woodrow Wilson,* ed. Arthur Link, 69 vols. (Princeton, NJ, 1966–94) [hereafter, *PWW*], 37:113–17. The liberal *New Republic* immediately dubbed this speech as a "Great Utterance" that "engineered a decisive turning point in the history of the modern world" (see Thomas J. Knock, *To End All Wars: Woodrow Wilson and the Quest for a New World Order* [New York, 1992], 77–78).

5. An Address to the Senate, January 22, 1917, in *PWW,* 40:533–37.

6. An Address to the Senate, January 22, 1917, ibid., 40:537–39. On the relationship between the domestic reform movement and the aspirations of wartime "liberal internationalism" to reform international society, see Alan Dawley, *Changing the World: American Progressives in War and Revolution* (Princeton, NJ, 2003).

7. An Address to the Senate, January 22, 1917, in *PWW,* 40:536–39. See also Lloyd E. Ambrosius, *Wilsonianism: Woodrow Wilson and His Legacy in American Foreign Relations* (New York, 2002), 129.

8. Knock, *To End All Wars,* 114; Arthur S. Link, *The Higher Realism of Woodrow Wilson and Other Essays* (Nashville, 1971), 106.

9. Knock, *To End All Wars,* 115.

10. An Address to a Joint Session of Congress, April 2, 1917, in *PWW,* 41:523–27.

11. Address from the Bolsheviks "To Peoples and Governments of Allied Countries," December 31, 1917, included in David Rowland Francis to Robert Lansing, in *PWW,* 45:412–13. See also Arno Mayer, *Wilson vs. Lenin: Political Origins of the New Diplomacy, 1917–1918* (Cleveland, 1964), 248, 298–303. For more on the Bolshevik impact on the postwar settlement, see John M. Thompson, *Russia, Bolshevism, and the Versailles Peace* (Princeton, NJ, 1967).

12. This address has been published as David Lloyd George, *British War Aims: Statement by the Prime Minister, the Right Honourable David Lloyd George, on January 5, 1918* (London, 1918). On Lloyd George's speech and its background, see Knock, *To End All Wars,* 142–43; Mayer, *Wilson vs. Lenin,* 313–28; and David R. Woodward,

"The Origins and Intent of David Lloyd George's January 5 War Aims Speech," *The Historian* 26 (November 1971): 22–39.

13. Address to a joint session of Congress, January 8, 1918, in PWW, 45:534–39.

14. The memorandum is reproduced in ibid., 45:459–75. Its authors were Sidney Mezes, president of the College of the City of New York; David Hunter Miller, an expert on international law; and a young Progressive journalist named Walter Lippmann.

15. Ibid., 45:552. On House's relationship with Wilson and his role during the war and the peace conference, see Alexander L. George and Juliette L. George, *Woodrow Wilson and Colonel House, a Personality Study* (New York, 1964); Inga Floto, *Colonel House in Paris: A Study of American Policy at the Paris Peace Conference 1919* (Princeton, NJ, 1980, © 1973); and Joyce G. Williams, *Colonel House and Sir Edward Grey: A Study in Anglo-American Diplomacy* (Lanham, MD, 1984).

16. See Mayer, *Wilson vs. Lenin*, esp. 329–67. The text of the Bolshevik peace initiative of December 1917 can be found in *PWW*, 45:411–14. For more on Wilson's policy toward Revolutionary Russia, see John M. Thompson, *Russia, Bolshevism, and the Versailles Peace* (Princeton, NJ, 1967); Betty Miller Unterberger, *The United States, Revolutionary Russia, and the Rise of Czechoslovakia* (Chapel Hill, NC, 1989); David S. Foglesong, *America's Secret War against Bolshevism: U.S. Intervention in the Russian Civil War, 1917–1920* (Chapel Hill, NC, 1995); and Georg Schild, *Between Ideology and Realpolitik: Woodrow Wilson and the Russian Revolution, 1917–1921* (Westport, CT, 1995).

17. On this point, see Knock, *To End All Wars*, 144–45; and Betty Miller Unterberger, "The United States and National Self-Determination: A Wilsonian Perspective," *Presidential Studies Quarterly* 26 (Fall 1996): 929–31. Knock has argued that it was Lenin's proclamations in the spring of 1917 that echoed Wilson's "Peace Without Victory" address in January of that year (Knock, *To End All Wars*, 138).

18. Address to Congress, February 11, 1918, in PWW, 46:321.

19. See Lloyd E. Ambrosius, "Dilemmas of National Self-Determination: Woodrow Wilson's Legacy," in his *Wilsonianism: Woodrow Wilson and His Legacy in American Foreign Relations* (New York, 2002), 125–43; and William R. Keylor, "Versailles and International Diplomacy," in *The Treaty of Versailles: A Reassessment after 75 Years*, ed. Manfred F. Boemeke et al. (Cambridge, 1998), 475 and 475n12.

20. See N. Gordon Levin, *Woodrow Wilson and World Politics: America's Response to War and Revolution* (New York, 1968), 247–51.

21. Address at Mount Vernon, July 4, 1918, in PWW, 48:515–16.

22. Robert Lansing, *The Peace Negotiations: A Personal Narrative* (Boston, 1921), 97–98.

23. Ibid., 101–2. See also Lawrence E. Gelfand, *The Inquiry: American Preparations for Peace, 1917–1919* (New Haven, CT, 1963), 229–30.

24. David Hunter Miller, *The Drafting of the Covenant*, 2 vols. (New York, 1928), 2:94.

25. Ibid., 1:53; Knock, *To End All Wars*, 214–16.

26. Robert D. Schulzinger, *Time for War: The United States and Vietnam, 1941–1975* (New York, 1997), 9.

27. Kristofer Allerfeldt, "Wilsonian Pragmatism? Woodrow Wilson, Japanese Immigration, and the Paris Peace Conference," *Diplomacy & Statecraft* 15 (September 2004): 545–72; Naoko Shimazu, *Japan, Race and Equality: The Racial Equality Proposal of 1919* (London, 1998).

28. Wilson to Tumulty, June 27, 1919, in *PWW,* 61:291. The Irish and Catalan petitions to Wilson are in Service Historique de l'Armée de Terre, Château de Vincennes, fonds Clemenceau, 6 N 74 & 75. On Irish expectations, see Ronan Brindley, "Woodrow Wilson, Self-Determination and Ireland, 1918–1919: A View from the Irish Newspapers," *Éire-Ireland* 23 (Winter 1988): 62–80.

29. Arthur Walworth, *Wilson and His Peacemakers: American Diplomacy at the Paris Peace Conference, 1919* (New York, 1986), 72–81; Gelfand, *The Inquiry,* 231–327. For a broader history of the mandate system as it operated in Africa, see Michael D. Callahan, *Mandates and Empire: The League of Nations and Africa, 1914–1931* (Brighton, UK, 1999).

30. This is evident in the protocols of the Paris negotiations and in Wilson's papers from the period (see *PWW,* vols. 53–57; Paul Mantoux, *The Deliberations of the Council of Four (March 24–June 28, 1919): Notes of the Official Interpreter,* trans. and ed. Arthur S. Link with Manfred F. Boemeke, 2 vols. [Princeton, NJ, 1992]; and Walworth, *Wilson and His Peacemakers,* pts. 2–4).

31. See, e.g., A News Report of a Campaign Speech in Phillipsburg, New Jersey, October 22, 1910, in *PWW,* 21:390–91. For an illuminating analysis of the impact of Wilson's racial views on his domestic politics, see Gary Gerstle, "Race and Nation in the Thought and Politics of Woodrow Wilson," in *Reconsidering Woodrow Wilson: Progressivism, Internationalism, War, and Peace,* ed. John Milton Cooper Jr. (Baltimore, 2008), 93–124.

32. A News Report of a Lecture on Constitutional Government, November 2, 1898, in *PWW,* 11:66; and A News Report of an Alumni Affair, January 14, 1899, ibid., 11:94. See also Allen Lynch, "Woodrow Wilson and the Principle of 'National Self-Determination,'" *Review of International Studies* 28 (April 2009), 423; and Niels Aage Thorsen, *The Political Thought of Woodrow Wilson, 1875–1910* (Princeton, NJ, 1988), 164–66, 174–80.

33. A Report of a Speech on Patriotism in Waterbury, Connecticut, December 14, 1899, in *PWW,* 11:298–99.

34. A Newspaper Report of a Public Address and an Alumni Meeting in Harrisburg, Pennsylvania, February 24, 1900, ibid., 11:440.

35. An Address to the Lotos Club of New York, February 3, 1906, ibid., 16:297–98.

36. Filipinos, he said on one occasion, "can have liberty no cheaper than we got it. They must first take the discipline of law, must first love order and instinctively yield to it. . . . We are old in this learning and must be their tutors" (An Address entitled "The Ideals of America" given in Trenton, NJ, December 26, 1901, in *PWW,*

12:217–18, 222). For more on Wilson's view of the relationship between progress and order, and on the gradual and "organic" nature of political progress, see Lloyd Ambrosius, *Wilsonian Statecraft: Theory and Practice of Liberal Internationalism during World War I* (Wilmington, DE, 1991), 8–9.

37. Wilson, "Democracy and Efficiency," published in the *Atlantic Monthly*, March 1901, in *PWW*, 12:17–18.

38. A Newspaper Report of an Address on Americanism in Wilmington Delaware, December 7, 1900, ibid., 12:44; A Newspaper Report of a Lecture in Waterbury, Connecticut, December 13, 1900, ibid., 12:47–48.

39. Wilson to Allen Wickham Corwin, September 10, 1900, ibid., 11:573.

40. On this, see Matthew Frye Jacobson, *Barbarian Virtues: The United States Encounters Foreign Peoples at Home and Abroad, 1876–1917* (New York, 2000), 164, 180–81, 222–23, 234–46. For the role of racist views among American anti-imperialists at the time, see Robert L. Beisner, *Twelve against Empire: The Anti-Imperialists, 1898–1900* (New York, 1968).

41. Kendrick A. Clements, *Woodrow Wilson: World Statesman* (Chicago, 1999, © 1987), 139. Harrison was recommended to Wilson by his secretary of state, William Jennings Bryan, a longtime pacifist and anti-imperialist.

42. An Annual Message to Congress, December 2, 1913, in *PWW*, 29:8–9.

43. On this point, see Lloyd E. Ambrosius, *Woodrow Wilson and the American Diplomatic Tradition: The Treaty Fight in Perspective* (Cambridge, 1987), 10–11. Ambrosius recognizes the ambivalence inherent in Wilson's views on Filipino self-government at the turn of the century but does not remark on the evolution apparent in his later views.

44. An Annual Message to Congress, December 2, 1913, in *PWW*, 29:8–9. In his last Annual Message to Congress, in December 1920, Wilson again reminded Congress that "the Philippine Islands have succeeded in maintaining a stable government since the last action of the Congress on their behalf," and thus "it is now our liberty and our duty to keep our promise to the people of those Islands by granting them the independence which they so honorably covet" (An Annual Message on the State of the Union, December 7, 1920, ibid., 66:490).

45. See, e.g., Mary Renda, *Taking Haiti: Military Occupation and the Culture of U.S. Imperialism* (Chapel Hill, NC, 2001).

46. Wilson to Bryan, April 6, 1915, in *PWW*, 32:487; Excerpt from House Diary, June 24, 1915, ibid., 33:452; Wilson to Lansing, August 4, 1915, ibid., 34:78–79; Wilson to Edith Bolling Galt, August 5, 1915, ibid., 34:89.

47. An Address on Preparedness in Topeka, Kansas, February 2, 1916, ibid., 36:94–95.

48. Wilson interview to Frank Worthington, December 28, 1918, ibid., 53:573–76.

49. A Statement to the American People, July 26, 1918, ibid., 49:97–98. See also "President Demands that Lynchings End," *New York Times*, July 27, 1918, 7; and "Mr. Wilson on the Mob Spirit," *New York Times*, July 27, 1918, 8. The latter piece echoed the president's perspective on the relationship between domestic atrocities and for-

eign affairs, concluding: "We are fighting arbitrary, cruel, law-scorning, and violent Powers. Let our hands be clean from any tincture of their iniquity."

50. An Address to the Senate, September 30, 1918, in *PWW,* 51:158–61. Wilson repeated the call for ratification of the amendment in his annual address to Congress, on December 2, 1918 (ibid., 53:277). For Wilson's attitudes toward the female suffrage movement, see Sally Hunter Graham, "Woodrow Wilson, Alice Paul, and the Woman Suffrage Movement," *Political Science Quarterly* 98 (Winter 1983–84): 665–79; and Christine A. Lunardini and Thomas J. Knock, "Woodrow Wilson and Woman Suffrage: A New Look," *Political Science Quarterly* 95 (Winter 1980–81): 655–71.

51. Jonathan Rosenberg, "For Democracy, Not Hypocrisy: World War and Race Relations in the United States, 1914–1919," *International History Review* 21 (September 1999): 592–93.

Contributors

JEAN HARVEY BAKER is Professor of History at Goucher College. She is the author of ten books, including *Mary Todd Lincoln: A Biography*, and *Sisters: The Lives of America's Suffragists*. She is currently writing a biography of Margaret Sanger.

DAVID W. BLIGHT is the Class of '54 Professor of American History at Yale University and the author of *Race and Reunion: The Civil War in American Memory*, and *A Slave No More: Two Men Who Escaped from Slavery, Including Their Narratives of Emancipation*. He is at work on a book about the impending Civil War Sesquicentennial.

JOHN MILTON COOPER JR. is the E. Gordon Fox Professor of American Institutions (Emeritus) at the University of Wisconsin–Madison. He is the author of *Breaking the Heart of the World: Woodrow Wilson and the Fight for the League of Nations*. His most recent book is *Woodrow Wilson: A Biography*.

ERIC FONER is the DeWitt Clinton Professor of History at Columbia University and the author of numerous books on American history, including *Reconstruction: America's Unfinished Revolution, 1863–1877*. He is currently working on a study of Abraham Lincoln's evolving views and policies regarding slavery.

ANNETTE GORDON-REED is the Wallace Stevens Professor of Law at New York Law School and the Board of Governor's Professor of History at Rutgers University–Newark. She is the author of *The Hemingses of Monticello: An American Family,* which won the 2008 National Book Award for Non-Fiction and the 2009 Pulitzer Prize for History.

THOMAS J. KNOCK is Altshuler Distinguished Teaching Professor at Southern Methodist University. He is the author of *To End All Wars: Woodrow Wilson and the Quest for a New World Order,* and co-author of *The Crisis of American Foreign Policy: Wilsonianism in the 21st Century.* He is currently writing a biography of George McGovern.

EREZ MANELA is Professor of History at Harvard University. He is the author of *The Wilsonian Moment: Self-Determination and the International Origins of Anticolonial Nationalism,* and co-editor of *The Shock of the Global: The 1970s in Perspective.*

MANNING MARABLE is the M. Moran Weston and Black Alumni Professor of American Studies, and Director of the Center for Contemporary Black Studies, at Columbia University. He is the author of *The Great Wells of Democracy: The Meaning of Race in American Life,* and co-editor of *The Autobiography of Medgar Evers.*

PETER S. ONUF is the Thomas Jefferson Foundation Professor at the University of Virginia. He is the author of many works on Jefferson and his period, including *Jefferson's Empire: The Language of American Nationhood,* and *The Mind of Thomas Jefferson.* In 2008–9 Onuf was the Harmsworth Professor of American History at Oxford University.

LUCIA STANTON is Shannon Senior Historian at the Robert H. Smith International Center for Jefferson Studies at Monticello. She is the author of many works on Jefferson, including *Slavery at Monticello* and *Free Some Day: The African-American Families of Monticello.*

Index